The Subscription Boom

ADAM LEVINTER

The Subscription Boom

Why an Old Business Model is the Future of Commerce

Figure.1

Vancouver / Berkeley

Cataloguing data is available from Library and Archives Canada
ISBN 978-1-77327-071-5 (hbk.)
ISBN 978-1-77327-072-2 (ebook)
ISBN 978-1-77327-073-9 (pdf)

Jacket design by Jessica Sullivan
Interior design by Naomi MacDougall
Author photograph by Laura Jane Brett Photography

Editing by Michael Leyne
Copy editing by Gillian Scobie
Proofreading by Melanie Little
Indexing by Stephen Ullstrom

Printed and bound in Canada by Friesens
Distributed internationally by Publishers Group West

Figure 1 Publishing Inc.
Vancouver BC Canada
www.figure1publishing.com

To my wife, Erika. Thank you for your endless support, love, and acceptance.

To my children, Loah, Hudson, and Ezra— my greatest sources of joy and happiness.

And, to my father Robbie, who passed away shortly before the release of this book. The greatest man I've ever known, and the father I aspire to be.

Contents

1   Introduction

ONE
9   Why Subscription Works

TWO
17   The Origins of Subscription

THREE
31   Amazon Pioneers
Customer Centricity

FOUR
51   Netflix Chills TV

FIVE
69   From Sales to Salesforce

SIX
85   Shopify Your Business

SEVEN
103   The Spotify Soundtrack

EIGHT
121   Booming Boxes

NINE

139   Dollar Shave Club
       Disrupts an Industry

TEN

153   Food, the Final E-Commerce
       Frontier

ELEVEN

173   A Fashion Industry Refit

191   **TWELVE**
       Bricks and Bytes—
       Online Hits the Streets

201   Conclusion

209   Acknowledgments

211   Notes

237   Index

Introduction

IT IS March 6th 2012, 9 AM EST, and Dollar Shave Club's web servers are unprepared for the surge of traffic about to descend on the California-based start-up's website. Michael Dubin, the company's founder, is scrambling, "terrified," in his words, "that, in that moment, my biggest dreams were turning into my worst nightmares."[1]

The quirky yet brilliant video he produced to magnify the company's official launch has fierce momentum on YouTube, the play count increasing more rapidly with each passing minute. A half hour in, the website crashes. At Dollar Shave Club's borrowed office space, a few individuals work frantically to get the over-heated servers back online.

When the smoke clears a few hours later, the promotional video has crushed all expectations: millions of views, and 12,000 new Dollar Shave Club subscribers.[2] If you haven't seen the video yet it's worth taking ninety seconds to watch it (https://www.youtube.com/watch?v=zug9qytjmsi) before reading on, but here's a small sample of the script:

[Mike is sitting at his office desk. Close-up shot of head and shoulders. Children's toys are hung up all over the background wall. Camera slowly zooms out as Mike begins to speak.]

Mike: "Hi. I'm Mike—founder of dollarshaveclub.com. What is dollarshaveclub.com? Well, for a dollar a month we send high-quality razors right to your door. [Mike stands up and begins moving around the desk towards the door.] Yeah. A dollar. Are the blades any good? No. [Stops in doorway and points at the poster to the right] Our blades are fucking great."[3]

Known to industry colleagues as a brilliant marketer with a savvy entrepreneurial frugality, Dubin took a DIY approach to the video. He starred in it himself, and used his existing fulfillment warehouse as a set for his smug yet humorous delivery. In all, he produced and shot the video for only $4,500—peanuts compared to what traditional ad agencies charge.[4] As I write this, the one-and-a-half minute sliver of marketing genius has over 26 million views.

Dollar Shave Club, or "DSC," as Dubin calls it, is an online company that sells razors and other men's personal grooming products by shipping them direct to consumers. Customers select a "shave plan" based on blade type, and subscribe for only a few dollars a month. The branding is slick, and framing the subscription as an opportunity to join a "club" puts a new spin on an old-school industry once dominated by legacy brands Gillette and Schick.

The barber shop aesthetic and irreverent humor might grab some initial attention, but that isn't enough to keep customers around long enough to build a billion-dollar business. The thing that really resonates for DSC subscribers is the same for most companies outlined in this book: a superior customer experience. That experience includes some obvious pieces, like great customer service, and convenience. But, ultimately, DSC used the subscription model as the business pillar to build enduring customer loyalty—a necessary requirement for success in today's new age of consumerism.

SHOPPING, IN the traditional sense, involves a buyer and a seller. A potential buyer learns about a product, usually from exposure to branded marketing, and if it's compelling enough to buy, they do so via a store or website. Following the purchase, the buyer's role shifts to that of a consumer (or user, if you prefer). If as a consumer, they are happy with the product, they might buy it again, or perhaps buy it for someone else; if not, they will likely try an alternative, and much of the initial marketing spend to move the buyer down the funnel from awareness and interest, to consideration, and, ultimately, to purchase won't amount to much profit over time.

Data geeks in corporate cubicles run spreadsheets and formulas attempting to dive deeper into this spectrum of consumer behavior, hoping to understand how to get buyers to make repeat purchases—and allow businesses to reap higher profits without constantly spending money to acquire new customers.

As brands claw at one another in an attempt to gain more market share, a new mode of retail commerce is on the rise, one largely driven by direct-to-customer brands generating repeat purchases via subscriptions. In recent years, the number of such businesses has grown significantly, from hundreds to thousands worldwide, prompting progressive thinkers to suggest that we are entering the age of the subscription-based economy.

Shifting to a subscription model fundamentally transforms how a company chooses to operate. While companies like Netflix, Spotify, IPSY, Amazon, and others may offer very different products and services, they are all pioneers in this changing world of digital commerce, where customers are being transformed from one-time purchasers into loyal subscribers. Spotify, the most successful music-streaming service globally, has over 200 million active monthly users, about half of whom are paid subscribers. Amazon Prime boasts over 100 million members. Netflix, the global leader in the world of video-on-demand, has garnered over 135 million subscribers across 190 countries since pivoting from its direct-mail DVD origins.

These sorts of consumer-oriented subscription businesses are seeing tremendous growth. Fueled by venture-capital investment, a plethora of start-ups have also launched and grown successful subscription money-makers in a wide range of categories, including food, personal care, baby, beauty, apparel, contact lenses, vitamins, and more.

IPSY, a cosmetics sample-box company that ships a "Glam Bag" to over 3 million subscribers each month, is widely considered to be one of the biggest subscription success stories to date. In 2015 the company was valued at $500 million, and recent reports suggest it could sell for as high as $2 billion.[5]

After Dollar Shave Club released its hilarious viral marketing video, its subscription razors propelled the men's grooming space to new heights, knocking Gillette and Schick back on their heels and prompting other new entrants to launch similar offerings. The company grew its subscriber count to just shy of 4 million subscribers by 2018, even as it faced competition from copycats like Harry's.[6]

Birchbox, IPSY's number one competitor, which sends samples of beauty products to its upmarket subscribers for about $15 each month, recently partnered with Walgreens to open stores-within-stores, a quick pivot from its own brick-and-mortar location in Soho. Stitch Fix curates a box of stylish fashion items which it sends directly to its dedicated customers, many of whom opt for recurring boxes, while UK-founded Graze ships monthly boxes of healthy snacks to its loyal followers. This kind of curation is a common theme across other subscription categories, such as food delivery, where meal kits, such as Plated and Blue Apron, send out recipes and all the necessary ingredients for a custom, cook-at-home experience.

There's also plenty of momentum beyond these types of curated subscriptions. Access subscription is another model that, though it has long been ubiquitous—in the form of gym memberships, country clubs, or online dating sites—has seen a resurgence. A new ramp-up of product-based companies like JustFab and Thrive Market are offering discounts on women's clothing and organic brands, respectively, to members only.

A growing number of subscription players now provide effortless replenishment of everyday items, automating the purchase-

and-delivery cycle of household staples such as diapers or laundry detergent. While Dollar Shave Club has mastered this subscription category with its razor offering, others, like Amazon, are operating similar business models. "Subscribe and Save" offers a 5 to 15 percent discount if consumers agree to regular deliveries of eligible goods like coffee and peanut butter. Jessica Alba's Honest Company applies a similar methodology to its subscription plans on things like diapers and wipes.

Some legacy companies have also pivoted from one-time purchase models to recurring subscriptions, especially in the realm of software-as-a-service, or SaaS. Microsoft is growing its subscription-based Office 365 offering for small businesses. LinkedIn, now owned by Microsoft, has focused heavily on its monthly subscription offerings like Premium, Sales Navigator, and Recruiter Lite. And perhaps most notably, in 2013 Adobe Systems stopped selling licences to its Creative Suite software (Photoshop, InDesign, etc.) in a bid to move everything to a $50-per-month Creative Cloud subscription plan.

Adobe's move looked risky at the outset, but is a perfect illustration of a successful rethinking of its business model. Executives were unsure about how subscription would work in place of traditional perpetual-licence sales, and skeptics figured profit margins would take a hit, since prices on Creative Suite products were high. While a small percentage of customers rebelled against the shift into cloud-based rentals, customer enthusiasm for the new Creative Cloud offering led the company to quickly move into subscriptions. Customers benefitted from a lower entry price point, and Adobe saw a steadier stream of income from recurring revenue rather than the typical peaks and valleys associated with continuing to rely on client software upgrades to hit sales targets. As a result, the software giant's revenue crossed $7 billion in 2017, up from $4 billion in 2013, with about 80 percent of that coming from subscriptions.[7]

Growth in the subscription space is everywhere, from SaaS, to retail, to e-commerce. Sephora, Walmart, Dunkin' Donuts, Under Armour, and Gillette have launched their own subscription programs. Sephora's subscription beauty sample box, Play!, and Walmart's Beauty Box are both efforts to establish a more connected customer experience in the cosmetics space. With a Regular Refills subscription, caffeine addicts can opt in to receive their favorite Dunkin' Donuts coffee products delivered at their preferred frequency. The Armour Box by Under Armour gives athletes a personalized box of UA gear every thirty, sixty, or ninety days. Gillette was famously late to the men's grooming subscription space but launched its On Demand subscription service in 2017 in an attempt to compete with Harry's and Dollar Shave Club.

And how many of you reading this have subscribed to a meditation app? Both Calm and Headspace offer free trials of on-the-cushion goodness before billing your credit card for subsequent access to further guided sessions. The "freemium" model has become ubiquitous among app developers as a viable monetization strategy.

Even industries like manufacturing or automotive are building subscription businesses. HP Instant Ink, from Hewlett Packard, is an auto-refill ink cartridge replacement service. Printers linked to the subscription program send ink-level information to HP; subsequent refills are automatically shipped. Japanese venture giant SoftBank Group recently invested $385 million in Fair Financial Corp., a company that buys used vehicles from dealerships and rents them out for a monthly fee. The investment values the Santa Monica, California, company at more than $1 billion. Legacy car companies are also getting into the subscription game, by testing offers in specific markets that allow customers to forego ownership and leases for the option to subscribe to a program, without the hassles of insurance or maintenance. Audi and Porsche both have new subscription-based services granting customers access to a fleet of cars for a set monthly fee. The Audi service is called Audi Select, which, for $1,395, gives subscribers the choice of a range of vehicles, including the Audi A4 sedan, A5 Cabriolet, Audi Q5 and Audi Q7 SUVs, and the S5 Coupe. The subscription includes two vehicle swaps per month. The Porsche Passport program allows unlimited vehicle swaps on the Cayenne and other models. And while these types of programs might seem novel, expect more automobile manufacturers to follow suit.

Zuora is a company helping incumbents evolve; according to its CEO, Tien Tzuo, "this shift can favor a disruptor, but it can also favor an incumbent. These big companies have big customer relationships, so they can learn a lot from them. In the last five or six years the conversation about digital technology is causing these guys to transform pretty quickly."[8]

Transformations are happening across the board, both big and small, not only through subscription innovation, but courtesy of several big acquisitions like Nordstrom's $350 million swallow of Trunk Club in 2014, Albertsons' $200 million-plus 2017 deal for meal-kit company Plated, and Unilever's $1 billion purchase of Dollar Shave Club in 2016.

IT'S SAFE to say that the subscription-based economy has now fully entered the mainstream. The companies noted above—and others, like Hulu, BarkBox, Apple Music, Dropbox, and many more—have all grown revenue and customer lifetime value by acquiring subscribers.

There's every reason to think there will be further growth ahead. The subscription e-commerce market more than doubled each year between 2011 and 2016, with total sales of the sector's leaders growing from $57 million to $2.6 billion.[9] From 2012 to 2018, businesses using a subscription model saw revenue growth that was about five times faster than that of American retail sales and S&P 500 company revenues; industry experts predict that by 2020 over 80 percent of software companies will use subscription models, and half of the world's largest companies will derive most of their business from "digitally enhanced products, services, and experiences."[10]

In the new era of retail, where Amazon looms large, companies like IPSY, Dollar Shave Club, Birchbox, and Stitch Fix, to name a few, have provided key insights into how brands should be thinking about the next chapter of selling stuff in the digital age. These names and many more are betting on the power of subscription

BY 2018, HALF OF ONLINE SHOPPERS WERE SUBSCRIBERS

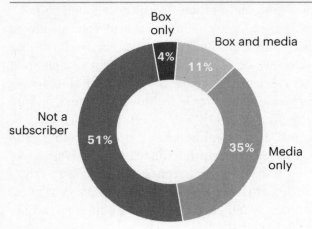

A survey in 2018 asked online shoppers if they had subscribed to product boxes (e.g., Dollar Shave Club, Ipsy, Stitch Fix) or online media services (e.g., Netflix, Spotify). (Note: percentages do not equal 100 due to rounding.)

Source: Tony Chen et al., "Thinking Inside the Subscription Box: New Research on E-commerce Consumers," McKinsey & Company, February 2018, https://www.mckinsey.com/industries/high-tech/our-insights/thinking-inside-the-subscription-box-new-research-on-ecommerce-consumers.

to control the buying cycle, stabilize cash flow and inventory, add recurring revenue, and, most importantly, boost customer loyalty.[11] Interesting times, to say the least.

In the pages that follow, you'll learn how each of these companies, and several others, achieved their success. Across many of these use cases, we see consumer-centric strategies that focus on better personalization, customer service, and product offering. We also notice a recurring pattern of winners moving away from broad market offerings in favor of going niche and narrow in a kind of anti-Amazon approach. Many of the other factors, capabilities, and lessons vary from company to company; but the common thread is the use of subscription as the core business model. It won't be long before that's the norm rather than the exception for companies that want to thrive and compete.

ONE

Why Subscription Works

WHEN I DUG into the companies profiled in this book, which vary hugely in what products or services they sell and how they sell them, I noticed that each one has a unique trait, whether it's an exceptional work culture, a visionary founder/figurehead, or outstanding marketing prowess. Despite these differences, the common thread, which each uses to achieve relationship-driven loyalty from customers, is subscription.

Amazon, Netflix, Spotify, IPSY, and Dollar Shave Club, for instance, recognize that as we enter the next chapter of consumerism, a customer can no longer be just a customer. They must be a loyal follower. A subscriber. A "true fan."

Subscribers as Fans

In 2008, Kevin Kelly, the founding executive editor of *Wired* magazine and a former editor/publisher of *Whole Earth Review*, wrote an essay called "1,000 True Fans." (Kelly recently rewrote the post, publishing a more succinct version on his website and in *Tools of Titans*, the 2016 book by Tim Ferriss.) When starting my first business, I referenced the essay. When I started the next business, I referenced the essay. And this year, when I began a set of new personal projects, including a podcast and this book you're reading, I referenced the essay.

The lessons in it apply to just about anyone wanting to make something of what they create, be it a business, a documentary, a book, a play, or an art project. As Kelly puts it in an introduction to the new version, "the concept will be useful to anyone making things, or making things happen."[1] The most important principles can be applied to not only individuals, but also to corporations with tens of thousands of people. Each company featured in this book is evidence of the wisdom of the 1,000 true fans concept.

Kelly's basic premise is that to be a successful creator you don't need to start with millions of dollars, or acquire millions of customers, clients, or followers. Whether you are a craftsperson, photographer, musician, designer, author, animator, app maker, entrepreneur, or inventor—you only need 1,000 true fans. A true fan is someone who is loyal to your brand, your company, your craft. Someone who will buy anything you produce. These are people who will drive miles to see you sing; buy the hardcover, paperback or audio version of your book; listen to your podcast; purchase the new organic soap you sell from your website. Not only that, they will emphatically share their admiration for your work with their friends, colleagues, and coworkers.

The Long Tail

As the internet became thoroughly entwined in most people's daily lives, it became increasingly easier to find and build an audience —and profit from it. This dynamic was magnified when companies like Amazon and Netflix realized that the combined sales (or views) of the lowest-selling items were equal to, or sometimes more than, those of a few bestsellers. The phenomenon was identified by Chris Anderson (Kelly's successor at *Wired*) when he looked at a graph of the average sales distribution curve. He saw "a low, nearly interminable line of items selling only a few copies per year," which forms a long "tail" on the X axis, as opposed to the "abrupt vertical beast of a few bestsellers" on the Y axis.[2] Anderson's crucial insight was that the total area of the long tail—i.e., its total sales—was as large as the more celebrated head.

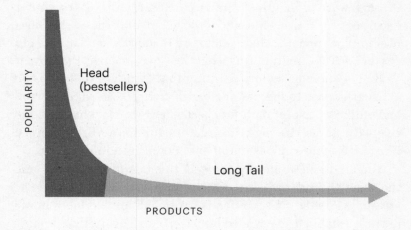

Products in the "long tail" are less popular but more numerous, so the total sales can rival those of the bestsellers. Somewhere in the curve lies the sweet spot of "1,000 True Fans."

Source: Kevin Kelly, "1,000 True Fans," The Technium, March 4, 2008, https://kk.org/thetechnium/1000-true-fans/.

And so Amazon and Netflix invented recommendation engines and other algorithms to channel attention to the less popular but more populous creations in the long tail—the titles, products, and content that brick-and-mortar retailers, with their fixed amount of shelf space, tended to shy away from. This meant that any creative pioneer, regardless of how peculiar their product was, now had a channel through which to find an audience.

As Kelly put it, "every thing made, or thought of, can interest at least one person in a million. Any one-in-a-million appeal can find 1,000 true fans."[3] Knowing they don't need to worry about securing precious space in traditional marketing and distribution channels, today's innovators, creators, artists, and entrepreneurs can use social tools like Kickstarter, Facebook, or Instagram to establish deeper connections with their early followers and fans.

The power of the fanbase lies in the multiplier effect. Fans become little marketing organisms that spread brand awareness through word of mouth at dinner parties, family affairs, conferences, networking events, and on social media. They write blogs, post product reviews, share photos on Instagram, and upload videos on YouTube highlighting what they love, and why they love it.

Kelly concludes by proclaiming that "1,000 true fans is an alternative path to success. Instead of trying to reach the narrow and unlikely peaks of platinum bestseller hits, blockbusters, and celebrity status," he suggests creators aim for a "direct connection" with a more modest number of potential admirers.[4]

You might be wondering what all this talk of "true fans" and the "long tail" has to do with subscription-based businesses. The answer is simple: subscription is a mechanism that lets a brand not only establish an engaged fanbase, but also turn that fanbase into potential profit—fast. As musician Robert Rich pointed out in response to Kelly, it's tough to make a living from only 1,000 fans if you're only selling them one album and concert ticket a year.[5] To generate real traction you need to sell them something several times over. Subscriptions are a great way to do just that.

The Problem with Retail

Retail is changing and incumbents are under pressure. So it's not hard to understand why a focus on customer loyalty is critical. Yet, still, very few companies get it: consumerism is no longer about the transaction; it's about the relationship. On the surface, this theory might feel opaque. But Kelly neatly underscores this very premise throughout his essay.

Kelly's theory is just as relevant to a legacy corporation as it is to a solopreneur, but still, we see evidence that big incumbents and their intermediaries aren't putting this kind of thinking into practice. For big corporations, what typically counts as a "win" is meeting quarterly sales results.

It's a different era—thanks to digital commerce, consumers have more power than ever before. Consumer-centric direct-to-consumer brands that have seen the paradigm shift are thriving. Legacy players that don't understand this new relationship-driven economy inevitably falter. This isn't a prediction. We've seen plenty of casualties of this ignorance already, not only with recent bankruptcies like Sears, Nine West, and Claire's, but also with older, more dramatic deaths that resulted from a failure to evolve: Blockbuster in the face of Netflix, for example, and most of brick-and-mortar retail in its repudiation of the new reality created by Amazon. J.C. Penney, Macy's, and Toys "R" Us are more examples of brands who've taken big swings in the past, but are no longer relevant. J.C. Penney closed 138 stores in 2017 while attempting to restructure its business to meet shifting consumer tastes. Macy's closed a number of its stores and laid off about 5,000 workers as part of an ongoing effort to stream-line.[6] Toys "R" Us filed for bankruptcy in September of 2017 amid mounting debt, joining a parade of other retailers that sought protection the same year, including shoe chain Payless and children's clothing retailer Gymboree.[7] From 2000 to 2014, over half of the companies listed in the Fortune 500 disappeared, an acceleration that is in large part due to this digital transformation.[8]

While these companies use euphemistic language like "shifting consumer tastes" and "streamlining the business" to explain the shortfalls, the truth is that their transaction-based strategies are being replaced by consumer-centric organizations like Amazon, who build revenue year over year by pursuing deeper relationships with their customer base. As an aside, Amazon now accounts for nearly half of all e-commerce purchases in the U.S., representing $200 billion in revenue or about 4 percent of total U.S. retail. About a third of Americans subscribe to Amazon Prime. Amazon—and others, like Netflix, Spotify, Shopify, and Salesforce—continue to dominate through the relentless pursuit of customer loyalty, using subscription as the foundational business model.

What seems obvious to pioneers like Jeff Bezos (Amazon) and Reed Hastings (Netflix), for instance, is missed by companies that still get caught up chasing quarterly targets. While they pay close attention to cost-cutting and other strategies "du jour" at the board table, the next wave of corporate trailblazers has already shifted—building customer-centric, loyalty-obsessed companies instead.

The Subscription Solution

Since 2012, the number of subscription-box companies has exploded. Pioneers like Dollar Shave Club have leveraged the power of subscription to make shopping online convenient, quick, and perhaps most important, innovative. At the core of their business is a recurring revenue model that attracts healthier business metrics than a traditional online business, while generating increased customer loyalty. According to John Warrillow, author of *Built to Sell* (2010) and *The Automatic Customer* (2015), subscription is "the perfect business model because it provides the greatest value to both the entrepreneur and the customer."[9]

From the entrepreneur's perspective, that value comes from the guarantee of recurring revenue, which Warrillow describes as one of the most compelling factors in a company's valuation. Tim Ray, founder of Carnivore Club (a gourmet charcuterie subscription service), agrees, saying he was attracted to the benefit of low-risk recurring revenue. "From a business perspective, it is the most efficient, flexible and easy to operate business model in e-commerce," he told the *Financial Post*.[10]

While recurring revenue is attractive, subscription also provides predictive cash flows, better inventory control, and juicy customer lifetime values—all while avoiding the volatility of a typical boom-and-bust product cycle. Most important, subscription creates better customer loyalty by building a relationship between brand and customer. A traditional model means a brand must go to great efforts to re-engage a customer to make a repeat purchase. Subscription, on the other hand, means that that onus shifts from merchant to customer, who, by default, is automatically opted in to repeats unless they sever the relationship by cancelling.

From the customer's perspective, with any product now available any time via a few clicks, expectations are higher than ever before. Competitors have Amazon to thank for much of this new reality. Even beyond the logistics of the sheer volume of stuff Amazon sells—their largest fulfillment center is over 1.2 million square feet, or 27 acres, and it's not uncommon for such centers to ship over 1 million items per day[11]— the company has made customer service its focal point since day one. Consider Prime's one-to-two-day free shipping, which has single-handedly raised the bar for other e-tailers hoping to compete on lead times. Thanks to the typical Amazon experience, consumers now expect all online sellers to offer both free shipping and product that gets to the front door fast.

This new customer expectation paradigm shift is bad news for most of Amazon's competition. Brands that can't adapt face steep challenges ahead. Instead of going toe to toe with Amazon, some are finding ways to leverage the beast. Using "Fulfillment by Amazon" (FBA), for example, many online sellers are tapping into Amazon's fulfillment centers to house inventory, and subsequently pick, pack, and ship online orders for a fee. Others have significantly cut back on in-house marketing and sales resources, choosing simply to use Amazon's platform as its primary sales channel. While removing marketing as a core function seems counter-intuitive, the result is often a drastic reduction in marketing costs on the P&L, alongside a boost in revenue stemming from the power and reach of Amazon.com.

In thinking through winning strategies in the Amazon age, there's plenty of talk in the C-suite about pivoting into subscriptions. But to execute, companies must first understand how their consumers are currently shopping, how they intend to shop in the future, and whether a subscription model fits their business objectives. Moreover, they need to quickly identify which items from their product (or service) stack are conducive to subscription, and how they intend to execute marketing, customer acquisition, billing, and last-mile fulfillment. Last mile doesn't mean just pick, pack, and ship, but a multi-pronged Amazon-like focus on speed of delivery, customer experience, and support throughout the process—all with the goal of building enduring loyalty from subscribers post-purchase.

TWO

The Origins of Subscription

SUBSCRIPTION IS experiencing a resurgence in the digital age. Yet the subscription model has been around for about 400 years, dating back to the sales of books and periodicals in the early seventeenth century.

Perhaps the first known direct-mail subscription business is the Book of the Month Club, which was started in 1926 by entrepreneur Harry Scherman, who arguably set the template for the current subscription-box model we see today.

Early iterations of the business began under the Little Leather Library (LLL) moniker, created in 1916 by Scherman, alongside Charles and Albert Boni and Max Saxheim, fellow members of a Greenwich Village literature group. After hearing of a tobacco company that included a volume of Shakespeare with each tobacco purchase, they were inspired to create a prototype version of *Romeo and Juliet*. Scherman shipped public-domain titles directly to consumers along with a selection of chocolates, a small gesture to delight customers. And delighted they were—by 1920, LLL had sold over 25 million volumes.

The seemingly simple strategy of sending an unexpected gift, message, or "ride along" is still widely used by several direct-to-customer brands, and has propelled many to the forefront of the customer satisfaction zeitgeist. BarkBox, for example, sends random toys as part of a regular monthly shipment of dog treats; and Chewy.com drove hundreds of millions in revenue not only by selling pet products, but by delighting customers with personal touches like handwritten cards—in 2017 alone, Chewy's "Hallmark" department mailed out 5 million of them.[1]

After the Little Leather Library was acquired in 1923, Scherman shifted his focus to his second venture, the Book of the Month Club (BOMC). While the business model was similar in certain respects, BOMC had larger-scale distribution and a mix of classic and newly published book titles on subscription. Subscribers choosing to enrol would receive at least four books a year, chosen in advance from the catalogue.[2]

To keep the quality of the titles high, Scherman's team engaged editorial experts—respected writers, editors, or journalists—to select the books each month. The curated selection provided readers with assurance that they'd be receiving recommendations from knowledgeable critics. Notwithstanding the value these critics provided, the key to the Book of the Month Club's early success was the subscription model. By subscribing to the club, readers could get premium titles conveniently, without having to travel to a store.

Scherman's direct-mail business managed 4,000 subscribers in its first year of operations, before climbing to 60,000 in year two. Incredibly, by the 1940s, in the aftermath of World War II, the number of subscribers had grown to 550,000. The company's growth came mostly from books, but also from other business lines, including Music-Appreciation Records, a classical music club for adults and a predecessor to one of the biggest subscription businesses in history, the Columbia Record Club (more on them later). By the mid-1950s, BOMC had 800,000 members—more than the total number of titles in all U.S. public libraries and universities combined. After Scherman's death in 1969, the club continued to grow under the stewardship of Scherman's son-in-law, who later helped BOMC orchestrate its sale to Time Inc. in 1977 for an estimated $63 million.[3]

Scherman's impact stretches beyond redefining marketing in the twentieth century. In fact, Scherman can be credited with introducing many literary classics to a broad audience of readers. Books like Ernest Hemingway's *A Farewell to Arms*, Margaret Mitchell's *Gone with the Wind*, and J.D. Salinger's *The Catcher in the Rye* might never have gained the popularity they did without the Club's recommendation and subsequent distribution to its loyal customer base.[4] In a way, the book club acted as the gateway for authors to reach customers in rural areas where few (if any) bookstores existed. Interestingly, BOMC is still operating, now owned by Pride Tree Holdings Inc., and although exact membership numbers are unknown, its Instagram page has over half a million followers.

As the Book of the Month Club grew throughout the 1950s, magazine publications were also growing revenues through more efficient distribution, sales from ad placements, and increased subscription rates. After a 200-year-plus history, the magazine industry was peaking.

While the subscription model seems synonymous with magazines, it took more than a century for the industry to reach full stride. The early roots of the industry point back to English printer Edward Cave, widely considered to be the first to release a magazine, *The Gentleman's Magazine*, in 1731, which contained everything from essays and poems to stories and political musings. Ten years later, the first two American publications were founded: Andrew Bradford's *American Magazine, a Monthly View of the Political State of the British Colonies*, and Benjamin Franklin's *The General Magazine and Historical Chronicle*.

It's not clear which publication was the first to attract a set of subscribers, or which first monetized its operation using the model. What we do understand, however, is that the industry had trouble attracting and keeping readers. That began to change when the U.S. Postal Service was established in 1775, helping to spark the first "golden age" of magazines, from 1825 to 1850, when better distribution coincided with "a general literary boom, rapid diffusion of the new practice of paying authors for their contributions, and expanding use of copyright law to defend publishers' exclusive rights to their magazines' contents."[5]

As magazine publishing blossomed, popular titles like *Harper's*, *McClure's*, *Vogue*, and *Cosmopolitan* began slashing prices to make publications more affordable for the masses. As circulation grew, so did revenue from subscribers, as well as revenue from advertising. For example, *Cosmopolitan* had advertising revenues of $5,000,000 from a circulation of 1,700,000 in the 1930s. These factors changed the economics of selling magazines, since the prospect of selling a magazine for less than the unit cost of production had now become a worthwhile growth strategy.

In 1953, Hugh Hefner—a University of Illinois psychology graduate who had worked for *Esquire* magazine writing promotional copy—endeavored to capitalize on the magazine boom, and launched a magazine of his own called *Stag Party*. He formed a corporation called HMH Publishing, recruited a friend to find investors (including his mother, who put up $1,000), and, after the publisher of an unrelated men's adventure magazine called *Stag* threatened a lawsuit, changed the name to *Playboy*. The first issue, which hit shelves in 1953, featured none other than Marilyn Monroe on the cover; the picture, taken at the Miss America Pageant a year earlier, complemented the magazine's racy centerfold photo of Monroe. The cover price at the time was fifty cents, and, as you may have guessed, the issue was an instant success—selling 50,000 copies in its first few weeks.

With photography expertise from Tom Kelley and promotional efforts that Hefner centered around Monroe, millions of male readers were hooked into subsequent subscriptions of Playboy magazine. By 1975, circulation had reached 5.6 million. By comparison, the iconic business and politics magazine *The Economist*, whose circulation in 1956 was similar to *Playboy*'s, took nearly thirty years to reach just 250,000.[6] Apparently sex sells better than economics.

Clubs, Exclusivity, and "Access"

Playboy was also leveraging its subscription model to expand into other business lines. In 1960, the business launched a new entertainment concept called The Playboy Club, a chain of exclusive nightclubs and resorts open to paying members only. A typical club featured a dining area, living room, bar—and occasionally a casino—where, for $25 per year (about $220 per year in today's dollars), members could hang out and be waited on by Playboy Bunnies who had appeared in the magazine—that is, if members actually visited. In fact, somewhat surprisingly, only about 21 percent of members ever set foot in a club after signing up.

For most, membership to Playboy Clubs offered a status symbol rather than any kind of tangible benefit; but for Hefner and company, the lack of membership usage helped boost the bottom line. As the chain expanded internationally, membership peaked at 750,000,[7] only to gradually disappear by the early 1990s. Interestingly, in 2018, Playboy opened a new club on Manhattan's West Side, the first in New York City in thirty-two years. Fees to this era's version of the club start at $5,000 a year and go up to $100,000—those who opt for the top tier get some cool perks, including chauffeur services to and from the club; ten complimentary nights at a local boutique hotel; ten VIP sports tickets per year in the Playboy seats for either Giants, Jets, Knicks, or Rangers games or the US Open; and a VIP table with bottle service at Playboy events. As of late 2018, women, allegedly, had bought 45 percent of all memberships.[8]

Playboy's current attempt at selling "bunnies" is questionable, given the failure of the initial chain and the brand's positioning in today's #MeToo era. But there are several modern-day iterations of this long-standing type of subscription model, running on the same chassis as *Playboy*, that are booming, including private health clubs, yoga studios, golf clubs, supper clubs, coworking spaces, and upscale business lounges.

While the core offering is different, each of these businesses operates on a member access model that relies on both analyzing subscription revenue from their exclusive enrollments and predicting "breakage"— revenue gained by a merchant through services that customers never claim (i.e., use).[9] Beyond industries like insurance products, home security, and most loyalty card programs—which make a killing off customers not redeeming their points—many lifestyle and fitness clubs have made fortunes using the access model, measuring overall business health by how little their members actually use what they've paid for.

Take a typical gym chain, for instance. It charges on average $50 to $75/month for dreams of a slimmer waistline. The big chains and the boutiques alike all rely heavily on passive consumer behavior (i.e., breakage) to generate profit. The statistics are pretty telling. Gym chains are inundated with new sign-ups in January, driven by New Year's resolutions to get in shape. Of the cohort of new entrants, 80 percent cancel their memberships within five months; only 20 percent use the gym consistently, while about half who sign up never even pass through the turnstiles, period.[10] Gym occupancy, or lack thereof, is therefore key to the business model. In fact, to be profitable, fitness chains need about 10 times as many members as they can actually fit through the doors.[11] In other words, the perfect gym customer is the one who intends to work out, pays to do so, but never does. Sound familiar?

The mix of subscription revenue and consumer laziness is big business. California-based LA Fitness logs about $2 billion in annual revenue. New York-based Equinox Fitness, which includes brands Equinox, Blink Fitness, SoulCycle, and PURE Yoga, does over $1 billion.

Although traditional private golf club memberships across the U.S. have declined since 2011, as aging baby boomers hang up their putters and five-irons, millennials are driving some impressive growth for a new generation of urban and athletic clubs, *sans* golf. Soho House, a group of private clubs founded by English entrepreneur Nick Jones, is one example: Jones opened the first location in London's Soho neighborhood in 1995 and now has almost two dozen clubs around the world, from Los Angeles to Mumbai.[12]

Soho prides itself on crafting a membership list that values creativity over financial success; industries like fashion, media, and the arts are well represented, for example, while membership committees purge applicants in banking and law who don't fit the image the club wants to portray.[13] This filtering strategy continues to drive consumer interest and long waitlists.

Soho has over 70,000 members worldwide who pay thousands of dollars in annual dues for access to a "House," its events and restaurants, the in-house Cowshed spas in certain locales, and more. The group posted $371 million in operating revenue in 2016 (up 20 percent from a year earlier), with about half of that coming from food and beverage sales, which of course are not included in membership fees.[14]

Record Growth

Back in the mid-1950s, another major industry was growing via direct-to-customer subscription: music. The music industry in the '50s was like a teenager going through a growth spurt. Record labels were experimenting with the product they were selling and the way they were selling it, motivated by a desire to capitalize on the emergence of new genres—jazz, funk, and, most important, rock and roll.

At the height of rock pandemonium, a few musical front-runners emerged, such as Chuck Berry, Little Richard, Fats Domino, Jerry Lee Lewis, Sam Cooke, Ray Charles, James Brown, and, of course, a guy named Elvis, who released his first album in 1956. Mainstream music had never heard or seen anything like Elvis Presley before. His pelvic gyrations, stage swagger, and hit-parade crooning would all have significant influence on the next generation of rock and roll, and on the music industry itself. With the flowering of the postwar baby boom, teenagers, especially ones with money, represented an enormous and largely untapped consumer group for record labels like RCA, Capitol Records, and Columbia.

At the same time, the gradual takeover of smaller record-distribution networks by major labels was changing the fundamentals of the music business. Indie labels that had launched the careers of many of these budding musicians quietly began winding down operations in the face of competition from the bigger labels.[15] As independents dissolved, Columbia Records began toying with new strategies and selling methods. When CBS Records formed a new direct-mail division of Columbia—the Columbia Record Club, in 1955—the new subscription club turned the industry upside down.

Columbia began as an experiment in selling music through the mail. To attract attention to the novel program, new members could choose one free monophonic record from a catalogue of jazz, easy-listening, and Broadway show titles. It was a great model that, by the end of its first year, had amassed 128,000 members. With unexpected success on their hands, Columbia management moved fulfillment operations from Manhattan to Terre Haute, Indiana, strategically located closer to major railway lines. Just two years after the move, the club was shipping 7 million records a year, and by 1963, accounted for 10 percent of the entire U.S. recorded music industry.[16]

By the mid-'90s, music clubs accounted for 15 percent of all CD sales worldwide.[17] Columbia captured a sizable portion of the market not only by offering a vast selection of titles, but by making it easy for subscribers to get them—not unlike Netflix, which began selling DVDs through direct mail decades later. In addition to selection and convenience, Columbia also invested in perfecting, analyzing, and optimizing customer preferences. In fact, the Columbia Record Club became one of the first companies to leverage data processing equipment to anticipate changing musical tastes when they invested in computers in 1962.[18] The club evolved over the years, selling various formats and later changing its name to Columbia House. At its peak in 1996, Columbia House was raking in annual profits of $1.4 billion.[19]

But, as Columbia House scaled up—to millions of members—so did the greed of its leadership team. The laser focus on customer acquisition that helped make Columbia House an early pioneer in subscription selling also contributed to its demise. Today, the company is among the most instructive examples for those seeking to understand where big subscription businesses fail.

In fairness to Columbia, there were some market fundamentals at play: by the late 1990s, new innovation in the form of MP3 technology and the rise of sharing software from services like Napster and Kazaa, for example, were chipping away at company market share; Columbia was also hobbled by internet-based retailers like Amazon, and big-box discounters like Walmart. But, while competition and innovation explain some of the company's challenges, the root cause of Columbia's failure was its brutal exploitation of negative option billing, supported by aggressive marketing tactics and a lack of customer service.

Negative option billing is the practice of providing unsolicited goods, and automatically, and often repeatedly, charging the recipient, until they cancel the service. A common example of the practice would be a traditional magazine subscription: after signing up for a fixed period, the reader is assumed to be satisfied with their subscription and can expect to automatically receive issues—unless and until they call to cancel. The tactics of Columbia House, while perhaps kosher in the early days, became increasingly questionable over time, as customer confusion around the company's offering and billing terms set in.

Columbia House was one of the first direct marketers to throw caution to the wind on things like clear and conspicuous messaging, terms and conditions, and customer service. Columbia's model of marketing music (and later movies) for a penny was, legally, onside, but the tactics it used to enrol new members were often deceptive and confusing, such as trumpeting "first eight albums for a penny" while downplaying or omitting the fact that customers were agreeing to receive further albums indefinitely at full price.

The "first album for a penny" incentives worked brilliantly. Dan Ariely, in his book *Predictably Irrational: The Hidden Forces That Shape Our Decisions*, clearly conveys why:

> Most transactions have an upside and a downside, but when something is FREE we forget the downside. FREE! gives us such an emotional charge that we perceive what is being offered as immensely more valuable than it really is. Why? I think it's because humans are intrinsically afraid of loss.... And so, given the choice, we go for what is free.

People took the bait in droves. Little did they know that as soon as they shared their credit card number, they had opted in to not only receive that first shipment of eight albums for a penny, but successive shipments—and subsequent billings at full price, which was even higher than record-store markups.[20] By the time they realized they didn't need or want the second, third, or fourth lot of CDs, it was too late; Columbia House had already dinged their card for $50 to $100. Attempts to dispute these charges were in vain—if a customer was even able to reach Columbia House in the first place.[21]

For years, Columbia executives got away with it. No governing body was paying much attention to how these music clubs were enrolling new customers. Regulatory enforcement by consumer protection watchdogs like the Federal Trade Commission (FTC) simply had other fish to fry; that is, until the late 1970s, when a changing and savvier consumer climate led to higher scrutiny, eventually placing Columbia House in the spotlight.[22]

While the effectiveness of consumer watchdogs helped in the short term, the emergence of online shopping in the '90s and 2000s led to a spike in internet charlatans exploiting the ugly underbelly of negative option billing. Direct mailers looking to take advantage of consumer buying behavior, for example, now had a cheap new platform to advertise shady incentives to hook consumers into recurring billing contracts. And they did just that, conjuring up clever landing pages to sell all kinds of stuff, using free-trial incentives to fix customers into long-term commitments to everything from teeth whitener, vitamins, and weight-loss items (remember Açai berries?) to business opportunity scams, free credit reports, and more. It was the Wild West of online selling.

Millions fell for these scams, typing in credit card information in return for a trial shipment of a diet powder for pennies on the dollar, for example, only to realize months later—usually by the shock value of their Visa statement—that they had been swindled into a monthly shipment of Açai at full price. Online scammers selling the stuff usually had no customer service number, formal address, or general company website. As soon as they began to see customer complaint and chargeback (a formal transaction dispute initiated by a credit card issuer) levels rise, they would shut down business operations, their registered PO box, and anything else tied to the underlying corporation—just in time to flee offshore with a bag full of cash.

In the late 2000s, consumers again began flooding the FTC with complaints of these types of fraudulent, deceptive, and unfair online business practices. As a result, a number of bad apples received significant fines. In 2009, for instance, the FTC accepted a $1 million settlement from an outfit called Commerce Planet, which had been offering a "free" online auction kit to trick customers into an "online supplier" program that came with monthly fees of $59.95.[23] Other FTC actions led to lawsuits that in rare cases even resulted in owner imprisonment; yet hundreds of other online merchants got away with shady business practices, vanishing without a trace to places like Panama or the Cayman Islands before the FTC could catch up with them.

The negative option billing practice itself isn't illegal. Several mainstream industries—such as insurance, financial services, web hosting, digital music subscriptions, and other online services like dating websites and paywalled news sites, etc.—operate using the same negative option umbrella.

Which begs the question: What's the difference between a mainstream corporation using the same billing model as the guy who's skipped off to Panama to avoid the FTC? The answer is tied to a legit product or service, supported by an acceptable level of customer service, governed by a company whose offer terms are fully transparent and understood by the customer it's selling to.

Customer complaints stemming from automatic billing are just as much a reality for blue chips like Verizon or Allstate as they are for online upstarts looking to build their business off the same billing model. The difference is in the company's inherent approach to customer service and satisfaction. Great companies make it easy for their customers to reach them.

I know, you're sitting there hemming and hawing over your cell-phone carrier and their overage charges. I'm not denying these annoyances exist. However, if you want to air your grievances, you can do it. Just call the toll-free number, and you'll get a poor agent on the line who has to listen to you vent. And, although it may not seem like it at times, given the dizzying array of plans and add-ons, their in-house legal teams make it a priority to communicate their billing plans transparently. It is their job, in fact, to ensure consumers know exactly what they're getting and how much they're paying for it.

When it comes to servicing the customer, transparency is key to staying out of trouble. Problems arise when companies like Columbia House and Commerce Planet abuse negative option billing by obscuring intentions. Contentious cases often center on solicitation lost in fine print, or the misinterpretation of what's on offer. Such was the case in the 1980s, when numerous cable companies got into trouble by ducking around required terms in order to automatically sign new subscribers up to additional tiers of service without consent, thereby ringing in substantial revenue.

In Canada, a national cable provider (as a nice Canadian, I won't name them, but any fellow Canuck can guess who I'm talking about) provided 7.5 million subscribers seven new specialty channels—for a free "trial period"—in 2014. However, when the trial period expired, the company began billing for the channels automatically, without subscribers' consent. At the peak of the ensuing outrage, the company was receiving 100,000 complaints a week, and several members of Parliament were swamped with calls from angry consumers.[24]

Concern about negative option billing is ongoing. The most fraudulent version (when recipients of wholly unsolicited products are then billed for them) is illegal in Canada; in the U.S., the FTC requires any business that offers a negative option plan to clearly and conspicuously indicate "purchase obligations, cancellation procedures, the frequency with which members must reject shipments, and how to eventually cancel a membership."[25]

But most subscription companies use negative option appropriately. They are forthright in their terms and conditions, marketing and promotional material, and FAQ pages. They also usually provide customer service at above-average to exceptional levels through live agents, live chat, support forums, email, and more. As a result, these companies benefit from lower than average complaint levels, low refund ratios, and low chargebacks, while garnering higher levels of customer satisfaction.

SO, WHAT happened to Columbia House? The company was the target of a number of lawsuits alleging fraudulent business practices, ranging from hidden shipping fees to fraudulent sale of debt to unauthorized credit card charges. It pivoted to DVDs-only in 2010 but filed for bankruptcy five years later, its assets of $2 million smothered by $63 million of debt. In 2011, a nation-wide class-action suit was filed against Columbia House seeking monetary damages and an injunction stopping the company's parent, Direct Brands Inc., from the alleged business practices of unauthorized credit card charges, inability to cancel, unwanted products being mailed to homes, and several other issues.

At the time, it attributed its decline to the rise of "streaming."[26] (Nice try.) Today Sony Music owns the Columbia House trademark, and Columbiahouse.com still sells DVDs for $9.95. I think the company still has one customer in Idaho.

THREE

Amazon Pioneers Customer Centricity

JEFF BEZOS launched Amazon.com from his garage in 1994, when the internet was still in its infancy. It seems unbelievable today, but at the time, selling things in "cyberspace" was considered a dicey proposition. Nearly twenty-five years later, shares of the Seattle-based juggernaut trade at nearly $2,000, contributing to a market cap of almost $1 trillion, making Bezos the world's wealthiest individual.[1]

You'd be right to attribute the incredible success of Amazon to Bezos's timing and foresight, and his ability to take big risks. But his (wildly profitable) genius wasn't just realizing that people would start shopping online. Bezos saw something deeper, before most. He saw that the internet would shift power away from big corporations, and into the hands of the consumer. He was right, and it's this kind of insight that remains the driving force behind Amazon's obsession with customer loyalty.

Since the beginning, Amazon has been relentless in providing customers with exactly what they want, lest they take their business somewhere else with just a click of a button. As the company has evolved they've managed to do it faster than anybody else, yet the focus on the customer has never wavered. As a former Amazon VP, Brian Krueger, explains it, "Jeff highly values the customer, probably more than any CEO I know, large company or small." [2] This fixation on the customer is the foundation of Amazon's rise to global dominance—and underlies the most successful subscription service in the world, Amazon Prime.

Customer Obsession

After graduating from Princeton, Bezos worked on Wall Street at investment firm D.E. Shaw & Co., where he was promoted to senior VP by the age of thirty. After four years at the firm he left in 1994 to move to Seattle, Washington. There he began putting together a business plan for what would eventually become a company worth more than Walmart, Target, Macy's, Kroger, Nordstrom, Tiffany & Co., Coach, Tesco, Ikea, Williams & Sonoma, and The Gap combined.

Although the internet was intriguing to some in the mid-1990s, it was still pretty esoteric—and a topic that journalists and business analysts seldom took seriously. Projections about e-commerce in general varied; Bezos, however, was bullish about the web's prospects and its probable impact on just about every business sector, including consumer retail.

Despite the general belief that Amazon was the first to sell books on the internet, a company in Silicon Valley called Computer Literacy actually began selling books via email in 1991. So credit for first category entrant doesn't go to Bezos. Yet unlike the first mover, Amazon did execute, scale, and ultimately pave the way for not only selling paperbacks, but just about every SKU (stock keeping unit) in existence, via a few clicks.

Initially, Bezos wanted to name the company Cadabra, but was advised against the moniker because it sounded too much like "cadaver." Playing with alternatives, he then purchased the URL relentless.com and incorporated under the same name, but to his dismay, some of his friends remarked that it sounded too sinister. (Relentless.com is still owned by Bezos and redirects to Amazon.com.)[3]

He finally settled on Amazon. Before Google's complex algorithms arrived in 1998, search engines would arrange links alphabetically, so Bezos thought having an "A" name would be advantageous. He also liked the fact that his company was named after the world's longest river, suggesting how big the company could become.[4]

He started making lists of products he believed would sell well online, then narrowed it down to 5 SKUS—CDs, computer hardware, computer software, videos, and books. He settled on books because they were cheap, easy to recognize, and lightweight— (still, by the way, a good formula for any entrepreneur thinking of starting an e-commerce business). The first iteration of Amazon.com launched in July of 1995 labeling itself as "Earth's biggest bookstore," with over 1 million titles in its catalogue.

The first transaction recorded through the web store was a copy of Douglas Hofstadter's *Fluid Concepts and Creative Analogies: Computer Models of the Fundamental Mechanisms of Thought*, purchased by Jon Wainwright, a computer scientist in California.[5]

What was interesting about Amazon, even from the beginning, was its promise to customers. Amazon's differentiating proposition (and what ultimately pushed Computer Literacy to the sidelines) was the promise to deliver any book, in any category, anywhere to readers. This "overpromise and overdeliver" strategy showed that Amazon was not just a bookseller, but a refreshing online company going above and beyond for the consumer.

Amazon drove orders almost immediately, relying on book distributors and wholesalers to rapidly fulfill purchases as they came in. Although the numbers grew quickly, bookstore chains such as Barnes & Noble and Waldenbooks still held stable ground, and the size of the online market in general remained uncertain. Financial columnists were divided on where Amazon fit into the whole equation. Skeptics couldn't make sense of Amazon or its business strategy; they claimed the online retailer was in too deep, and would ultimately lose out to big-box paperback sellers.

The lack of company profits in the early days seemed to justify the skeptics' position, but Bezos dismissed doubters, pointing to a lack of understanding of the massive potential of the internet. He argued that to succeed, a company like his needed to "get big fast," and that meant scaling quickly, reinvesting every last dollar into the business, and ignoring profitability in the interest of growing the top line.

Despite pessimism from the media, along with the high infrastructure costs of pre-broadband internet, Amazon grew fast. By December 1996, it had nearly $16 million in sales and 180,000 customer accounts—astounding figures for a young company entering its second full year of operations.

Seeing an opportunity to capitalize on Amazon's early momentum, Bezos gathered his top executives, underwriters, and lawyers to get an IPO rolling in 1997. Amazon went public that May, less than two years after opening its virtual doors. Settling on an opening price of $18 a share, Amazon raised $54 million on the NASDAQ, giving the company a market value of $438 million.[6]

Now a public company, Bezos was even more insistent on building Amazon with certain core principles in place:

1. Customer Obsession
2. Frugality
3. Bias for Action
4. Ownership
5. High Bar for Talent
6. Innovation[7]

As Amazon has grown into one of the biggest global success stories in retail history, customer obsession, at the top of the list, stands out time and again. In a recent letter to shareholders, Bezos wrote about the benefits of a business centered on customers, rather than on products, technology, or competitors:

> There are many advantages to a customer-centric approach, but here's the big one: customers are *always* beautifully, wonderfully dissatisfied, even when they report being happy and business is great. Even when they don't yet know it, customers want something better, and your desire to delight customers will drive you to invent on their behalf. No customer ever asked Amazon to create the Prime membership program, but it sure turns out they wanted it .... Experiment patiently, accept failures, plant seeds, protect saplings, and double-down when you see customer delight.[8]

The Dot-Com Bubble

In 1998, the year after its IPO, Amazon expanded beyond books. With the addition of music and video, sales leapt to $610 million. The next year it broadened the product line again, this time adding consumer electronics, video games, software, home-improvement items, toys and games, and more.

It was the beginning of the dot-com boom. Times were good for online companies like Amazon. So much so that Bezos landed himself a spot on the cover of *Time* magazine, as 1999's Person of the Year. Many online companies, perhaps inspired by Bezos's new celebrity, sprang into being, determined to take advantage of the influx of venture capital and the ramp-up in dot-com valuations.

To paint a relative picture, Apple stock wasn't in favor; it was a struggling hardware company. Facebook didn't exist. Google and Netflix were around, but weren't publicly traded yet; Google had just landed a $25 million round of funding and Netflix was building its business on the back of DVDs by mail.

As investor exuberance swelled, dependable companies like Oracle, Intel, Cisco, and Microsoft saw stock prices soar. Though of course, so too did a boatload of worthless stocks. Times were good for just about anybody willing to register a URL and draft a slide deck with some projections.

Soon it became apparent that many of these companies, including names like eToys and Pets.com, had no real business model. The NASDAQ began to reflect as much, dropping from 5,132 in March of 2000 to 1,470 a few months later. Many investors had taken a round trip from zero to unimaginable heights and back down again. The dot-com bubble had burst.

Most of the big names of that era, such as Lycos, Netscape, Infoseek, and CDnow, turned into colossal failures. The complete list of bankruptcies is too long to feature here, but highlights include fashion retail site Boo.com, which burned through $135 million of venture capital in eighteen months; food delivery failure Webvan, created by Louis Borders (of Borders bookstore fame); and Mark Cuban's baby, Broadcast.com, which was acquired by Yahoo! for $5.7 billion.[9] Sadly for Yahoo!, the company never took off—although Mark's career as a TV celebrity and NBA owner certainly did. Talk about selling at "the high."

Unique among the carnage, Bezos and Amazon not only survived but flourished in the wake of the tech disaster. How? One of the reasons was that Amazon raised money at just the right time—only a month before the crash—which helped insulate the company from further financial exposure. Former Amazon CFO Warren Jenson decided the company needed a stronger cash position as a hedge against the possibility that suppliers might request more favorable payment terms. Tapping into overseas markets, Amazon sold $672 million in convertible bonds to investors, even as the global economy teetered on the brink of recession.[10]

The importance of Jenson's foresight and bond issue can't be overstated. Sure, Amazon was already changing e-commerce while converting traffic to dollars. Moreover, its revenue growth and cash conversion cycle indicated it had a working business model—a delight compared with the basket of other dot-coms whose CEOs were, according to many accounts, spending VC (venture capital) money on lavish parties, sex workers, and private jets (not kidding). But most of what made Amazon into the behemoth we know today—namely, Marketplace, Prime, and Amazon Web Services—was invented after the bubble. Suffice it to say, without Jenson's bond issue, Amazon might not be here today.

Prime and the Flywheel

Today, Amazon Prime is one of the best-known subscription models in the world. The service launched back in 2005, offering members free and unlimited two-day shipping on over 100 million items. In most countries, membership now also includes unlimited Kindle ebooks, and access to streaming music and video (among other benefits).

The introduction of free two-day shipping transformed fast, affordable delivery from an occasional indulgence to an everyday experience, helping Prime to quickly attract tens of thousands of members. As Amazon expanded into international markets like Japan, the United Kingdom, France, Canada, and others over the next decade, Prime membership numbers grew to tens of millions. As of April 2018, more than 100 million people worldwide can call themselves Prime subscribers, including as many as 60 percent of U.S. households, according to some estimates[11]—that's more than the 44 percent that have a gun.

A few years ago Bezos famously said that his goal with Prime was "to make sure that if you are not a Prime member, you are being irresponsible."[12] It appears he's well on his way to making that statement an undisputed fact. The *business* of Prime is staggering:

- Of Americans who earn over $150,000 a year, 70 percent of those who shop online have Prime memberships.

- Globally, Prime shipped more than 5 billion items in 2017.

- Prime members spend an average of $1,400 a year on Amazon—nearly twice the average of a regular Amazon customer.

- 73 percent of 30-day-trial subscribers pay for the first full year of membership; 91 percent of first-year paid subscribers renew for a second year, and 96 percent of second-year paid subscribers renew for a third year.[13]

While member loyalty continues to drive a good portion of the growth, the average ticket of a Prime subscriber (approaching $1400 per year) is key to Amazon's ability to offer more, for less.

WHEN SUBSCRIPTION-BASED businesses fail, it's often due to high customer acquisition cost, poor retention, low customer lifetime values, and a lack of loyalty. (These factors kill off many traditional retailers too.) The brilliance of Prime is that it creates a flywheel effect, boosting all these metrics simultaneously.

Once on board, Prime subscribers not only order more often, but they also start buying things they probably wouldn't have otherwise, to justify their membership cost (in the U.S., currently $119 a year). This phenomenon, by design, of course, boosts Prime retention and loyalty. And with Amazon.com being the principal driver of Prime memberships, Amazon capitalizes on another advantage—low customer acquisition costs.

There are more advantages to the Amazon flywheel. Prime members not only spend more on Amazon than its regular customers do, but they use more of Amazon's services, such as Prime Video and Amazon Fresh. This Amazon cycle, let's call it, also works in reverse: customers come in the media door, for instance, via Prime Video, and ultimately spend more across the general marketplace.

In essence, Amazon Prime is one of the most effective physical/digital hybrid membership programs globally—where users enter through whatever door is open—be it Prime Video, Marketplace, or otherwise—only to find themselves right at home in every room. Sheer genius.

Video in Demand

Not content with reshaping the retail world, Amazon is also turning itself into a media giant. The move into digital media isn't just a cool thing to offer millennials; it is a highly calculated strategy. More Prime Video subscribers means more revenue for Amazon, in the form of more purchases made on the Amazon platform. Even in isolation, Prime Video is a huge catalyst for current and future growth: forecasters predict that by 2022, Prime Video subscribers will number 56 million in the U.S. and 122 million worldwide.[14]

Prime Video was created in 2006, the perfect time to capitalize on two evolving and interconnected trends: the increasing popularity of television (shows, that is), and the changing ways viewers consume content.

For decades, A-list movie actors shunned TV. Movies were the pinnacle of success, and actors caught slumming on TV shows were seen as "has-beens." That phenomenon began to change over a decade ago. As TV on demand evolved, Hollywood heavyweights were changing their tune and gravitating toward serialized television: Kevin Spacey and Robin Wright in *House of Cards*; Matthew McConaughey and Woody Harrelson in *True Detective*; Jessica Lange, Kathy Bates, and Angela Bassett in *American Horror Story*, etc. Bezos took notice—TV shows were beginning to steal the spotlight.

As individuals across North America tossed popcorn and movie tickets aside for binge-watching sessions of *Breaking Bad*, streaming television gave consumers the flexibility and wealth of content they desired. Amazon saw an opportunity to capitalize on the changing behavior, and in turn, doubled down on Prime Video, knowing that the media business would grow over time.

As media relationships go, Amazon and Netflix have an interesting one. Although Prime Video and Netflix bid against one another on the supply side for content, they don't necessarily compete for consumers. Bezos suggests the two platforms can easily live side by side. And so far, the data says he's right.

Since Prime Video debuted, both platforms have continued to grow their subscriber base. More telling is research that says there is "high overlap" among subscribers to Netflix and other streaming video services, especially Prime Video. In the U.S. and U.K., half of subscribers to Netflix also subscribe to Prime Video.[15] Fees to both are modest and most popular content is exclusive to a single platform, so if customers want to watch *House of Cards* (on Netflix) and *Patriot* (on Prime Video), for example, it's easy for people to justify signing up for both.

While both Netflix and Amazon are profiting from the shift to on-demand viewing, only Amazon can leverage its additional assets to boost overall customer-lifetime-value dollars. Netflix has a ton of members and a slick recommendation engine, but it can't sell you a purse after you've watched *Stranger Things*. Capitalizing on this flywheel effect provides Amazon with a distinct and impenetrable advantage over the long term.

Subscribe and Save

As Amazon attempts to migrate more and more users over to Prime, the company's subscription tentacles extend to the general online marketplace as well. In fact, the company has been tinkering with the automation and delivery of household goods for over a decade.

Amazon's "Subscribe and Save" program is basically a milkman for the twenty-first century. Introduced in 2007, the subscription play lets consumers sign up to have everyday consumables delivered regularly, with a price discount of 5 to 15 percent. Customers choose from a list of eligible items, set a desired frequency from one to six months, and Amazon automatically creates and sends orders. It's convenient for those who prefer to have paper towels or diapers sent regularly, rather than having to think about monitoring and replenishing if they run out. You might not have known you could do this, or even that you wanted automatic shipments of things like milk and baby wipes, but the idea is likely to cross your mind the next time you have to run out at 10 PM to get 'em. It's no surprise that the offering has quietly ballooned over the last decade into one of the largest subscription programs globally for consumer staples.

More recently, Amazon added another subscription service to its impressive mix, called Prime Pantry. Available only to Prime members, customers pay an extra $5 a month for the ability to shop for non-perishable household items in "everyday package sizes" (one box of cereal, a box of Oreos, etc.) and ship orders of over $10 for free.

Programs such as Subscribe and Save offer a broader indication that shopping behavior, in general, is changing even with boring items like detergents, body soap, peanut butter, and gardening seeds (all things you can "subscribe to" on Amazon). It's all part of a shift toward subscriber-based consumerism.

RETAILERS SEEM to cringe every time Amazon introduces a new business line like Prime or Subscribe and Save, and rightly so— Amazon is the bully in the retail schoolyard. As Bezos prioritizes Amazon Prime and uses other business lines like Subscribe and Save to drive more of its growth, the rest of retail can only hope to stay afloat.

The most worrying research from the competition's point of view suggests that once Amazon's Prime members are hooked, they tend to stop shopping anywhere else. They assume Amazon's prices are competitive, and don't bother to search for comparisons. In fact, if they spot something at another retailer, they are more likely to see if Amazon sells the item first, rather than buy it elsewhere.

It doesn't stop there. The list of perks that comes with a Prime membership is growing, and current members (an engaged bunch) still register low on the consumer awareness scale. Things like Prime Wardrobe, Prime Reading, and lengthy free trials to the *Washington Post* (which Bezos now owns) are all value-adds that Prime consumers typically don't know about—yet. So as Amazon turns up the marketing volume to highlight these additional benefits, Prime's value proposition increases.

Notwithstanding the above, Amazon has yet to fully exploit several other ways Prime can evolve and add value. Awareness is still low for Amazon Music, its Spotify-like streaming service, which grants Prime members free access to well over 1 million songs. The same is true for Amazon channels, where users can watch shows and movies from HBO, SHOWTIME, and STARZ. And the potential of Amazon Echo, the smart speakers, in combination with Alexa, the virtual assistant, is vast—both technologies are sure to become more sophisticated in enabling (and motivating) customer orders. Even with a third of the U.S. on Prime, the upside for further growth is still significant.

The retail industry has grown by about 4 percent over the past few years. Yet Amazon Prime's compound annual growth rate is roughly 21 percent in the U.S. and a whopping 58 percent internationally. Amazon reigns supreme in retail e-commerce, owning 38 percent of online sales over the holiday season; the next nine companies on the list account for 20 percent combined.[16] If retail is a zero sum game, and Amazon is growing at this kind of a clip, who is losing? Just about anyone trying to compete.

AWS—Another Amazon Weapon

A year after launching its Prime program, perhaps the most successful subscription program for consumers to date, Amazon launched Amazon Web Services (AWS), the platform-as-a-service arm of Amazon.com, with little fanfare. Even Bezos himself, who had the early vision of turning a book idea into the "Earth's biggest store," couldn't have foreseen the trajectory his cloud services business would take. It's clear now, though, that AWS was a monumental shift for a company focused initially on retail e-commerce.

AWS allows individuals, companies, and even governments to buy storage space to hold a database, bandwidth to host a website, or processing power to run complex software remotely. It lets companies like Netflix and Airbnb, as well as individuals like you and me, host complex software or large amounts of data without having to buy, house, and maintain costly hardware. The AWS technology lives at server farms across the globe. Subscribers can reserve virtual computers or dedicated real-life machines, individually or in clusters, and Amazon manages, upgrades, and provides industry-standard security to each subscriber's system. Fees are based on factors like usage, chosen features, required availability, redundancy, security, and service options.

Although the cloud infrastructure play flies under the consumer radar, it is a killer whale: as of 2018, AWS was the fifth-largest business software provider in the world, and "far and away the leading provider of cloud infrastructure technology."[17] In mid-2018, AWS was responsible for 34 percent of "the entire cloud-computing services market," according to Synergy Research Group, well ahead of Microsoft at 11 percent, Google at 8 percent, and IBM at 6 percent.[18] AWS revenue for 2018 was astonishing, about $26 billion (up 30 percent from the previous year).[19] Even more notable is the balance of Amazon's total revenue—AWS accounts for about 10 percent of the top line, and nearly 70 percent of its bottom-line profit.[20] As one analyst put it, AWS provides Amazon with "a level of profitability that it can't find anywhere else."[21]

The Birth of AWS

One of the tropes in the business zeitgeist is "take what's already built and see if you can sell it to others." Such was the case for Amazon, which first began allowing outsiders to access its internal services in 2000 with the launch of Amazon Marketplace, a platform for third-party retailers to sell goods via Amazon.com.[22] Amazon was a far different company back then, struggling with the operational challenges that stem from scaling up. As a small part of its coping strategy, the company began building more internal systems to deal with the hypergrowth.

With the precedent of Marketplace, and the infrastructure in place, the seeds of AWS were planted a few years later, in 2003, during an executive brainstorming session at Bezos's home. The team did an exercise to identify the company's core competencies. Beyond the obvious e-commerce strengths (massive product selection, quick and cheap fulfillment, customer-centric service), they identified a set of capabilities the company hadn't properly considered: the sophisticated technological infrastructure it had built to power Amazon.[23]

The team didn't fully articulate a business plan at that meeting, but they did realize that the company was proficient at running the tech infrastructure for its internal business. As Andy Jassy, the current CEO of AWS, recalls, "In retrospect it seems fairly obvious, but at the time I don't think we had ever really internalized that." Later that year they fleshed out the idea to carve out a separate business line that would provide this same service to others—essentially an operating system for the world of the internet. According to Jassy, "We realized we could contribute all of those key components of that internet operating system, and with that, we went to pursue this much broader mission, which is AWS today, a platform that allows any organization or company or any developer to run their technology applications on top of our technology infrastructure platform."[24]

In 2006, Amazon's S3 (Simple Storage Service) and EC2 (Elastic Compute Cloud) were the first of its cloud infrastructure services to hit the market. Amazon now offered scalable, hassle-free storage and computing, the foundation for pretty much anything a company or individual could do on the web, from hosting web pages to training artificial intelligence.[25]

Before sophisticated cloud infrastructure, companies had to find a server provider, choose a machine, and pay for the data and the bandwidth that accessed it. It was inefficient and expensive, and sites would notoriously crash amid surges in traffic—as Twitter experienced during the 2010 World Cup, when the site crashed several times due to a lack of server power.[26] Dropbox, an AWS customer until 2017 when it moved onto its own bespoke server infrastructure, experienced similar woes before moving some of its needs over to Amazon.

According to aws.amazon.com, AWS now offers over 125 fully featured services—for computing, storage, databases, networking, analytics, machine learning and artificial intelligence (AI), Internet of Things (IoT), mobile, security, hybrid, virtual and augmented reality (VR and AR), media, and application development, deployment, and management, all from fifty-five "availability zones" within eighteen geographic regions around the world, including the U.S., Australia, Brazil, Canada, China, France, Germany, India, Ireland, Japan, Korea, Singapore, and the U.K., with locations slated to open in Bahrain, Cape Town, Hong Kong, and Milan.

Friends of AWS

Earlier, we touched on the supposed potential rivalry between Prime Video and Netflix, especially from the viewpoint of consumer behavior and original content. However, Bezos's suggestion that Netflix and Prime Video are complementary has another intriguing component: Netflix is an Amazon customer.

Unknown to most, Netflix is the most prominent user of AWS. It began using the platform for much of its back-end infrastructure in 2009, and in 2015 moved the remainder onto AWS servers, going "all-in."[27] Netflix stores and streams its content from the same servers as Amazon Prime Video. That means that the 35 percent of network traffic in North America that is coming from Netflix is ultimately coming from Amazon servers.

Beyond Netflix, the AWS customer list consists of enterprises like Intuit, Hertz, and Time Inc., which all trust Amazon with their entire IT operations, including transactions and customer databases. In July 2018, 21st Century Fox announced that it would migrate the vast majority of its key platforms to the Amazon cloud, and leverage AWS's machine learning and data analytics services across its brands. Other trusted clients include Adobe, Airbnb, Yelp, the U.K. Ministry of Justice, NASA's Jet Propulsion Laboratory, and even Salesforce, another dominant force in the world of cloud services.

The media got wind of a partnership between the two cloud kings in 2016, when both companies announced that AWS would become the official "preferred public cloud infrastructure provider" to Salesforce.[28] The deal would see Salesforce spend about $400 million on AWS services over the next four years. The exact shape of the deal has since become clearer, with Salesforce announcing in 2018 that its products would be connected to various AWS products, including the integration of Service Cloud Einstein with Amazon Connect to allow Salesforce customers to "set up and manage a customer contact center in minutes."[29]

On the flip side, Amazon, which has less to lose in all of this, has extended an olive branch to Salesforce's chief Marc Benioff by choosing Salesforce as its company-wide customer platform.

Salesforce has stated that it is moving away from developing and providing cloud infrastructure that would compete with AWS, due to the overwhelming success of Amazon's foray into the space and the limits of its own capabilities in the face of Amazon growth. In a bit of a "if you can't beat 'em join 'em" play, Benioff smartly got into bed with Bezos before there was any real threat to his own long-standing cloud business. A year after the partnership was announced, Benioff said, "At Salesforce, we really strongly believe that the enemy of my enemy is my friend, and I think that makes Amazon Web Services our best friend."[30]

A Cloudy Forecast

Making predictions is notoriously difficult given how the tech world loves to move fast and break things. But there are a few broad trends we can expect to see develop with AWS and cloud computing: growth from government clients, the expansion of digital assistants, a renewable-energy push, and the increasing prominence of Chinese competitors.

As more American departments follow the lead of the U.K. Ministry of Justice and move their data into the cloud, AWS is poised to capture a major chunk of the expanding market. The U.S. government currently spends about $80 billion each year on technology. AWS has positioned itself to take advantage, in both a tech and physical sense. The largest number of AWS employees outside of Seattle is in the town of Herndon, Virginia,[31] less than a ten-minute drive from Washington, D.C.'s Dulles Airport—and that's even before Amazon announced that its second "headquarters" would be partially in Arlington, Virginia, even closer to D.C.

There's a lot of excitement around AI-powered digital assistants such as Salesforce's Einstein, Google Assistant, and, of course, Alexa, which is seeing heavy investment from Amazon. Although Alexa "isn't the brightest assistant in the room," as one pundit says, it is already superior to Apple's Siri, and in the same league as Google Assistant.[32] But in the long run, expect Alexa to come out ahead. After all, it's Amazon.

We can expect Alexa to continue to evolve by drawing on the artificial intelligence and machine-learning platforms of AWS. With such a powerful resource, Alexa is likely to leave the confines of the home and start chipping away at Skype, Cortana, Einstein, Watson, and others as it infiltrates offices everywhere. Richard Windsor, an analyst at Edison Investment Research, predicts that "Alexa for Business will allow businesses to build their own skills for the digital assistant that can be used in a work context.... This has the scope to both generate more skills and applications for the Alexa digital assistant but also to generate increasing loyalty to AWS."[33]

As it works to expand Alexa's capabilities, AWS will also continue its push into new areas like energy. The company already operates numerous solar and wind farms, and will move to build on its vision to achieve "100% renewable energy usage for our global infrastructure footprint."[34] AWS already has partnerships in place with renewable energy providers including Community Energy Solar in Virginia and Tesla.

Can AWS hold on to its dominant market share as the cloud sector grows? There are other big names gunning for market share in the Western Hemisphere, like Microsoft, Google, Oracle, and IBM, to name a few. With $26 billion in annual revenue, growing at 40 percent plus per year, it's hard to see Amazon slowing down on domestic soil.[35] But, while Jassy and team aren't likely to get disturbed at home, there's a new kid on the cloud block that could chip away at global market share.

Alibaba Cloud is growing at a faster clip than not only Amazon, but Microsoft, IBM, and Google. The cloud-computing arm of the Chinese e-commerce giant now has regional headquarters in Dubai, Frankfurt, Hong Kong, London, New York, Paris, Sydney, and Tokyo, in addition to its base in Singapore. It grew over 100 percent in 2017, with an annual run rate around $4.4 billion.[36]

That figure may pale in comparison to AWS, but Alibaba didn't dedicate substantial resources to its cloud business until 2015. Since then, however, the company has kicked things into high gear in the face of favorable market conditions, which should compel competitors to take Alibaba Cloud president Simon Hu and his team seriously.

The sheer potential of Alibaba's total addressable market is vast. Most of its business is in China and the surrounding region, a huge and underexploited market certain to foster continued growth for the company, as well as the two other Chinese cloud leaders, China Telecom and games giant Tencent. Unlike in the West, where AWS built its cloud business with start-up clients, the Chinese cloud began almost in reverse, with larger companies like Taobao and Alibaba's e-commerce marketplace. As the small-to medium-sized business market continues to grow in China in sectors like financial services and emerging tech, a move to the cloud is inevitable. While Chinese companies have so far been slow to the cloud, the nation is now third in the world for venture capital investment in advanced tech like artificial intelligence.[37] Alibaba is likely to capitalize on this funding momentum.

And then there's the public sector. The cloud will be a key part of China's Belt and Road Initiative, President Xi Jinping's ambitious infrastructure plan to connect his country with other parts of Asia, Europe, and Africa.[38] Moreover, the Chinese Ministry of Industry and Information Technology said in 2018 that it planned to increase the cloud industry more than two-and-a-half times over 2015 levels by 2019.[39]

While Alibaba is enjoying the spoils of exponential growth in its home market, foreign rivals like Amazon will be kept to the sidelines. As it stands, Chinese law forbids foreign cloud companies from building data centers in the country unless they link up with Chinese-owned partners.[40] While not insurmountable, it is an obstacle that's sure to slow Amazon's efforts in China.

As the global market for cloud services spreads, Chinese and Western providers are bound to run into each other eventually. Simon Hu says he's confident Alibaba will be able to surpass AWS in due time, but even in the face of that kind of hubris it's hard to take a short position on Amazon. Jassy has come a long way since 2003's brainstorm at Casa de Bezos. He's not likely to give up pole position.

FOUR

Netflix Chills TV

WHAT DO THESE popular TV shows have in common? *House of Cards*, *Stranger Things*, *Ozark*, *Orange is the New Black*, and *Chef's Table*. Correct—they are all on Netflix. They are also Netflix Originals.

Netflix was expected to spend $12 to 13 billion on content in 2018, as much as a one-third increase from the year before.[1] The streaming giant now produces shows in twenty-one countries, in multiple languages. Globally, it is producing or procuring 700 new or exclusively licenced television shows, including more than 100 scripted dramas and comedies, dozens of documentaries and children's shows, stand-up comedy specials, and unscripted reality and talk shows. Netflix now produces more television than any other network, and was slated to produce eighty-two movies in 2018, more than any studio in Hollywood—the next most was twenty-three from Warner Brothers.[2] It's an incredible evolution for a company that began in 1997 renting DVDs through the mail.

Thanks to the vision of CEO/co-founder Reed Hastings, Netflix has continually evolved its business model, and successfully executed several critical business pivots along the way. Shortly after launching the novel mail-order DVD business, it broke new ground with its no-late-fee subscriptions in 1999, six years before

Blockbuster introduced a watered-down version of the promise. As broadband technology improved, Netflix began offering downloadable movies, and evolved again when it pivoted into online streaming. The move to original content production started with Netflix exclusives like the Emmy Award–winning *House of Cards*, the first season of which was released in 2013 in its entirety—an innovative move at the time.

Producing *House of Cards* and signing Kevin Spacey and Robin Wright back when broadcast television had all the clout was seen as something of a coup for Netflix. Today, Americans aged twelve to twenty-four watch less than half as much broadcast TV as they did in 2010, and those between the ages of twenty-five and thirty-four are watching 40 percent less.[3] In other words, millennials, the largest demographic segment driving the company's growth, spend more time watching Netflix than they do all network or cable TV combined. If Netflix had rested on its laurels, the company would no doubt be alongside Blockbuster as a thing of the past.

The current value proposition Netflix peddles is simple: a massive, effectively unlimited selection of movies and TV shows—increasingly, many of which you can't get anywhere else—for about $10 a month. The mix of quality and quantity is working, not only at home but abroad: at the end of 2018 Netflix reported 139 million subscribers across 190 countries, with less than half (60 million) in the U.S.[4] In the fourth quarter of 2017, the company notched its most subscriber additions ever for a three-month period, 8.33 million, only to add another 7.4 million subscribers in the first quarter of 2018.

By comparison, Netflix's closest streaming competitor, Hulu (jointly owned by Disney, Fox, Comcast, and Turner) has about 20 million subscribers, about one-third of Netflix's U.S. base.

Netflix is now part of the FAANG club (with Facebook, Apple, Amazon, and Google), the exclusive class of world-dominating tech companies whose market cap as of March 2019, according to online sources, was U.S. $3.1 trillion. And arguably, it's done better than all of them at managing its brand reputation, so far eluding the criticism or scandals that have plagued the others, such as privacy intrusions (Facebook and Google), elitism and a "walled garden" mentality (Apple), links with depression (Facebook), labour violations (Amazon), and promotion of hatred and propaganda (Facebook again—there's not enough room in this book to slam Facebook properly). In 2004, Netflix was sued for false advertising in claims of "unlimited rentals" with "one-day delivery," and there have been some copyright violations, but overall, Netflix has steered well clear of controversy to focus on its core objective of filling everyone's leisure time.

Investors have noticed. Although there was some volatility in the third quarter of 2018, the NASDAQ-listed stock price has seen compound annual growth rates (CAGR) of approximately 52 percent over a five-year period.

SEVERAL FACTORS have contributed to Netflix's success. It benefitted from years of uncontested leadership in the OTT (over-the-top, i.e., direct-to-consumer, streaming) sector. The company inked some good deals with suppliers to gain access to large volumes of high-quality content, and also produced great originals that subscribers love. Most important, they built a great business by making bold predictions on consumer trends, and then tailoring their offering through iterating on personalization algorithms, informed by intensive analysis of reams of user data. The result is a stable cash flow–generating subscription machine with minimal member churn.

Hastings has done well to make his brand both valuable and likeable. But, as always, there's way more to the story of how Netflix turned a subscription-based business model into a global entertainment giant.

Kibbles 'n' Discs

In the late 1990s, the DVD (digital video disc) began to replace the ubiquitous VHS tape as the format of choice for home movie watchers. People took notice of its superior picture and sound quality, and began to trade their clunky old VCRs for DVD players.

In California, Reed Hastings and Marc Randolph, two software engineers who had previously worked together, wanted to replicate the Amazon model of listing products online and shipping them direct to consumers.[5] Hastings recalls tinkering with packaging to see if DVDs sent through USPS would arrive intact: "I went out, bought a whole bunch of CDs and started mailing them to myself to see how quickly they would come back and what condition they would be in. I waited for two days—and they all arrived in perfect condition. The pieces started to fall into place after that."[6]

Rather than sell books, the two founders decided DVDs would be the right primary product. The discs being lightweight meant they could ship them easily, and at low cost. It was a good combination for a potentially viable direct-to-customer business model.

The guys were taking a real gamble. It wasn't clear whether the market would adopt the DVD as a mainstay format; both Betamax and laser discs had failed to gain traction in previous decades. But, like Bezos, Hastings was bullish on the role the internet would play in shifting shopping behavior, which gave him the confidence to continue to push the hypothesis.

At the time, the movie rental business was dominated by Blockbuster, still largely facilitated by its in-store experience. Decisions to rent movies were often last-minute, with customers picking up a flick on their way home from work. Blockbuster's success throughout the '90s hinged on a unique combination of this kind of last-minute impulse mixed with the desire to watch a new release. Although anybody could rent *The Matrix* for $5 from one of Blockbuster's 9,000 stores in the U.S., Hastings and Randolph were convinced that the market would soon shift, and instead respond to convenience and selection over brick-and-mortar release-radar ubiquity.

Kibble, Inc. was incorporated in August 1997. By the time they officially launched the business on April 14, 1998, with a vision to disrupt how Americans rented movies, Hastings and Randolph had (wisely) changed the name to Netflix. The pricing was initially similar to Blockbuster's: customers could choose on the website from a catalogue of about 925 films, and rent one for roughly $4 plus shipping. Renters had to return the movies by a specific due date or they'd be charged.[7]

Like Amazon's early online advantage over the incumbent brick-and-mortar retailers, Netflix touted itself as the world's first online DVD-rental store. The big competitive differentiators for Netflix were convenience and selection. For the first time, Americans could forgo a trip to the store and instead receive in the mail an odd documentary their spouse had read about in a local paper. Beyond the film, the Netflix delivery model had "water cooler" appeal—it was an innovative customer experience buyers wanted to tell their friends about.

And while 925 titles doesn't sound like a lot today, in 1998 it represented almost the entire catalogue of DVDs in print, including rare titles Blockbuster didn't carry. Like any big-box retailer, Blockbuster had a fixed amount of usable shelf space, so most of its stores were dedicated to new releases. What Netflix decided to do, much like Amazon, was go after the long tail, complementing popular selections with esoteric titles that you couldn't find in stores. Film enthusiasts loved it.

While customer counts rose to north of 100,000 subscribers by the end of 1999, Netflix was not without operational struggles. The appeal of convenience was undercut by lagging delivery times. As the business grew, the company also battled through rounds of layoffs and additional costs associated with building its extensive DVD library.

The turning point came later that year, with the introduction of a new, no-late-fee subscription model—perhaps the most important pivot in the company's history.

Pivot into Subscription

Neil Hunt, the company's chief product officer, describes the thinking behind the move:

Our original model didn't work—we needed to overcome the shipping delay. It just wasn't a high enough value product to overcome the delivery waiting time. We spent a lot of money to market to and attract new customers, and they wouldn't be repeat renters. We were spending $100 to $200 to bring in a customer, and they would make one $4 rental. There was no residual value.[8]

To overcome the delivery lag and improve the overall value proposition, Hastings devised the model of a prepaid subscription service. As told by Barry McCarthy, the CFO at the time, "it was Reed's insight that the subscription model would resonate with consumers in a compelling way."[9] Hunt explains that with the move, Netflix "turned the disadvantage of delivery time into having a movie at home all the time. The value to Netflix of having our movies in the customers' homes at all times was our key insight."[10]

In December of 1999, Netflix announced the company's new foray into subscription, the "Marquee" program, a "DVD-on-demand" service that offered members "four DVD rentals per month with no due dates or late fees" for a $16 monthly charge.[11] Prepaid return envelopes were sent with each delivery. The program also featured an "automatic replenishment" option: members would select a list of films and, each time they returned one, the next in the queue was automatically shipped. Because the number of DVDs in the customer's possession was limited to four, the ensuing title was mailed out only when the previous disc was returned, allowing Netflix to better manage its supply chain.

The new model paid off immediately, setting Netflix on a trajectory that led to its exalted position today. Revenue increased sevenfold the next year, from $5 million to $35 million, and according to McCarthy, hit $500 million three years later and $1 billion another three years after that.[12]

The press release announcing the Marquee program, claiming it would "transform the movie rental marketplace," turned out to be an understatement. The move to subscription was a disruptor, to say the least, one that would redefine what home entertainment would look like in the twenty-first century.

Even as the subscription model led to skyrocketing revenue and user counts, other challenges needed to be dealt with. Customers still had to walk to the post office to return viewed titles, which began to hinder the company's convenience play. And despite fast growth, cash was still an issue.

Putting pressure on financials was the lack of discounts from small distributors. To populate its film library, Netflix sought titles from small distribution partners rather than the studios themselves, and as a result received limited discounts. Higher costs meant the company had to choose carefully, and were unable to stock enough copies of the popular stuff.[13]

To solve the distributor dilemma, Netflix recruited a key hire in Ted Sarandos (from Video City, a large rental chain) as chief content officer in 2000. Although Sarandos recognized the hurdles, he was impressed by what the company was doing—particularly with respect to the subscription model.

Tapping some of his old relationships, Sarandos made an early mark by negotiating revenue-sharing agreements with nearly all the major studios. In exchange for discounts on DVD unit costs, Netflix agreed to pay the studios a negotiated fee based on how many times a title was rented in a fixed period—royalties, essentially. Hastings explained that the deals resulted in more money for the studios, but a much better overall product for Netflix to offer subscribers: "We spent more money, not less, with the studios but got bigger customer satisfaction. It was like paying 20% more and getting two times the number of copies."[14]

A Blockbuster Deal

With more favorable terms from the studios, Netflix's content improved. Customer satisfaction increased. Sarandos was on a roll, and the company was improving. But despite its unique and compelling model, most of the market still opted for in-store rentals. Ultimately, how successful Netflix could (and would) become depended on customers changing their behavior and adopting direct delivery—again, a bold prediction.

Without retail locations, the Netflix experience wasn't "touchy-feely," and despite the improved selection of titles, delivery lag meant the absence of instant gratification—a cornerstone of Blockbuster's value proposition.

In 2000, 70 percent of Americans lived within a ten-minute drive of a Blockbuster store. The company held firm market share, with millions of customers holding a Blockbuster card in their wallets. Nevertheless, Netflix executives believed Blockbuster had a few gaping holes.

For starters, Blockbuster's model wasn't personalized. The extent to which the company understood its customers depended on a store clerk's ability to interact with one in person. Netflix, on the other hand, had a proprietary system for personalizing movie recommendations via its rating system. Like Amazon, Netflix could build a profile of each person's movie preferences to inform and refine subsequent recommendations.

The other significant weakness in the Blockbuster model was its reliance on due dates and late fees. The company's profits were largely driven by the penalties it levied on customers.[15] So you had an interesting phenomenon whereby the thing that was most likely to piss off a customer was the very thing that was creating the margins.

In late 2000, with Netflix still considered the brash upstart and Blockbuster the undisputed incumbent, Hastings, along with co-founder Randolph and CFO Barry McCarthy, flew down to Dallas to meet with Blockbuster CEO John Antioco. Hastings proposed a deal, a merger of sorts: Blockbuster would acquire Netflix for $50 million, and represent the brand in their stores, while Netflix would manage Blockbuster's presence online.

While the strategy made intuitive sense on paper, Blockbuster viewed Netflix as a start-up riddled with uncertainty as to how its business model would mature. Antioco's company, on the other hand, was the established rental titan, with thousands of stores and a long-standing history. Hastings was "laughed out of the room," according to one account.[16]

Reports suggest Hastings attempted to sell Netflix to Blockbuster not once, but a few times in 2000.[17] If not for Antioco's lack of strategic vision, a flipped script would see Hastings's portrait as one of the great CEOs of our time look a bit different—a $50 million sale to Blockbuster could have gone down in Antioco's favor as one of the best bargain-priced acquisitions in history. (Lucky for Hastings, Antioco gets to play the fool. The decision to walk away from the deal is notorious as one of the biggest lost opportunities in corporate history.)

With Netflix all but doubling its subscriber count every year, the company decided the timing was right for a public offering. On March 29, 2002, shares of Netflix began trading at U.S. $15 per share on the NASDAQ. An excerpt from Hastings's first letter to investors shows the visionary nature of the company:

> At Netflix, we are encouraged by a number of market trends that indicate strong demand for our service in both the immediate and long-term future. For starters, consumers are becoming increasingly comfortable with the internet. The widespread adoption of broadband technologies means a smoother web experience for more people across the U.S. In particular, people are coming to appreciate the more personalized recommendations that are enabled by software (compared to, for example, recommendations from video store clerks who may know nothing about their customers' movie tastes) as well as the ease and security with which purchases may now be made online....
>
> Our vision is to change the way people access and view the movies they love. To accomplish that, on a large scale, we have set a long-term goal to acquire 5 million subscribers in the U.S., or 5 percent of U.S. TV households over the next four to

seven years. By then, we expect to generate $1 billion in revenue and $100 to $200 million in free cash flow.

In the shorter term, a year from now, I expect to be able to report to you that we ended the year 2003 with twenty-five operational U.S. distribution hubs, initiated international expansion into Canada, and generated total revenue of more than $235 million.[18]

By the end of 2003, Netflix had generated over $270 million in top-line revenue, amassed 1.5 million subscribers, and reached profitability for the first time in its short history.

Another Pivot

The technology to enable dependable, high-quality streaming video was still a few years away, but Hastings could see it on the horizon as early as 2005. He told *Inc.* at the time, "movies over the internet are coming, and at some point it will become big business. We started investing 1–2 percent of revenue every year in downloading, and I think it's tremendously exciting because it will fundamentally lower our mailing costs. We want to be ready when video-on-demand happens. That's why the company is called Netflix, not DVD-by-Mail." Of course, he was right— although the future came sooner than he predicted—thanks to YouTube.

YouTube launched in February of 2005, supposedly inspired by one of the founders, Jawed Karim, being unable to find videos of Janet Jackson's infamous "wardrobe malfunction" at the 2004 Super Bowl. Karim uploaded the site's first video, (a vid of himself at the San Diego Zoo) on April 23, 2005. A few months later, a Nike ad became the first video to reach 1 million views. It didn't take long for YouTube to become one of the fastest-growing sites online.

The increasing popularity of YouTube prompted another Netflix pivot, this time to a service that allowed users to watch movies that were hosted remotely, rather than requiring down-loaded files. The pivot took about two years to perfect, given the complexities of rebuilding technological architecture to host and serve content.

The new tech requirements were in addition to Netflix's continued efforts to perfect its personalization algorithms, which the platform relied on to predict customers' movie preferences. Interestingly, in a bid to improve one of its great competitive advantages, Netflix put together a mandate to promote a $1 million prize to anyone who could improve the recommendation system by 10 percent: the winning team comprised mathematicians, computer scientists, and engineers from the United States, Canada, Austria, and Israel.

True to its internet shift, Netflix officially began offering streaming movies and television shows in addition to the DVDs by mail in 2007. The company later partnered with various companies to enable streaming to devices like gaming consoles and Blu-ray players. In 2010 it offered its first streaming-only subscription plan, initially in the United States, then Canada, Latin America, the Caribbean, the United Kingdom, Ireland, and beyond. By 2016, it was available in 190 countries.

As mentioned, the debut of *House of Cards* in 2013 was another turning point. The serial drama was Netflix's first original video content, and went on to earn thirty-three Emmy nominations and several Golden Globe nominations before its final season in 2019. Since *House of Cards*, Netflix's annual spend on original content over the past five years has outpaced its own subscriber and revenue growth—in fact, content spending has shot up an average of 39 percent each year, while subscribers and revenue grew at 29 percent and 35 percent, respectively.[19]

The impact of this continued rise in content spending has led to some broader questions about the company's current business model. Since Netflix has embraced streaming, cash losses have ballooned. With nearly 140 million active paying users watching an average of two hours per day, the costs of the content it feeds outweighs the revenue coming in. In 2014, Netflix ran a modest surplus of $16 million from operating activities, but in 2018 it burned through $3 billion in a single year, and was planning to do the same in 2019; in true Bezos fashion, Hastings has promised the negative cash flow will persist for "many years," though the company expects the amount to dwindle after 2019.[20]

While Netflix's volumes and viewership have eclipsed the competition, it commands a fraction of the total market, and competitors like Amazon, Apple, Disney, and Hulu are not going away. Consequently, the Netflix spending spree is sure to continue, driven by not only competition, but the company's ultimate goal—to not just compete, but to be the world's dominant subscription video service, to in effect "become TV."[21]

Netflix does have a few monetization options if cash-flow woes persist. The company can continue to increase its prices (which it has started to do) to afford to produce more content, and thus gain even more subscribers. Should Netflix opt for more tepid price increases, it can explore alternate ways of generating cash through strategic partnerships with companies like Tesla—which, in the summer of 2019, announced it would work toward showcasing both Netflix and YouTube content on its vehicle screens. According to Elon Musk, the videos will only play while the car is parked, or while moving "when full self-driving is approved by regulators."[22] Musk didn't announce a specific date for the new feature. And then there's advertising. Historically, Netflix has stayed away from monetizing viewership through in-home advertisements on the platform. However, as negative cash flows remain on the short-term horizon, ad placements seem probable at some point.

Data is Crucial

Unlike Facebook and Google, who generate a ton of revenue from advertisements, or traditional television, where viewership ratings are directly reflected in the advertising the networks themselves sell, Netflix's subscription-based business model means it doesn't need to sell user data or bandwidth to make money. A different business model, in this case, means different success metrics.

Netflix may not sell your data, but the data it collects on viewing behavior is essential to the continuous execution of its business model. In Netflix's ad-free subscription environment, customer retention is paramount, so member data is carefully leveraged to categorize individual preferences into "taste clusters," used to serve up targeted recommendations—which help to boost revenue and retention in the absence of ads. The robustness of its data science is often overlooked. But make no mistake— Netflix's algorithms are as technologically sophisticated as those of Facebook's or Google's. However, unlike those two ad-selling engines, the sole mission of the Netflix algorithms is to improve the user experience.[23]

Aside from the recommendation engine, the technology includes proprietary video compression algorithms (which optimize for bandwidth and the context-specific needs of the content); distribution (Netflix's apps are available fully featured on more devices worldwide than any other video provider's); engagement functions such as auto-play trailers, vertically oriented trailers, personalization, recommendations that rely on 80,000 micro-genres, the ability to skip opening theme songs—the list goes on.[24]

The obsession over data science is driven by a few factors, but the most important is the need to constantly boost engagement numbers. Hastings identifies hours per subscriber per month as the most important key performance indicator of customer retention.[25] The company's catalogue, which consists of licenced rerun content as well as premium original TV and movies, is optimized at every level to push this number up.

This fixation on engagement is indicative of a best practice in running a subscription-based business. Engagement leads to renewals, renewals lead to greater retention, greater retention leads to customer loyalty, customer loyalty leads to recurring revenue, and recurring revenue leads to growth and profits. On the flip side, subscription companies with high churn rates typically have low engagement, low retention rates, and no real loyalty. Plain and simple. Those who *don't* obsess over engagement—Columbia House for example—get into trouble, don't last, or both, because their subscribers stop seeing the value of their subscription.

As a subscription business, Netflix is just as much about delivering value as it is about optimizing for high-quality content. The question for any subscriber when they gaze down at their credit card statement is not necessarily whether or not they were satisfied with the last particular movie or show they watched on the platform, but rather, did they get enough value for $13 a month? To that end, the company serves up not only quality, but quantity of content to lift the value proposition. Given that Americans watch on average 5.5 hours of video each day, Netflix can throw some garbage onto the platform to fill the cracks between great shows like *House of Cards* and *Ozark*. As users scroll through the seemingly endless list of options, they can't help but feel good about the actual available "amount" of content they're getting in exchange for the low monthly fee they're paying.

Next for Netflix

As capital markets go, the massive cash outlays on content make investors nervous. Hastings sees the spending as necessary to keep growing subscriber count. But that doesn't allay outside concerns, especially when Sarandos, the CCO, says the strategy is "more shows, more watching; more watching, more subs; more subs, more revenue; more revenue, more content."[26] To some, that sounds like a Ponzi scheme, with the company going into debt to broaden its catalogue to attract more paying customers to pay off that debt, etc.[27]

NETFLIX REVENUE GROWTH VS. EXPENDITURE GROWTH

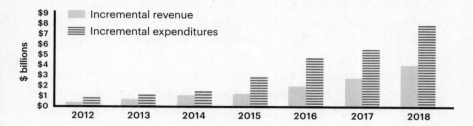

Netflix continues to spend massively on original content, but subscriber revenue is not keeping pace.

Source: Kyle Guske, "Reality Is Closing in on Netflix," New Constructs, January 28, 2019, https://www.newconstructs.com/reality-is-closing-in-on-netflix/.

And if what the company is after is our leisure time, it will be battling not only with other networks and streaming platforms, like HBO and Disney, but social media and content platforms like Facebook, Twitter, YouTube, LinkedIn, and Instagram. It's conceivable that to get to where Netflix wants to be, it would have to surpass Facebook in terms of overall engagement—and that will be difficult.

Concerned investors can take comfort knowing Netflix can play with certain levers to turn the heat down, such as reducing marketing efforts, raising prices (it remains relatively cheap), or opening the network to targeted advertisers. These are all tactics the company has yet to properly tinker with.

To date, the investor consensus still seems to be that Netflix is the real deal—a 20+ year-old business selling arguably the most valuable entertainment bundle in history. What's more, the actual business model remains envied by corporations seeking to build sizeable recurring revenue and consumer loyalty. The overall fundamentals still look promising, even as competitors copy the Netflix model, and attempt to compete. As of mid-2019, Comcast, AT&T, and Disney have announced plans to launch streaming subscriptions of their own.

Comcast, which boasts 54 million cable subscribers, will introduce NBCU in April of 2020. Unlike the incumbents', NBCU's app will be free for its cable TV subscribers. A fee-based model will be available to non-Comcast consumers, although pricing details are vague.

AT&T/WarnerMedia, home to Warner Brothers and HBO, plans to bundle content from HBO, Cinemax, and Warner for about $16/month. The streaming service, which is also expected to be live in 2020, will feature shows like *Game of Thrones* and *The Sopranos* as part of its offering. Given that the estimated pricing is still more expensive than Hulu, Netflix, or Prime, and much more expensive than the soon-to-be-launched Disney+ service, it's hard to see AT&T's competitive advantage—HBO Go is already an option at $15/month for those wanting on-demand selections of HBO content.

Disney+, in addition to the platforms it already operates like Hulu and ESPN+, is Disney's "Netflix." It is slated to launch in the U.S. in late 2019, starting at $6.99 a month, or $69.99 a year, and will allow users to stream material from its archives as well as original content hooked to Pixar, Marvel, and the Star Wars franchise.

Although Disney is certain to capture much of its loyal fanbase, most analysts don't view the fresh competition as a real threat. "We do not view Disney+ as a strong alternative to Netflix," Matthew Thornton, a tech analyst at bank holding company Suntrust, said. J.P. Morgan analyst Doug Anmuth agreed, saying that "while we expect Disney+ will likely be the most competitive streaming offering to Netflix, we still do not view it as a major threat to Netflix subscriber numbers given Netflix's quality & quantity of content."[28] Moreover, while Disney is aggressively removing some of its best content from Netflix as it gears up for launch, such a move represents hundreds of millions in lost licensing revenues coming from deals it hand-inked with Netflix. Investors are not likely to applaud the strategy if subscription dollars can't bridge the gap.

Perhaps the only real object in Netflix's rear-view mirror is Amazon, whose growth-at-all-costs approach means the company will spend the cash it needs to to compete for content. The online retailer spent somewhere between $4 and 5 billion on original content in 2018, more than NBC, ABC, or HBO.[29] Given Amazon's access to cheap capital and its ability to compete with Netflix on the supply side, it is conceivable that Amazon might become somewhat of a thorn in Hastings's side. Though, as mentioned earlier, Netflix is also an AWS customer—so there are politics at play that may make for a friendlier coexistence.

It won't be easy for Bezos if he decides to put on the gloves and double content spend. Notwithstanding the billions it has at its disposal, Amazon still faces a unique brand association hurdle that Netflix doesn't. When consumers think Amazon, they think online commerce, not entertainment—and that's not easy to overcome.[30] One thing is certain: the world of streaming, especially with Amazon in the mix, is about to get even more interesting. Only time will tell if Prime Video is enough of a catalyst for boosting the rest of the Amazon flywheel to justify Bezos taking a more aggressive approach in 2020 and beyond.

FIVE

From Sales to Salesforce

"Clayton Christensen wrote a book called *The Innovator's Dilemma*. It illustrated how a start-up company—by employing innovation that disrupts existing business models—will always beat established big companies. It validated us for what we knew was right: the future wasn't about simply improving on what was already done; it was about being bold enough to make big, sweeping, dramatic changes." [1]

MARC BENIOFF, FOUNDER, CHAIRMAN, AND CO-CEO OF SALESFORCE

YOU CAN GET a degree in just about anything these days, including one in "Adventure Education" from Plymouth State, one in "Bagpiping" from Carnegie Mellon, and even one in "Puppet Arts" from the University of Connecticut. I don't know anyone with the aforementioned diplomas, but I do know plenty of graduates with degrees in accounting, law, computer programming, information systems, and political science. To date, though, I don't know one person with a degree in sales.

Of the over 4,000 universities in the U.S., fewer than 200 have a sales program, let alone a sales course. There is no such thing as an MBA in sales. Despite this lack of academic training in "influence," about one in nine people enter the workforce in some kind of sales role. That's roughly 11 percent of folks employed in some kind of sales gig, without any real formal training in how to persuade people.

What's interesting is how the sales industry has changed in the last couple of decades. Direct door-to-door selling is old hat; cold calling is all but done. Marketing channels are now dominated by Facebook and Google. Facebook is perhaps less of a social network than it is an advertising platform that hordes of marketing teams use to ultimately drive sales.

Ahead of Facebook, Google is now the biggest media owner in the world. It attracted $116.32 billion in ad revenue in 2018 (the majority of the online company's total revenue pie), which represented more than twice Facebook's $55 billion haul, and over 40 percent of the $283.35 billion global advertising market.[2] Google makes vastly more money from digital ads than any other company on the planet. Together, Facebook and Google account for about sixty cents of every dollar companies spend on online advertising. It's an astounding shift from the days of traditional selling.

While post-secondary institutions may be excited about the idea of introducing the first real MBA in sales, the next era of selling won't be driven by academic pedigree—instead, corporations and their industry leaders will leverage search tools, social media, machine learning, and, most important, customer relationship management software (CRM) to create better sales teams.

This shift is happening in real time, with cloud-based CRM systems like HubSpot, Oracle's NetSuite, Infusionsoft, and Salesforce making it more efficient for sales teams to manage prospecting, marketing, and relationship building. Top salespeople are combining these tools with their unique ability to build relationships in person. It's all part and parcel of the modern-day approach to selling, where business cards and business lunches seem irrelevant. Does anyone even have a business card anymore?

In addition to the one in nine in a formal sales role, the rest of us, perhaps unwillingly, are also in sales. Our personal brand is becoming increasingly important. Job seekers are eschewing résumés and cover letters in exchange for personalized web pages, tailored social media silhouettes, and well-crafted blogs. Reference checks from employers are now part of a broader, more important Google search, Instagram audit, and deep dive on a potential candidate. We are in a truly unique time where the business of selling—whether it be a product, a service, or one's self—is very different than it used to be.

How did we get here?

A Brief History of Sales

The concept of managing the customer relationship is likely as old as the idea of exchanging money for goods or services—sales as a profession probably started with the first Mesopotamian to try to talk his buddy into giving him a couple of shekels of barley for his spare goat. Let's fast-forward, through the fifteenth-century Grand Bazaar in Istanbul, quite possibly the world's first shopping mall; to nineteenth-century book peddlers trading on the strength of teaser chapters; to cosmetics companies like Avon and Mary Kay; to 1920, when a professor emeritus of psychology, E.K. Strong Jr., published *The Psychology of Selling Life Insurance*, allegedly the first work of its kind to focus on specific selling techniques; all the way to 1936—when Dale Carnegie, already famous for his courses in salesmanship, public speaking, and interpersonal skills, published *How to Win Friends and Influence People*.

This was a big turning point in sales psychology—the first, and perhaps the best, depiction of the relationship-based approach to sales. To date, Carnegie's masterpiece has sold over 30 million copies, making it one of the bestselling books of all time. I've often listed it as required reading for courses I've taught at the University of Toronto.

Leap ahead a few more decades to the 1980s, which saw (in addition to big hair, Atari games, and Michael Jackson videos) the first versions of digital rolodexes. ACT!'s software product, introduced in 1987, allowed users to organize contact information more efficiently, and was perhaps the first CRM system on the market. Other vendors quickly followed with similar management software for businesses, spurred on by the explosive growth of personal computers and advances in server architecture.

In the early 1990s, Tom Siebel founded Siebel Systems, which quickly grew to become the largest provider of sales force automation tools, and by the late 1990s controlled almost half the broader CRM market. Other software giants noticed, and companies like Oracle and SAP began offering new applications and services to compete. The pressure was on to innovate and retain a share of a growing market.[3]

The rise of the web throughout the 2000s sped things up, as the sheer volume of available information slowly chipped away at any kind of seller's advantage. Armed with more intelligence, prospective buyers were introducing a new equilibrium, which meant another new role for technology—one in which software would help salespeople to not only manage sales funnels, but also deepen their understanding of buyer behavior. This drive to better understand the psychology of a prospective buyer forced CRM companies to introduce even more sophisticated software tools.

The CRM market has grown by leaps and bounds to become a household acronym across almost every industry. Worldwide, CRM became the largest software market in 2017, according to Gartner, Inc., with total revenue amounting to roughly $40 billion—and that number is set to rise to over $52 billion in 2019, with 75 percent of the market expected to be issuing such tools via a SaaS (software-as-a-service) model.[4] Today, SaaS companies crossing $1 billion in annual recurring revenue are almost commonplace, with Atlassian, Box, HubSpot, and Zendesk all well on their way. And leading the pack is Salesforce.[5]

The Rise of the Biggest "Sales" Company on Earth

Marc Benioff had an entrepreneurial spark from an early age. At fifteen, he began creating games for the Atari 800 computer. By sixteen, he was pulling in about $1,500 a month—enough to pay for his tuition at the University of Southern California.

Following USC, Benioff took a job at technology giant Oracle, a company specializing in software, cloud systems, and enterprise software. He fit in nicely at Oracle, rising up the ranks in a variety of positions, and working closely with the company's boss, Larry Ellison. At twenty-six, Benioff was promoted to senior vice president, the youngest person ever to hold the title at the company.[6]

Benioff clearly had a very bright future at Oracle, yet he couldn't shake the urge to try something entrepreneurial. Without much of a plan, he took a sabbatical in 1996, opting to get clarity on what was next from Hawaii and India. Benioff's time away was transformative.

As he details in his memoir *Behind the Cloud*, Benioff came to two clear convictions during this period. He didn't want to spend the rest of his career working in a traditional corporate job. And the internet would change everything, not only for consumers, but businesses as well.[7]

These two eerily Bezos-like epiphanies led Benioff to pursue the idea for Salesforce.com—a world-class internet company for salesforce automation. Benioff's idea was to "make software easier to purchase, simpler to use, and more democratic without the complexities of installation, maintenance and constant upgrades."[8]

Benioff's goals were ambitious, but also timely. In a 2015 TED talk, Idealab founder Bill Gross shared what factors matter the most to start-up success.[10] Sure, ambition plays a role. So do other factors like idea, team, execution, business model, and funding. But, as Gross makes clear, *timing* trumps everything. And Benioff's timing was perfect—launching Salesforce in early 1999, not only at a time when there were several existing technology

SALESFORCE'S FIRST "V2MOM" (VISION, VALUES, METHODS, OBSTACLES, AND MEASURES), 1999[9]

Benioff credits his V2MOMs with helping to clarify, communicate, and achieve his goals.

Vision
Rapidly create a world-class Internet company/site for Sales Force Automation

Values
1. World-class organization
2. Time to market
3. Functional
4. Usability (Amazon quality)
5. Value-added partnerships

Methods
1. Hire the team
2. Finalize product specification and technical architecture
3. Rapidly develop the product specification to beta and production stages
4. Build partnerships with big e-commerce, content, and hosting companies
5. Build a launch plan
6. Develop exit strategy: IPO/acquisition

barriers when it came to software tools, but also when the overall business landscape was shifting under a new wave of sociographic and psychological factors that had never been addressed or even understood.

Business, and more specifically sales, had historically been transaction-driven. The average '90s salesperson came equipped with an aggressive churn-and-burn mindset. Picture Gordon Gekko, Michael Douglas's character in the 1987 film *Wall Street*, imploring his audience to believe/agree that "greed, for lack of a better word, is good." Or Alec Baldwin, playing a pompous salesman in 1992's *Glengarry Glen Ross*, screaming at a room full of underlings about the law of ABC—"always be closing." That was the dominant portrait of what successful salespeople were supposed to be like in a corporate setting—it usually meant an amoral pursuit of a single goal: more sales.

Existing software of the '90s fit perfectly with what a Gordon Gekko might use. Oracle, Microsoft, and IBM had plenty of tools to load and manage lead contacts so cold callers could pound the pavement—Gekko-style. But they didn't help salespeople understand prospective buyers on a deeper level.

There were also cost barriers. Most software was purchased outright—i.e., paid for up-front and installed on a corporation's internal servers. Market tools were slow and difficult to navigate, and typically only large corporations could afford them. That left a pretty big gap between the Fortune 500 types and what the rest of the market was looking for.

Benioff looked at enterprise software through the prism of these small-to-medium-sized players, as well as online businesses such as Amazon and eBay—both early inspirations. He wrestled with a key question: Why were software companies selling systems that cost millions of dollars and took up to a year and a half to install from CD-ROMs, rather than something that could be delivered online, and used on demand?[11]

Benioff, perfectly poised at the intersection of three key trends—the renewed interest in sales psychology, the rise of the internet, and the underserved small-to-medium-business market—began planting the early seeds of cloud computing. He outlined a software concept that could be used on a pay-per-user services model rather than the cumbersome purchase-and-install format that companies were used to.[12] The goal was to remove up-front costs by instead allowing users to pay a monthly fee for employees to access the tools. Users of Benioff's software would, simply, "rent," rather than "buy." Wisely, Benioff targeted businesses that were struggling with sales force automation and CRM, mostly small-to-medium-sized firms.

Investors were skeptical. Benioff writes of being rejected by multiple venture capital firms before finally securing funding from some key individual investors, including Dropbox investor Bobby Yazdani, CNET founder Halsey Minor, and, not surprisingly, his old pal and mentor, Oracle's Larry Ellison. Once Benioff had some initial working capital, he immediately brought in former Oracle colleagues Parker Harris, Frank Dominguez, and Dave Moellenhoff to begin working on Salesforce out of an apartment in San Francisco.

The environment was Amazon-like: raw and bare-bones. The original server room was a bedroom closet. As Benioff tells it in his memoir, "It was an archetypical California start-up scene with a dog in the office and a mass of young and energetic people wearing Hawaiian shirts, working hard, and subsisting on pretzels, Red Vines licorice, and beef jerky."[13]

Bare seemed to be the theme early on. When the team churned out the first prototype, built in about a month, the software was simple, featuring only necessary information fields. To test out the UI (user interface), Benioff invited friends and colleagues to visit the apartment, which he called the Laboratory. It's worth pointing out that most software companies (both then and now) work surreptitiously at this stage, but Benioff knew that the value of feedback far outweighed the risks of a ripped-off version of his prototype, so he allowed just about anyone to check out what the guys were working on: "When a group of Japanese businessmen were in town, they came to see what we were creating. We eventually became a stop on a tour for visiting Korean businesspeople who were interested in seeing an American start-up. Being inclusive of potential users from large and small companies across the world helped us gain valuable insight. After all, our goal was to build something that could serve as a global CRM solution for the masses."[14]

As the company grew, Salesforce portrayed itself the way Benioff himself is portrayed: different, unique, and definitely going against the grain. This deliberately Amazon-like approach

cast Salesforce as the underdog in the software world, with
notable legacy players, like Siebel and Oracle, as the reigning
corporate Goliaths. Salesforce embraced its underdog status,
picking up organic PR through various attention-seeking stunts
like hiring bicycle rickshaws to offer free rides to attendees of a
conference held by rival Siebel Systems. As a perk for riding a
Salesforce rickshaw, each attendee was given a Krispy Kreme
doughnut and a coffee mug with a quote by a U.S. Bancorp analyst
that said: "Wake up Siebel, Salesforce.com is a disruptive technology and is slowly moving in on the CRM prize." The press ate it up.[15]

In 2004, Salesforce IPO'd on the New York Stock Exchange.
Trading under the apropos ticker symbol CRM, 10 million shares
of stock priced overnight at $11 put $110 million in the company's coffers. The stock quickly appreciated, selling at $15 for most
of the day before shooting up to $17.20 on day one of trading—a
more than 55 percent first-day gain.[16]

Despite the early skepticism, the success of the IPO indicated
that investors were now betting on not only Salesforce's perfect
market timing and vision, but also the relatively certain revenue
stream generated by the company's subscription pricing model.
While traditional software companies could sell some big-ticket
contracts, Salesforce's recurring revenue play could garner higher
valuations than a traditional licenced software company.[17]

Today, the company Benioff started out of that apartment at
1449 Montgomery Street in San Francisco is headquartered in
a new 1,100-foot tall skyscraper, Salesforce Tower (still in San
Francisco), the highest building in America west of Chicago. It
is the global leader in cloud-based CRM services. It is the world's
fourth-largest software firm, after only Microsoft, Oracle, and
Germany's SAP, all of which were founded in the 1970s. About
one-third of the company's $10 billion in annual revenue comes
from large companies like Dell, Cisco, E*Trade Financial, and
Starbucks. And the company plans for even more ambitious
growth, expecting to double annual sales in four years on its climb
to Benioff's "dream" of $100 billion in revenue by 2038.[18]

Given the new digs and immense shareholder value generated by Salesforce over the last twenty years, the climb to 100 billion dollars seems possible. If it gets there, it will be in large part due to two key factors that inform Benioff's every move: the Salesforce culture, and its relentless focus on the customer.

A Culture of Success

Like Amazon, Salesforce is led by a big personality. Benioff is a famously gregarious individual and cocky marketer who remains front and center as the force driving the company forward. He is also a philanthropist, and a political activist who has taken progressive public positions on gay rights and equal pay for women and faced off with leaders in the American Bible Belt over issues like state bathroom laws. Recently, on CBS's *60 Minutes*, he said that "as political leaders become weaker, chief executives have to become stronger." [19]

Not everyone loves Benioff's left-wing activism. Some say a partisan CEO isn't a good thing for shareholders. According to former executives, Mr. Benioff's fondness for influencing policy discussions by tweeting—which he's done to cancel events in states that have passed anti-gay laws, for example—can create chaos within the company. In fact, Salesforce's annual 10-K filing listed the company's political positions as a *risk*. But Salesforce's left-leaning customer base seems to appreciate Benioff putting a few stakes in the ground. Some customers go so far as to say that they "feel they are not only buying software but doing good for the world." [20] However one feels about his politics, Benioff is comfortable in his role as lead C-suite salesman, and doing it the way he knows how: with bold, left-wing swagger, at the head of a company reflecting the same.

Salesforce's workplace culture, which is undeniably influenced by its salesman-in-chief, has helped it attract and retain some of the best talent in the world. In 2018, Salesforce topped *Fortune*'s annual "100 best companies to work for" list, which noted that it spent "$8.7 million over three years to address differences in pay across gender and race." The company slipped to second in 2019 (with Hilton assuming the top spot), but has spent eleven years on the list—a testament to its company-wide commitment to upholding its core values over the long term.[21]

Joining Salesforce as an employee starts with baseline compensation and benefits, but also includes, among other things, company-paid gym memberships, yoga classes, discounted airline tickets, and free massages; there are also lavish rewards for performance—for example, anyone who makes their quota gets an all-expenses-paid trip for two to Hawaii.[22]

Community involvement is a core value, and employees play an important part. As Benioff notes, goodwill and sincere intentions won't cut through the profit imperative unless they are "woven into the fabric of an organization"—to truly make a difference, a company's philanthropic program must be "part of a company's DNA."[23] Backing up that statement, the company has a number of initiatives contributing to the company's philanthropic energy, including a system it uses for its own foundation, Salesforce.org, called 1-1-1, which requires a pledge to donate:

- 1 percent equity—to be used for grants and monetary assistance to those in need;
- 1 percent time—employees can take a certain number of paid days each year to volunteer in their community; and
- 1 percent product—donated to non-profits to help them operate more efficiently.

There's also the "Power of Us" initiative, which encourages the company's vendors and partners to engage in their own philanthropic efforts. Then there's BizAcademy, "a four-day entrepreneurial workshop designed for high school students in underserved school districts"; "Future Ready," a series of "education and workforce development initiatives" offered to K-12 and post-secondary students; and "Pro Bono," where the company donates time and resources to help non-profits improve their operations—the list goes on.[24]

Since the company's inception, Salesforce has worked with over 40,000 non-profits or educational institutions, donated more than $260 million in the form of grants, and paid for its employees to volunteer over 3.8 million hours. When Salesforce reached the 1 million subscriber mark, it celebrated the milestone by giving away $1 million to ten non-profit organizations.

What has all this done for company morale? According to Benioff, "The foundation has made us a better company. It has served as a tool for collaboration with other companies. It has made our employees more fulfilled, more productive and more loyal. It has made us happier. Customers have rallied behind our cause. This is not why we do it, but the opportunity to work on something bigger together has positively affected our bottom line."[25]

Salesforce is perhaps one of the few for-profit software companies of its size to leverage corporate philanthropy as a distinct competitive advantage. But from the company's point of view, it's a sound strategy that adds to the bottom line over the long haul. A reduction in overall poverty levels translates into a more skilled workforce, which then feeds more worthy recruits into the job pool. Moreover, giving back enhances the Salesforce brand by generating lots of favorable press—resulting in more exposure, more customers, and more profits.

An Obsession with Customers

In 2018, Benioff told *Forbes* that "nothing is more important to Salesforce than customer success . . . I believe being so committed to the customer is more important than it's ever been."[26]

A big part of that commitment has been to smaller businesses, which were ill-served before Salesforce. Today, one-third of Salesforce customers are small businesses. The company has made it easy for this section of its client pool to seamlessly integrate with programs like Google Cloud's G Suite and other valuable software, such as Slack and Mailchimp. Salesforce's app marketplace allows clients to customize CRM functions, and to tie in systems like Dropbox and Outlook as well as external social media platforms like Facebook and Twitter. Other advantages include access to Einstein, Salesforce's artificial intelligence (AI) software. With Einstein, businesses can automate basic sales activities to reduce the waste that small-to-medium businesses typically spend manually inputting data.[27]

Salesforce is also hedging its bets by not only developing its own products, but by helping other companies to develop theirs. Salesforce Ventures, the company's own venture capital arm, has invested in more than 275 enterprise cloud start-ups since 2009. Its impressive global portfolio includes names like Dropbox, Zoom, HubSpot, Evernote, Survey Monkey, and Automattic, among others.[28] And the VC team's focus is not just on home soil—it's active in seventeen countries, including Canada, where Salesforce Ventures recently launched its Canada Trailblazer Fund, a $100 million fund looking to capitalize on forecasts that point to rapid growth in Canada's public cloud software market.[29] It's a bet on the future of technology not only coming from much of Salesforce's own products, but the entire ecosystem it's helping to fund.

Then there's Dreamforce, one of the biggest technology conferences worldwide. Dreamforce 2018, Salesforce's sixteenth annual tech "Superbowl," brought together over 200,000 thought leaders, industry pioneers, and thousands of IT professionals from eighty different countries. The conference, held in San Francisco, included more than 2,700 breakout sessions, roughly 100 hours of hands-on training, and over fifty workshops available to attendees.

Using the 'Force

In his memoir, Benioff says, "I know that markets are more receptive to change in challenging times. We are now in a time of extraordinary opportunity. People always ask me, what's in store for the future? The future is whatever we imagine. We all must think three years out, five years out, ten years out. What's ahead of us is whatever we create. Seize the opportunity in front of you."[30] Benioff was reflecting on the opportunities inherent in the 2008–09 financial crisis, but his thoughts are equally relevant in today's world roiled by the ongoing American political crisis, and to the future of his company. It also provides insight into his 2018 purchase, with his wife Lynne, of *Time* magazine, for $190 million in cash.

There are some obvious reasons why Benioff purchased the ninety-five-year-old asset: for one, *Time* is a Salesforce client. More important, it is profitable—a rarity for a media company— complete with the world's largest circulation for a weekly news magazine, and a readership of roughly 26 million. And, of course, there are plenty of synergies with respect to understanding *Time*'s long-standing subscription model. But, beyond the veil of the front page, are there covert political motivations?

The deal itself stoked further comparisons to Jeff Bezos, who bought the *Washington Post* for $250 million in 2013, prompting Donald Trump to disparage the iconic newspaper as an "expensive lobbyist" for Amazon.[31] Like Amazon's figurehead, Benioff created an innovative online business, pushed an early narrative to stir up free press, outlined customer obsession as a cornerstone of his business model, and has now put his stamp on the media world. This recent move could be seen as another Bezos-like play, perhaps an attempt to inflate his political influence beyond California. Regardless of the fact that Benioff has said that daily operations of the New York–based publication won't change, the deal comes in the wake of the magazine featuring Trump on the cover almost two dozen times since he announced his bid for the presidency—each time accompanied by left-leaning criticism. The political influence of the paper certainly isn't lost on Benioff, who himself has been an outspoken critic of Trump. Whatever's in store for Benioff and *Time*, the newest tech CEO/media baron has added yet another unique marketing channel for Salesforce.

ON A two-week retreat across the South Pacific in the middle of 2018, Benioff unplugged to do some soul-searching. When he returned, he decided that Salesforce would move forward with a "divide and conquer strategy" and that Keith Block, his long-time colleague and ex-Oracle software vet, would join him as the company's co-CEO.[32]

Block's ascension comes at a good time. The market has adopted CRM as a mainstay, and the $56 billion category is still growing. CRM software has moved from luxury to necessity across organizations of all sizes, including small business, the section of the market that has historically been squeezed out because of high up-front costs.

As CRM technology begins to merge with artificial intelligence, the industry continues to evolve. For instance, Salesforce.com users can purchase plug-ins that are powered by "Neuralytics," a "predictive engine powered by over 90 billion sales interactions," to record, store, and analyze phone calls.[33]

With more sophisticated AI-driven CRM tools, companies can aggregate client data, including things like social media postings and interaction history (e.g., emails sent, voicemails left, text messages sent, etc.) and rank a lead database according to the probability of securing a deal from a prospect. Moreover, sales managers can more accurately predict which members of their team will hit their monthly quotas, and conversely, who might not make the grade.

AI is also helping companies simply sell more stuff. For example, an AI algorithm can help a merchandising operation to price-optimize so discount rates can be applied strategically across a subset of SKUS. The same technology can also forecast next month's revenue, or help identify which clients are more likely to upgrade a product they already own and which ones may want to purchase a new one.[34]

And, as the "tech within tech" improves, Benioff continues to expand Salesforce globally. In mid-2019, Salesforce announced a new partnership with Chinese e-commerce giant Alibaba, one that would see the company make inroads into the Chinese SaaS market, with Alibaba as the exclusive provider of Salesforce software to China, and Salesforce the only CRM product suite Alibaba would sell.

More growth is likely, as Salesforce continues to incorporate leading-edge tech into what's already a best-in-class subscription-based product, operating in a healthy demand-driven market and webbed in a corporate culture defined by employee satisfaction, customer obsession, philanthropy, and progressive political ideals. It's tempting to call this software giant unstoppable.

SIX

Shopify Your Business

TRIANGL.COM IS the brainchild of Australian couple Craig Ellis and Erin Deering, who launched the line of neoprene bikinis in 2012 after Deering couldn't find affordable swimwear she liked. The next year, Ellis and Deering, who had some previous experience working in e-commerce and design, sold all their belongings and moved to Hong Kong to grow their online-only swimwear label. With a social boost from celebrities like Kendall Jenner and Miley Cyrus sporting the company's swimwear, Triangl quickly grew to $60 million in revenue within a few years of its online launch.[1] Beyoncé even wore one of its tops in a video. Celebrity endorsement and beautiful models make the brand worthy of an Instagram follow, but from a business perspective the web engine that powers Triangl's online store is way sexier. Shopify, founded by CEO Tobias Lütke in Ottawa, Canada, in 2006, powers Triangl as well as about 800,000 other merchants, including brands like Red Bull, Tesla Motors, General Electric, Penguin Books, and Nestlé.

Merchants who use Shopify to run their online store can design, set up, and manage their entire e-commerce business across multiple sales channels, including web, mobile, social media, and even brick-and-mortar locations. Its affordable SaaS model means a tiny start-up in rural Rhode Island can begin sell-ing custom apparel online in twenty-four hours, and trust that the engine behind the website and its transactions is not only reli-able but affordable. In simple terms, Shopify is to an e-commerce business what electricity and plumbing are to a house—it pro-vides every essential service, tucked out of sight behind the walls.

Notwithstanding its robust offering, Shopify knows switch-ing platforms is complicated and costly. And so each merchant represents a predictable client with a relatively high lifetime value. Shopify's focus on growing its recurring revenue through subscription services, and its broader strategy to attract more enterprise-level clients, adds to the long-tail customer base Shop-ify has historically served.

Shopify Plus—its enterprise-level service—continues to gain traction, and now powers over 2,500 large businesses. As more big corporations seek to upgrade legacy infrastructure typically built on platforms like Magento or BigCommerce, Shopify Plus is increasingly seen as a viable alternative despite packages start-ing at around $2,000/month. With names like Tesla and Red Bull using Plus, Shopify has officially shed its old reputation as simply a platform for start-ups.

Enterprise-level technology and robust reliability are two key factors that make this subscription/SaaS company, which began as an online snowboard equipment store in 2004, a giant in the technology space. At 4,000 employees and climbing, Shopify supports approximately 800,000 merchants across 175 coun-tries, who in 2018 collectively processed over $43 billion in transactions on the platform (Shopify reports in U.S. dollars). Subscription revenues grew 50 percent in 2018 over the previ-ous year, to $465 million. That represents nearly half of Shopify's $1.073 billion in revenue for 2018. In Lütke's words, "No other SaaS company has crossed the $1 billion-dollar revenue mark at a faster growth rate."[2]

As the cloud-based, multi-channel SaaS e-commerce platform has grown into one of the largest companies of its kind, Lütke and his leadership team have had to make some decisions about how to expand globally. While there was early pressure from institutional investors to relocate its head office from Ottawa, Canada's capital, to glittery tech epicentre Palo Alto, Lütke instead chose to double-down on the company's Canadian footprint, hiring more local employees and expanding its already impressive headquarters at 150 Elgin Street to a total of 170,000 square feet. Shopify has added an additional 325,000 square feet nearby, in a former Export Development Canada building, and increased its presence in Toronto. It plans to double its workforce in Canada's biggest city to 1,500 by 2022.

The company's chosen headquarters is both purposeful and advantageous. "Ottawa may be one of the best places in the world right now to build a multibillion-dollar business," said Harley Finkelstein, Shopify's chief operating officer. "In fact, we consider Ottawa to be one of Shopify's competitive advantages."[3]

In a city where Prime Minister Justin Trudeau is a pretty big deal, "Tobi" Lütke isn't far behind on the status ladder. But, for a tech titan whose net worth is nearly $3 billion, and whose company is one of the biggest Canadian-based success stories of the post-internet era, he's done a good job of keeping a low profile. Unless you've made a career in Canadian tech, you're not likely to know who "Tobi" is. Shopify's Ottawa-based footprint allows the company to fly under the radar, and the German-born Lütke wouldn't have it any other way.

Lütke prefers Zuckerberg work attire to a three-piece suit. The only thing flashy about him is the Tesla he owns, which he often leaves at home in favor of his bicycle. People who know him say he enjoys the limelight about as much as a raccoon likes a flashlight in its eyes. Instead, Harley Finkelstein, the company's coo and a more naturally animated personality, welcomes the role of media bobblehead as part of his job description. That has proven to be a killer combination since the two met in 2009.

In many ways, Lütke's approach as ceo is the opposite of a typical tech company executive. In an age where big personalities like Bezos, Branson, and Musk rule the front pages of *Forbes*, Lütke makes a concerted effort to avoid any kind of media and fame, focusing instead on what the company has done successfully, and how it will manage its next phase of growth.

To make sense of Shopify, one must understand Lütke's influence as well as his personality type, both of which are woven into the firm's fabric. The result is a unique culture and company stemming from not only the German native's leadership style and perspective, but his childhood, his connection to Canada, and all the lessons he's learned along the way.

How to Grow a Billionaire

From the beginning, Lütke didn't fit the mold of a typical German schoolkid. As a child growing up in Koblenz, Germany, he took academic shortcuts where possible so he could spend more time working on computer programs. Teachers didn't appreciate his extracurricular efforts: "They diagnosed me with all sorts of learning disabilities and started to medicate me," he recalls on his blog. "I wanted to leave it all behind."[4] Despite being concerned about their son's desire to retreat to screens, Lütke's parents gave him a computer, the equivalent of a Commodore 64, at the age of six. By the time he was twelve, he was rewriting Commodore code to build new games for the system.[5]

Like Bill Gates and Mark Zuckerberg, Lütke made an ostensibly bold decision to drop out of school to pursue his passion for computers. "School was not for me," he says in that same 2013 blog post. "To me, computers were so much more interesting. Right or wrong, I felt like I wasted my time there and my real education was starting when I came home." Lütke quit traditional education at the age of sixteen and decided to follow the apprenticeship path to become a *Fachinformatiker*, or computer programmer. "This might sound like a stupid decision to people in North America, who often go to College or University to get a degree in something like computer science," he explains, "but in Germany leaving high-school for an apprenticeship is not out of the ordinary. It is called the dual education system, and it is likely one of the main reasons for Germany's success." [6]

Germany's apprenticeship system is based on the idea that many professions are best entered through experience rather than theoretical understanding. Apprentices can develop their craft primarily through on-the-job training and spend as little as one day a week in vocational school, with a choice of roughly 350 different occupations, ranging from business to trades—everything from bankers, hairdressers, and oven builders to software developers and computer programmers. It's this German system that gave Lütke a viable alternative to classic curriculum-based learning.

Lütke completed an apprenticeship at BOG Koblenz, a subsidiary of Siemens, under the watchful eye of a mentor named Jürgen. "Jürgen was a long-haired, fifty-something, grizzled rocker who would have been right at home in any Hell's Angels gang," Lütke recalls. He was a rebel when it came to things like company attire and formal language, but what Lütke gravitated toward was his commitment to nurturing the next generation of workers. "Jürgen was a master teacher. He created an environment in which it was not only possible but easy to move through 10 years of career development every year. It is a method and an environment which I am fiercely trying to replicate at Shopify." [7]

Jürgen's influence, and Lütke's desire to reproduce it, is evident in Shopify's work culture, which fiercely pushes its people to learn and grow through experience. If you visit one of its offices, it's clear the company embraces a diversity of opinion and background through a mosaic of personality types and ethnicities. Employees wear what they want, share ideas openly, and are encouraged to express themselves authentically under a culture rooted in both personal and professional growth.

Lütke's admiration for this kind of experiential learning over academic study could be considered the hidden DNA of his success, and that of Shopify's. As he explains it, "My apprentice-ship and the dual education system in general taught me [that] experiencing and learning things quickly is the ultimate life skill. If you can do that, you can conjure up impossible situations for yourself over and over again and succeed."[8]

THE SUCCESS of this apprenticeship-based system in a field as influential as tech should prompt reflection in any organization attempting to change its internal culture—but it also poses a broader set of questions about North America's educational ideals. With a long history propped up by alumni, endowments, and a closed-minded narrative, the current North American college/university system doesn't just discourage students from pursuing experiential learning—it scoffs at those who drop out, often label-ing those who take an alternate path as failures without a future.

We can make sense of this traditional viewpoint from an ROI (return on investment) perspective: after all, academic institu-tions need a steady flow of students paying high tuition fees if they're to survive. And so, to lure applicants, schools tout pro-gram rankings, a vast alumni network, and high expected average salaries out of school. Celebrating the "dropouts" like Lütke, who achieve tremendous success by forgoing that path, erodes the value proposition.

But, what if we were to ask ourselves the question, What is the purpose of a formal educational institution? If the answer is a variation on something like "to develop students' capacity to learn a set of skills in order to bring value to society and be happy doing it," we are then left with an even more important question: Is the current North American educational framework the most effective at fulfilling that purpose?

Germany isn't the only country that has built a successful education system that bucks North American expectations. In his book *Antifragile*, Nassim Nicholas Taleb describes how Swit-zerland, "perhaps the most successful country in history," has "traditionally had a very low level of university education com-pared to the rest of the rich nations. Its system, even in banking...

was based on apprenticeship models, nearly vocational rather than the theoretical ones. In other words, on *techne* (crafts and know how), not *episteme* (book knowledge, know what)."[9]

If kinesthetic learners like Lütke, Jobs, Zuckerberg, Gates, Ellison, Mackey, and Dorsey, who thrive on "know how," not "know what," had been compelled to follow the so-called normal path, it would likely mean a world without Shopify, Apple, Facebook, Microsoft, Oracle, Whole Foods, or Twitter, respectively.

As more graduates enter the workforce with degrees in the liberal arts, and an average of $37,172 in student debt (a $20,000 increase from 10+ years ago), apprenticeship-based learning seems not only practical, but inevitable—and this predictable shift is certain to affect both educational institutions and corporations competing for talent.[10]

Canadian entrepreneur Carl Rodrigues, founder of SOTI, one of Canada's largest mobile solutions and IoT providers, has a similar perspective. He believes the education system must change, especially for software programming and related tech. "We have to change how we're teaching technology. Technology is constantly changing and moving—there's new stuff going on every day. People are teaching this stuff who aren't as passionate as those working in the field. So, there has to be more direct involvement from the private sector, so we're teaching what's relevant."[11]

In the face of a rapidly expanding "gig economy," companies with deep visionary-founder roots, like Shopify, are at a distinct advantage. What Lütke and leaders like him bring is a unique openness to challenging the status quo. This kind of long-term thinking on an evolving economy certain to be ruled by data science, artificial intelligence, quantum computing, and autonomous transport shapes a company's mission and "raison d'être" in a way that traditional firms seem to miss.

Is there a place tomorrow for today's traditional school curriculum and post-secondary system? Maybe, but the argument for its relevance is waning. One thing is for certain: North America should soon feel a little more like Germany if it wants to compete and evolve.

A Snowdevil of an Idea

By the time he completed his apprenticeship, in addition to his passion for programming in various languages like Rosie, SQL, and Delphi and hacking languages like Java, Lütke had another significant interest: snowboarding. His winter hobby would prove to be an important piece in the puzzle—both personally and professionally.

This book isn't a romance novel, so I'll keep this part short. While on a snowboarding trip to Whistler, B.C., Lütke met Fiona McKean, an Ottawa native who, as the daughter of diplomats, had grown up travelling the world. After pursuing a bachelor's degree, she joined Lütke in Germany for a while before they decided to move to Canada to build a future together.

Shortly after moving to Ottawa with Fiona (Tobi and Fiona are now married), Lütke met Scott Lake, an Ottawa local with a solid academic pedigree. Lake, a natural relationship builder with a PhD in political science and a master's in international relations, had a valuable network in Canada's capital. Conversations between him and Lütke quickly turned into a business idea built on a mutual passion for hitting the slopes. In 2004, Lake and Lütke launched their new online business, selling—you guessed it—snowboards.

They called it Snowdevil. There was no grand vision for the start-up, and no real long-term plan. More than anything, the business was simply a cool project that tapped into both their personal interests. They each had defined roles and responsibilities, with Lake taking the business reins, and Lütke handling all the technology.

Coding up the first iteration, Lütke developed the snowboard store in an application framework called Ruby, then switched to a newer framework called "Ruby on Rails," devised by Danish programmer David Heinemeier Hansson, to improve the website's efficiency. On online forums, Lütke shared his hacks and certain software components he was creating for the store, and quickly became part of a core group of up-and-coming Rails developers.

As the snowboard business trucked along, Lütke and Lake both realized that the e-commerce software Lütke had customized for the store could potentially be its own stand-alone product that other merchants could use to sell stuff online. There wasn't much in the way of competition. Lütke had tried all the other software solutions and found them lacking, in quality if not in quantity of options. "I sometimes liken the landscape to what MP3 players were like before the iPod," he wrote on Quora. "They had tons of 'advanced features'... but they just sucked." [12]

Excited by the prospect of a new business pivot, Lake and Lütke persuaded a group of ten friends and family members (McKean's father and Lütke's uncle among them) to help fund the new vision—which they called Jaded Pixel. Before long, Lake changed the name to a Sean Parker–style moniker: Shopify.

In 2006, its first year of operations, Shopify reported revenues of $96,000. Revenue increased the next year, but not before Shopify quickly developed cash flow problems. On January 1, 2007, Toronto-based Klister Credit, an early-stage angel investment firm under the stewardship of John Phillips, wrote Shopify a check for $250,000—the company's seed round, valuing Shopify at $3 million. [13] While the cash provided a little breathing room, it wasn't enough.

Lake knew Shopify needed more funding if it was to survive. He was adamant about pushing for a proper injection of venture capital. But Lütke was conflicted: raising venture money meant a totally different path for Shopify, one that didn't necessarily resonate with Lütke's personality and aspirations as a product developer. He questioned whether it made sense to turn Shopify into a growth company (inherent with any VC investment), or keep it more of a "lifestyle" play, small and dividend-rich. "I think Scott was frustrated with me, based on me changing my position on this so often," said Lütke. [14]

Things came to a head in 2008. Lake left Shopify, leaving Lütke to play the role of company frontman. Picking up the reins of CEO meant a crash course in various aspects of business operations Lütke knew nothing about—like what to do about the company's dire need for cash and how to keep its operations afloat.

Lütke's first instinct following Lake's departure was to book a trip to San Francisco to earn a so-called real-world MBA, by picking the brains of every venture capitalist who would take a meeting. While the prospect of learning some business chops was top of mind, the urgency to find funding, and replace himself as CEO, were also key priorities for Lütke. While he did learn about customer lifetime value, conversion funnels, and churn rate, his mission to find cash and a CEO was an utter failure. Silicon Valley was still licking its wounds from the dot-com crash, and no one was ready to take a leap back into e-commerce just yet. As for leadership, the overarching feedback from the VC panel was that Shopify was Lütke's offspring, a project that only he could oversee—sobering news for a founder who wanted someone else to take over.

Lütke turned to Fiona's father for help. Luckily for him, Bruce McKean not only lent an ear, but covered Shopify's payroll while Lütke agreed to bridge any financial gap with his personal savings. It was a desperate time.

Things began to change in early 2009, with the release of Shopify's new API platform and app store. In a press release, Lütke said, "E-commerce is a highly individualized business. Every store wants to offer a unique buying experience but providing too many features makes the software cumbersome and difficult to use. The Shopify API solves this by allowing merchants to install exactly the features they need to get the most out of their store."[15] By offering an app store, essentially a marketplace for third-party developers to sell their apps to Shopify merchants, Shopify now offered a new, widespread set of tools the company could not otherwise create at scale, thereby bolstering the entire value proposition of the platform. It was a key turning point.

Shopify Becomes a Growth Company

In 2010, Bessemer Venture Partners caught wind of Shopify's momentum. Bessemer, one of Silicon Valley's largest venture capital firms, was surprised that Shopify was able to grow so quickly out of a city as un-Silicon-Valley-like as Ottawa. In fact, it's not clear whether the firm's partners could even point to the city on a map at the time.

VCs unfamiliar with Canada's tech sector didn't know it, but the 2008 financial crisis and subsequent recession, which had hurt most of the American tech sector, had benefitted Shopify in a couple of unique ways. First, individuals who had recently lost their corporate jobs were becoming more entrepreneurial, launching online stores to sell home-grown products like cookies and biscuits, wine, surfboards, apparel, accessories, artwork and graphic novels, and more. And many of them flocked to Shopify.[16] Second, the collapse of Canadian corporate telecom giant Nortel, and, similarly, layoffs at IBM's office in Ottawa, had spilled a pool of talent into the region, which became filled with thousands of capable and unemployed software engineers just as Shopify was scaling. Lütke's team took advantage.

Bessemer was convinced that Lütke and his Ottawa-based company had something compelling. In December of 2010, it organized a Series A funding round of $7 million, purchasing 20 percent of the company and two board seats. Series B quickly followed for another $15 million in 2011, followed by a Series C in 2013, led by OMERS Ventures and Insight Venture Partners, bringing in an additional $100 million.[17] Cash positions had turned a corner; revenue as well as employee count was climbing.

Merchants, however, were having a hard time navigating Shopify's complex payments setup. The platform made it easy to set up an online store, but its third-party payment integration requirements were a total mess by comparison. At the time, the general payments ecosystem was (and still is, to some extent) a notoriously complex web, with each company playing a nuanced role in the payments value chain. Companies like Visa, Mastercard, or American Express worked with banks to issue credit cards, keep an eye on card activity, and approve transactions. Acquirers for these companies, such as Chase and Bank of America, provided merchant accounts and lines of credit, sometimes directly, but often through ISOs or other third parties. Point-of-sale (POS) technology companies such as Ingenico were busy selling hardware to retailers, while companies like Square were introducing modernized POS equipment and software for mobile computing devices like smartphones and tablets (among other things). Online sellers, who simply wanted to accept credit cards on their website, needed merchant accounts that they had to source themselves—a process that could take up to four weeks.

For Shopify's clients, the payment side of things was, to put it politely, a total shitshow. There were alternatives—mainly through closed loops like PayPal or Bitcoin, which independently manage all steps of the transaction process between consumer and merchant—but these options weren't, and still aren't, considered "mainstream" when it comes to accepting online payments. PayPal-only merchants would quickly get pushed out of the credibility ring.

Given all the complexities, Shopify set out to find a solution through a strategic partnership with the most innovative disruptor in the payments space to date: Stripe. To make things easy for merchants, the Irish company was busy removing all the inefficiencies of acquirers, card-issuing banks, and credit card brands. As a result, it played two primary roles in the payments ecosystem: "payment processor" and "e-commerce payment provider." Stripe was a one-stop shop for merchants just wanting to accept a Visa or Mastercard.

Shopify noted that Stripe could remove the headaches associated with accepting payments, and provide its merchants with faster onboarding in the process. Shopify also smelled plenty of business upside through a new potential revenue stream stemming from funds that traditionally went to other payment acquirers. By inking a deal with Stripe, the two companies could bypass the "middlemen," and capitalize on a portion of these interchange fees and related charges.

Midway through 2013, Shopify announced the new partnership: Shopify Payments, "powered by Stripe." Merchants could set up and accept credit card payments within minutes, instead of weeks—right on Shopify. It was a seamless addition to the platform. Shopify tied in all kinds of cool payment features such as real-time payment tracking, inventory tie-in, chargeback recovery, and more. Pricing too was easy to understand, with a simple discount rate of 2.9 percent plus $0.30 applied to each transaction. Incumbent pricing models were significantly more complicated, with additional fees tied to processing American Express or international credit cards, and for PCI (payment card industry) compliance.[18] With Shopify's new offering, none of this applied.

The partnership with Stripe helped boost Shopify's total value proposition, which then saw the company capitalize on the momentum with an IPO in the spring of 2015. The company's public offering raised more than $131 million.[19] In 2018, Shopify's share price on the NYSE rose by 66 percent, joining Twitter, Intuit, Salesforce, and Amazon as an overall top stock market performer for the calendar year.[20] By September 2019, the share price had broken the $300 threshold.

Critics like Andrew Left, an analyst with Citron Research and a famous Shopify short-seller, is not only skeptical of Shopify's lofty valuation and business model, but says the company's ethics are questionable. He points to the hundreds of thousands of customers the company claims it has, and says that many of them are smaller online players marketing shady products and business opportunity scams. He also disparages the company's use of third-party marketers (known as affiliates), which it compensates through its partnership program, who often use banner advertisements with nebulous terms like "become a millionaire" to lure traffic and, ultimately, sign-ups to Shopify's platform. Left says these types of advertisements violate U.S. Federal Trade Commission marketing standards, making Shopify complicit in its participation in such tactics.[21]

Based on traditional valuation ratios, Left might be right to suggest that Shopify's stock is overvalued. The company's price-to-sales ratio, for example, hovered around 30x in mid-2019—while leading tech giants like Adobe and Salesforce run at about 14x and 9x respectively.[22]

If you're a profit-first pundit, there's an easy bear case here. Shopify's relentless focus on growth at the expense of its bottom line has meant the company has never actually turned a full year of profit, and it looks like it won't for a few more years to come.[23] Moreover, competition has heated up, with more new entrants as well as mainstream acquisitions, such as Adobe's purchase of rival Magento, which counts Coca-Cola Co., Intelligentsia Coffee, Canon Inc., and Burger King among its customers. Wordpress is also a threat, given that the open-sourced platform can be totally customized in the hands of the right developer. In fact, its e-commerce plug-in, WooCommerce, was the market leader as recently as 2018, ahead of both Magento and Shopify, with a 21 percent global market share.[24] Automattic, its parent company, just raised $300 million in Series D funding from Salesforce Ventures to boot.

Left's short-selling position could come to fruition over the long term if competition starts to chip away at Shopify and investors refocus on industry multiples to fairly valuate the stock price. Yet his claims lambasting the company for ethics violations go too far. Shopify, like any company with an affiliate program, faces the near-impossible task of policing all of its publishers. Certainly Shopify could improve its ability to clean up its marketing and communication strategy by circulating preapproved banner ad messaging and associated creative, while keeping a watchful eye on offenders—but claiming the company can sterilize its partner program to remove all such harm isn't realistic; there will always be bad apples. Judging by the company's stock performance in 2019, investors tend to agree.

High Expectations

Shopify has played the long game since it pivoted away from snowboards, building a business off servicing the long tail first. With a goal of allowing anyone, anywhere, to set up a digital store without technical expertise, the company has made good on its vision to make online commerce accessible to any entrepreneur. As of late 2019, it was the most-used e-commerce technology across the global internet.

DISTRIBUTION OF E-COMMERCE TECHNOLOGY AS PERCENTAGE OF ALL E-COMMERCE WEBSITES

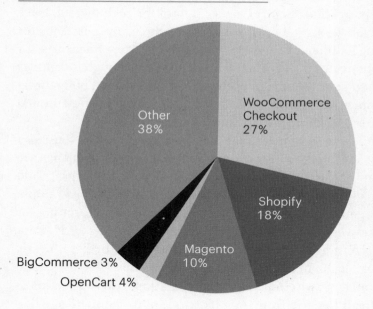

As of September 2019, Shopify was used on over 1 million websites—nearly a quarter of all websites that used e-commerce technologies.

Source: "eCommerce Usage Distribution on the Entire Internet," BuiltWith, accessed September 24, 2019 https://trends.builtwith.com/shop/traffic/Entire-Internet.

By servicing previously neglected merchants with enterprise-grade infrastructure, Shopify has developed a substantial customer base that includes both small merchants (that long tail) and, more recently, enterprise-level clients, who represent a growing slice of the pie. Boasting clients like Google, GE, and Tesla, the company is sure to add more to its bottom-line enterprise profit margin through pricier subscription tiers.

Shopify's business seems more robust than ever before, stemming from the simplicity and reliability of its platform, its accessible subscription model, and its ability to create and foster a great company culture. More important, though, is Shopify's ability to retain customers. Client retention is rooted in a kind of business philosophy, often called the "lock-in effect," where a company (like Shopify) makes it hard for customers to leave once they've signed on. Banks, for example, are notorious for making it difficult to move to another bank. The same is true for cell-phone providers, who tie up customers through incentives like a $0 smartphone, in exchange for contractual obligations. Customers who want to leave for another provider before the end of a contract's term are penalized financially.

In the B2B (business-to-business) world, companies like Salesforce and Shopify, which maintain several enterprise clients, are masters of the lock-in. Once Salesforce deploys its software and trains employees on using it, clients like Adidas, for example, aren't going anywhere. The operational costs of searching for alternatives, committing to a new provider, moving legacy data, and retraining everyone on using a new system, makes it nearly impossible for an executive to justify such a move.

Similarly, switching costs and operational disruption make it difficult to move from Shopify to one of its competitors, like Magento. Let's keep on this point about switching costs for a moment, using Netflix as an example—this time, from the perspective of a B2C (business-to-customer) company. If, as a Netflix customer, I want to cancel my subscription and sign up for Hulu instead, it doesn't take much effort. So a B2C player like Netflix doesn't garner the same lock-in advantage as a B2B company like

Shopify or Salesforce. As a result, Netflix must devote an extraordinary amount of effort to keeping content relevant and engaging, ensuring it is boosting its value proposition over time. In highlighting this stand-alone example, we can say that as a general rule, switching costs for businesses are much higher than they are for consumers, and B2B companies who understand this phenomenon, and subsequently nail their value proposition, are rewarded by retaining most of their client base.

Shopify's lock-in is a key factor contributing to a rosy forecast. But given our earlier mentions of the competition, there's an urgency to innovate that Lütke cannot ignore—and isn't. Not only is Shopify investing in improving its existing technology, it's also creating new channels to reach customers, like physical stores. Shopify opened its first brick-and-mortar location in Los Angeles in a bid to attract—and keep—more retailers on the platform. The first store provides Shopify product training and education, guidance for growing one's business, and community events designed to bring business owners and entrepreneurs together.[25] The Shopify store announcement came just after the company announced its new "dynamic checkout," a point-of-sale product that allows brick-and-mortar merchants to offer contactless payment systems like Apple Pay, and will soon include features like tipping, in-store pickup, and "multi-channel return and exchange options."[26] Technology innovation is also underway to better serve the cashless payment space overseas for merchants running operations in other languages, such as French, Spanish, Italian, German, Japanese, and Portuguese.

Perhaps most exciting, though, is Shopify's horizontal expansion strategy to align itself with the Canadian cannabis industry, a crafty move since the Government of Canada legalized marijuana on October 17, 2018. Shopify signed an agreement with the Government of Ontario to power the province's online sales of recreational weed in partnership with the newly created Ontario Cannabis Retail Corporation.[27] Shopify later signed on with British Columbia in a similar arrangement.[28]

The opportunity extends beyond government contracts to local cannabis dispensaries in the private sector as well. As the industry takes shape in Canada, plenty of emerging cannabis distributors will demand robust point-of-sale and inventory tracking systems. Licenced producers will soon need robust systems to run direct-to-consumer sales channels. Shopify is sure to be the de facto option, having already teamed up with licenced tier-1 producers such as Canopy Growth Corp. and The Hydropothecary Corp.

Shopify has made itself the Canadian technology pioneer in the emerging cannabis economy, with no "bud" left unturned, as they say. Lütke continues to make good on his ties to innovation, with Canadian culture courtesy of cannabis now front and center in Shopify's home-grown growth story.

SEVEN

The Spotify Soundtrack

APPLE AIR PODS, introduced in September 2016 alongside the iPhone 7, have largely supplanted wired audio. The next generation of the over-the-ear headphones are likely to be noise-cancelling, water-resistant, and certainly more expensive.[1] Beyond the cult of loyal Mac followers, Apple is also introducing products that continue to take advantage of the next wave of the music industry—which is experiencing a new revival, thanks to streaming.

Be it music, movies, TV shows, or podcasts, streaming is growing exponentially. Global revenues from music streaming alone have more than tripled in three years, to an estimated $9 billion in 2018—47 percent of the entire industry.[2] Before 2014, the music industry was slowly declining, due in large part to piracy issues. Since then, we've witnessed a resurgence led by companies like Amazon, Pandora, Apple, and the biggest driver and market leader, Spotify.[3] Spotify owns two-thirds of the streaming pie, with revenues climbing from $3.6 billion in 2016 to over $6.3 billion (USD) in 2018, making it one of the most important companies in the music business, largely responsible for resuscitating a dying industry.[4]

Founded by Daniel Ek and Martin Lorentzon in a suburb of Stockholm in 2006, Spotify is now widely considered the king of music streaming. As of June 2019, the company had notched roughly 230 million active monthly users, about half of whom were paid subscribers—approximately double that of Apple Music.[5]

Spotify's basic version is free, supported by a traditional advertising-supported business model. Users can stream whatever they want as long as they're willing to tolerate the occasional paid advertisement. For those willing to spend $10 a month, Spotify Premium provides unlimited, ad-free access to more than 35 million songs via any device connected to the internet. Music on the platform is searched using parameters such as artist, album, genre, playlist, or record label. Spotify users can create, edit, and share playlists and tracks on social media platforms like Facebook.

While DJs used to routinely populate our eardrums through radio airplay, Spotify's 2 billion playlists (most of which are curated by subscribers) have pushed pancake spinners aside while garnering millions of followers. Data generated through machine learning allows Spotify to use listener behavior to suggest complementary playlists and daily mixes. Its ability to personalize the user experience makes Spotify that much more valuable.

So, how did we go from buying music in physical format, to sharing and pirating MP3 files, to a streaming-crazed audience consuming audio through platforms like Spotify? There is some great innovation and a few very smart creators involved, but Spotify's success is rooted in a deeper history that links the Swedish company to Facebook, and a critical x-factor, Napster.

The Napster name still carries some stigma owing to piracy and a questionable "free music" model, but the disruption and innovation that Napster unleashed in 1999 has lifted the industry to new heights. Suffice it to say, if it weren't for Napster, Spotify and its constituency wouldn't exist.

The Napster Revolution

For several years, CDs were the ultimate showcase of musical taste and appreciation of high fidelity. In addition to superior audio quality, compact discs came in a case complete with album liner notes, pictures, and, at times, pages of song lyrics.

The discs themselves were fragile, requiring lots of attention and constant care. If one wasn't careful, a scratch on the bottom side could ruin a whole album, meaning collectors like me regularly cleaned their discs and used creams to smooth any visible nicks. At one time, the CD collection I owned was the most important thing in my life. However, the hundreds of titles I gathered over years are nowhere to be found—gone, poof, like Kansas's "Dust in the Wind." They evaporated courtesy of internet innovation, the advent of MP3, broadband, the rise of streaming, and the controversial company that made it all happen.

To understand how the music industry has evolved in the last two decades, we need to go back to 1999—a year that saw the launch of the BlackBerry, talk of Y2K, impeachment proceedings against Bill Clinton, and, perhaps more consequential than all of the above, the launch of Napster.

The peer-to-peer music sharing platform was founded by Shawn Fanning, the enigmatic visionary who *Time* and *Fortune* have called the greatest computer hacker of all time; Sean Parker, who went on to serve as Facebook's first president; and a lesser-known but critically important programmer named Jordan Ritter.

Before Napster, Fanning had developed an interest in coding when his uncle, John Fanning, bought him an Apple computer. John had a foggy business history but was something of a father figure to Shawn, and would later allow the early Napster team to work out of his struggling Chess.net office. By the late 1990s, Fanning had developed a passion for computer hacking and joined an exclusive IRC (Internet Relay Chat) channel called w00w00, where web junkies shared their mutual programming interests. He sent messages under the moniker Napster.

In 1998, while at Northeastern University in Boston, Fanning spent much of his time on a pet project geared at enabling audio file-sharing online. At the time, formats for compressing CD-quality music into digital data had shortcomings, and websites that had attempted to simplify the process required users to know things like File Transfer Protocol (FTP) commands and other esoteric conventions—which a layperson, of course, knew nothing about. Excited by the possibilities, Fanning turned to some fellow hackers on woowoo for feedback on his project in the spring of '99. One of them was Jordan Ritter, a software engineer employed at a firm called BindView. Ritter liked what we he saw. With a fellow woowoo member, he provided Fanning with some feedback and helped fix bugs as the project took shape. Fanning soon asked Ritter to officially join him, and oversee development of the server. Ritter quit his full-time gig and dove in.

Reflecting twenty years later on his decision to work with Shawn Fanning, Ritter recalled realizing "there's something here .... People loved this service. All those things were wonderful and attractive for me. I didn't know what to expect from this start-up experience, but there was nothing that had skyrocketed like this." [6]

Although there were similar networks facilitating the distribution of files, such as Hotline and Usenet, Napster's technology had a specific appeal buoyed by an interface that enabled its users (mostly students) to easily download and share MP3 audio files for free. If an individual wanted to listen to *The Miseducation of Lauryn Hill,* say, they could simply search for the album on Napster and download it to their hard drive in minutes. The platform was revolutionary, and in short order infected college campuses everywhere.

As Napster spread across the country and beyond, Ritter worked to enhance the back-end, adding some critical features such as load balancing, which helped level internet server weights as the company scaled to avoid downtime. As the platform attracted more and more users, the business side needed tending to. So Fanning brought on Sean Parker, another chat room friend whose charisma complemented Fanning and Ritter's desire to work behind the scenes. Parker, who joined as a partner, seemed to round out the team's skillset, but questions about corporate structure hung in the balance. Smelling an opportunity to take advantage of his nephew's early run, John Fanning had swiftly incorporated Napster Inc. before Parker came on board, in the process sneaking his way into owning 70 percent of the company. Parker, who had some business savvy, was shocked at the share split. But, given the momentum, he and the team pushed forward.

As Parker started networking, he soon landed a deal with Yosi Amram, Napster's first outside investor. Amram not only cut a check, but recruited Napster's first CEO, Eileen Richardson, a veteran Silicon Valley venture capitalist, to step in and help with additional stewardship.

In its first year of operations, without any advertising or promotion, Napster went from 50,000 users to nearly 20 million. The sheer volume of users put unforeseen pressure on networks in college dormitories, with as much as 61 percent of external traffic consisting of MP3 file transfers—causing some colleges to go so far as to block Napster's use.[7]

Things looked good, but as more users embraced the platform, the music industry was singing a different tune. Controversy struck when popular metal band Metallica discovered a demo of their song "I Disappear" circulating across Napster before its official release. Metallica filed a copyright infringement suit against Napster in early 2000, dealing a big blow to the brand's reputation. A month later, rapper and producer Dr. Dre did the same after Napster refused to remove his music from circulation.

In the wake of the suits, Richardson stepped down as CEO, replaced by venture capitalist Hank Barry, who was chosen to help navigate the muddying legal waters. In his testimony before the senate judiciary committee, Barry said:

> Lawsuits against Napster contend that our 20 million users, the recording and music publishing industry's best customers, are guilty of copyright infringement. We strongly disagree.

Copyright is not absolute. It has limits. Companies that hold copyrights on behalf of creators, and which control distribution of creative works, have a strong inclination to change the copyright laws from a balanced vehicle for public enrichment to an unbalanced engine of control. Copyright holders traditionally are reluctant to allow new technologies to emerge.[8]

Despite Napster's efforts to work with industry incumbents to cut some sort of distribution deal, an appeals court ordered Napster to stop allowing copyrighted material to be shared. In a somewhat desperate final attempt to save the company, Napster held a press conference to promise record labels $1 billion over five years from a new subscription service it had in the works. The offer was refused, of course, and, unable to comply with court demands, Napster ceased operations in 2001, and filed for bankruptcy in 2002.

DESPITE ALL the negative backlash against Napster and its supposed impact on the recording industry, the company revolutionized music accessibility. Without its vision for the way music would live via the internet, the industry would not have evolved the way it has.

While bands like Metallica led the recoil, others, like English alternative "prog-rock" icons Radiohead, saw Napster's model as progressive. They even credit the platform for some of their commercial success—citing as a specific example the premature leak of songs from their fourth studio album, *Kid A*, on Napster before the official release. When the album hit the market in late 2000, *Kid A* skyrocketed to number one on the Billboard 200 chart in its debut week. As the band explains, the early slip acted as a promotional tool. But Ray Lott, president of Capitol Records, the band's label at the time, dismissed the industry's panic over Napster. "I'm trying to sell as many Radiohead albums as possible. If I worried about what Napster would do, I wouldn't sell as many albums."[9]

Parker Finds Napster 2.0

In the wake of Napster's demise, the resolute Sean Parker re-emerged onto the scene in 2002 with the launch of Plaxo, a networked address book that helped influence companies such as LinkedIn, Zynga, and Facebook. "Plaxo is like the indie band that the public doesn't know but was really influential with other musicians," Parker said.[10] Two years after founding the company, Parker was ousted by its venture financiers, Sequoia Capital and Ram Shriram, in an acrimonious exit that certain sources say involved the company's investors hiring private investigators to prove misconduct.[11]

In 2004, when Parker stumbled on "The Facebook" on the computer of a roommate's girlfriend at Stanford, he immediately knew that his expertise from Napster, Plaxo, and social network pioneer Friendster (where he played an advisory role) could bene-fit the fledgling social network. He set up a meeting with founders Mark Zuckerberg and Eduardo Saverin, and in true Parker fash-ion was soon networking hard around the Valley on behalf of Facebook. One of his first deals was securing the company's first outside investment, $500,000 from Peter Thiel, the PayPal co-founder who served as that company's chief executive officer until its sale to eBay in 2002. Parker's swagger resonated with Zuckerberg. "Sean was pivotal in helping Facebook transform from a college project into a real company," said Zuckerberg.[12] In short order, Parker found himself the founding president of the social network. But in 2005, after an incident involving a rented beach house, cocaine, and the police—though he wasn't arrested or charged—Parker was forced to resign. After the dust settled, he remained in contact with Zuckerberg from his new post with Thiel's vc firm, the Founders Fund.

While sniffing around for investment opportunities for the fund's portfolio, Parker came across a technology entrepreneur named Daniel Ek who was doing some interesting things in Swe-den. Ek had a solid tech pedigree from several previous roles, in particular as CEO of µTorrent, another popular P2P (peer to peer) file-sharing platform. He was working on something akin to Napster—a peer-to-peer music service called Spotify, whose mission was to solve piracy issues, compensate the industry, and still allow end users to share files.

In the wake of its successful launch at home in Sweden in October of 2008, Spotify slowly rolled out its offering in the U.K., and then to other markets across Europe. While business expansion was slow by North American standards, Spotify use cases in markets like Sweden, Norway, Denmark, the Netherlands, and the United Kingdom were promising, prompting music buffs to take notice.

Spotify's release was well timed. The industry was still mired in piracy problems, courtesy of Napster substitutes that had popped up in its absence. As Ek's platform began to spread, music execs caught wind of a potential lifeline in the form of not only a free, but a legal alternative. Parker, who had been following Spotify from California, emailed Ek and Shakil Khan, one of Spotify's advisors.

The email sparked a phenomenal string of events, linking Spotify to Parker, then to the Founders Fund, and finally, and most important, to Facebook. Parker's ability to make connections and spot unicorn potential was on full display. If you have time, it's worth reading the entire email.[13] But here are the core paragraphs, where Parker recognizes the power of Spotify's value proposition:

> What's clear is that the labels never quite understood the way people really consume/share/experience digital music. And they couldn't admit to themselves that this behavior pattern wasn't changing anytime soon. Rather, to create the right experience, the business terms of their standard licensing deals would need to change.
>
> And change they have (in subtle but important ways) to enable the user experience that you've created with Spotify. Perhaps it was wishful thinking to believe that these deals

could have been implemented in the US first... so I'm not surprised that the Spotify "experiment" had to be conducted elsewhere.

. . . . I've waited nearly a decade for a product that could match the standard set by Napster on three counts:

(1) convenience
(2) speed/responsiveness
(3) sampling/discovery of music

. . . . We find ourselves in an odd place. The iPod monopoly has effectively stifled innovation in the market. The investor bias towards web applications over desktop applications has lead [*sic*] to a broken user experience and poor implementation of streaming music solutions.

You guys have changed all that. You've distilled the product down to its core essence and implemented the right basic set of features. As product designers we can never have exactly what we want, when we want it. We have to start by understanding the really important parts and building that core functionality first, then building additional features around that core. When you're building consumer products, getting serious leverage in the marketplace (distribution) is the most important first order goal, so you need to accomplish this as quickly as possible and then shift gears to build second generation features.

You guys nailed the core experience: it's at least as good as Napster for search and listening, and everything else can be built from there.[14]

Parker's email sparked an €11 million investment from Founders Fund and solidified a new board seat for Parker himself, who Ek recruited to assist Spotify's business development efforts in the U.S. market.

However, the real turning point came in September 2011, at Facebook's annual F8 conference, just two months after Spotify's

U.S. launch. During his keynote speech, Zuckerberg presented an overview of Facebook's open graph—a technology enabling a new class of integrated social apps—and said that "eventually all apps that you use will be social." [15] Zuckerberg then discussed Spotify as a prominent example, showing attendees how Facebook users could listen to songs from their Spotify account within Facebook, with one click. To cap off the speech, Zuckerberg invited Ek on stage to announce an official partnership between the two companies. "Today is a big day for Facebook, and a big day for Spotify," Ek said. "We spent the last few years building a service which fairly compensates artists. Put that on top of Facebook's 800 million users and the world will light up with music." [16]

The collaboration with Spotify meant some new added features to Facebook, like the ability to automatically share what you were listening to in your newsfeed—but it was a game-changer for Ek's platform. Facebook users who didn't have Spotify installed now had a hell of an incentive to download it. Within twenty-four hours of the announcement at F8, Spotify had over 1 million new sign-ups. Within a month, they had doubled their user base, from approximately 3 million users to over 6 million. Thanks to Facebook, and specifically Parker, Spotify was on its way to the moon.

SPOTIFY'S MONTHLY active user base continues to grow, reaching over 230 million; global subscriptions recently passed the 100 million mark. Total revenue eclipsed $1.7 billion in the first quarter of 2019, though the company still recorded a loss of over $150 million. [17]

The company has crushed the competition in terms of customer engagement. Subscriber stickiness is about five times that of Apple's. Spotify users rack up sixty-one monthly sessions on average—or around two sessions per day—while Pandora's user base and that of Apple Music engage forty-three and twelve sessions per month, respectively. [18]

Spotify has renegotiated licensing deals with Sony Music, Universal Music Group, and Warner Music Group, thus giving the

MUSIC STREAMING USERS WITH PAID SUBSCRIPTIONS

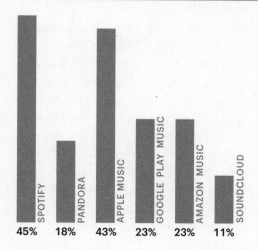

By 2018, nearly half of Spotify users were paying for the service, ahead of Apple, Amazon, and other competitors.

Source: "Understanding Spotify: Making Music Through Innovation," Goodwater Capital, March 15, 2018, https://www.goodwatercap.com/thesis/understanding-spotify.

company a break on royalty payouts, which in turn helps to boost its operating margins.

Spotify is currently testing plenty of new products, such as the Apple Watch app that hit the market in early 2019. It's the first time users have been able to directly access Spotify playlists/song control on the Apple Watch without using an iPhone.

Savior or Snake?

Despite all the positive momentum surrounding Spotify's growth and its ability to pave the way forward for both musicians and listeners, the company still gets Napster-like flack from record labels and artists who question whether Spotify is an industry poison.

Spotify's business model, which is driven by subscriber revenue, differs from that of physical album sales, or even downloads, where artists are paid a fixed price per sale. Instead, the amount Spotify pays out, which is based on a per-stream of a song, varies according to several factors, including the proportion of total streams that the artist represents. Consequently, royalties range from $.006 and $.0084 per play, depending on the artist, and are paid to whoever holds the copyright. In the aggregate, approximately 70 percent of Spotify's revenue is paid to rights holders, a handsome sum of the company's top-line revenue, to be clear. It's then up to those rights holders, be they a big music label like Sony, Universal, or Warner, or a smaller independent house, to distribute the revenue accordingly based on individual agreements.

David Crosby (of Crosby, Stills, Nash & Young fame) says Spotify royalty payments are unfairly low. "They rigged it so they don't pay the artist," he told *Rolling Stone* magazine. "I've lost half of my income because of these clever fellas. I used to make money off my records, but now I don't make any."[19] Crosby is not alone—top artists and producers like Taylor Swift and Thom Yorke are not fans either. A common argument is that Spotify's model sends the lion's share of revenue to the top pop stars, who are able to negotiate up to 40 percent of royalties, whereas older or unknown musicians settle for much less—approximately 12 to 15 percent.

The problem is bigger than revenue sharing. Wixen Music Publishing, which controls copyrights for songs by artists who include Tom Petty, the Doors, and Neil Young, filed a $1.6 billion lawsuit against Spotify in late 2017, alleging that it used compositions without proper licences and dodged related royalty payments. Jeff Price, the founder of Audiam, a company that helps artists retrieve unpaid streaming royalties, said, "It didn't matter who the songwriter was—for Bob Dylan, there are 700 versions of 'All Along the Watchtower,' and almost none are getting paid."[20]

In Spotify's defense, the company has no affiliation with or control over independent agreements between rights holders and artists. As Richard Jones, manager of the Pixies and Teenage Fanclub, notes, "there are very apparent differences in the amount of income coming from streaming. The labels are certainly getting the money—how they're paying the artists is the debatable point."[21] Jones's point is key: what needs more scrutiny is how record labels are adjusting to the industry, and how they are paying their artists.

Consumer preferences for music genres also affect royalties. What artists like David Crosby miss is that classic rock as a genre isn't as popular as it used to be. Classic rock radio as a format has been replaced by Top 40. "Radio has become homogeneous that way," says Daniel Goldenberg, a partner with law firm Goldenberg Nahmias LLP in Toronto, whose practice focuses on commercial transactions in the areas of entertainment, media, and intellectual property. "Crosby used to make higher royalties from radio play. But radio has changed . . . Q107 [a classic rock radio station based in Toronto] doesn't play much CSNY [Crosby, Stills, Nash & Young] anymore so he is feeling a hit there. Moreover, most listeners who are using streaming services like Spotify aren't streaming classic rock—it's just not what younger people are listening to—the raw data doesn't lie," Goldenberg explains.

And what does the raw data say? According to Goldenberg, as of fall 2019, the Rolling Stones had 15.6 million monthly listeners on Spotify—as listenership rankings go, that's good for 156th in the world. And, while impressive, Taylor Swift's 41.5 million monthly listeners puts her at 13th. Ed Sheeran, at 67.3 million monthly listeners, is 1st in the world. Sadly for Crosby, CSNY has 2.5 million monthly listeners. No world ranking attached.[22]

Regardless, Spotify doesn't seem to be dodging the indie narrative. In fact, its newest venture, Spotify for Artists, cuts out the middleman by allowing independent artists to upload directly to the platform and receive 100 percent of revenues. Should individual artists not want to go this route, they can outsource digital music distribution, publishing, and licensing to services like CD Baby and Tunecore—both of which use Spotify to manage and collect royalties.

SPOTIFY GENERALLY responds to its critics by citing the $10 billion in royalties it's paid out. In its recent modified public offering, the company claims it has helped save the record business from online piracy.[23] Judging by the industry's near-demise from 2001–08, give or take, the company is spot-on.

While the discrepancies may anger a few, a sobering aspect of this phenomenon is that most artists on any streaming platform, be it Spotify or otherwise, simply don't get the listens. Music is no different than any other industry: it follows the laws of supply and demand. Consumer demand, and consumer preferences, are generally validated by dollar spend; in this particular case, the voting mechanism has changed from album sales in stores to streams and downloads on the web. In other words, the music people want to listen to gets the streams.

The benefits of streaming revenue, albeit controversial in many cases, are still very real for artists who otherwise would have to rely on their own marketing vehicles to draw attention to their music and consequently pull in dollars. With access to Spotify, musical newcomers now have a global platform for listener discovery, and a plausible monetization channel in addition to YouTube and the bar around the corner. There's also the benefit of long-tail revenue from streaming—it's not a one-time revenue grab. Hundreds of millions of streams are happening every day, which multiplies potential revenues over the long term.

Notwithstanding the David Crosbys of the world, there are plenty of artists who are staunch supporters of Spotify's model, specifically those not signed to major labels. Without access to traditional mass media such as radio and television, this bucket of up-and-coming talent has claimed that Napster and successive internet file-sharing platforms like Spotify have helped get their music heard. Will Toledo, the frontman for the band Car Seat Headrest, told *Rolling Stone*, "Some artists are making money off Spotify. It is not an across-the-board negative experience." Howard King, an attorney for Kanye West, Pharrell, and, ironically, Metallica, adds that "Not only the record labels but the composers have a whole new income stream they've never had before, and in large part may have replaced what they used to earn on albums."[24] And after taking a three-year hiatus from Spotify, Taylor Swift has since relisted all her music on the platform. I suppose Swift has decided the nearly $400,000 she makes in weekly royalties from Spotify is sufficiently fair.[25]

Most important, Spotify offers a compliant way for music lovers to listen to what they love. It's all in the spirit of Spotify's core maxim, as expressed in the company's public offering in 2018: "Spotify was founded on the belief that music is universal and that streaming is a more robust and seamless access model that benefits both artists and music fans."[26]

What's Next on the Playlist

As Spotify pulls away from Apple, Pandora (now owned by SiriusXM), and others, Ek can't ignore Amazon's new premium music-streaming service, which unlocks millions of songs, thousands of playlists, and personalized stations for a similar price. Amazon is already causing some commotion, with about 12 percent of the global music-streaming subscriber pie, behind Apple's 19 percent and Spotify's leading 36 percent. And the company indicates more focus on music to come, as it integrates with its popular Echo speakers and smart assistant, Alexa.

Amazon Music Unlimited, at $9.99/month, has surpassed Spotify in terms of sheer volume of music. The company boasts 50 million songs[27]—Spotify has just over 35 million. Amazon's music service is available in thirty countries vs. Spotify's sixty-five.

While Amazon does have playlists, they don't compare to Spotify's plethora of highly curated genre- and mood-based ones. The critical mass of Spotify's library, along with its daily mixes, playlists, and music-discovery tools is killer, making for a competitive advantage that is not only hard to replicate, but would take even a company the size of Amazon a considerable amount of time to do so.

Spotify has another competitive advantage: its use of granular data (i.e., accumulated data points based on listener habits) from its listeners, which it accumulates over time based on listening habits. As highlighted earlier, user engagement is among the highest in the industry—so as monthly sessions go up, so too does the personalization meter. For example, Spotify curates daily mixes for me, as a Steely Dan listener, based on artist and genre derivatives such as Fleetwood Mac and the Eagles. A recent marketing campaign put this data to novel use when billboards were erected with messages like "Dear person who played 'Sorry' 42 times on Valentine's Day, What did you do?" Spotify's head of marketing, Seth Farbman, said "there has been some debate about whether big data is muting creativity in marketing, but we have turned that on its head . . . For us, data inspires and gives an insight into the emotion that people are expressing."[28]

We can't be sure Spotify will emerge the winner at the end of the streaming marathon; Bezos has proven Amazon can not only enter a market, but soon dominate it. But, rather than push Spotify to the sidelines, expect Amazon's Music Unlimited to play a supporting role in helping the company bring more awareness to the general Amazon ecosystem. Confusing the issue is Amazon Prime—which has its own Prime Music service with 2 million songs (yes, Amazon effectively has two music-streaming services) free to members. Since Amazon's Music Unlimited, the real potential rival, isn't free with Prime, expect music fans on Spotify to stay put, and hold a Prime membership in addition to Spotify, rather than dump the Swedish platform for a Seattle-based alternative altogether.

Another cause for Spotify optimism is podcasts, which continue to surge in popularity. Spotify is poised to benefit from the momentum: it now streams over 250,000 podcasts through a variety of fixed and variable deals, much like with music, and it recently acquired podcasting companies Gimlet Media, Anchor, and Parcast.[29] Around $14 billion is spent on U.S. radio advertising annually, but podcasts are devouring the listenership of

FM, and dollars typically reserved for radio airwaves are increasingly moving online. As a result of its infancy, podcasting advertising revenue is still only a fraction of radio's, but it's growing fast, up 86 percent in 2017 to $314 million.[30] As time goes on, the balance is certain to shift.

Objectively speaking, Spotify's advertising revenue is still pretty low; it makes up less than 10 percent of the company's total revenue. However, as the podcast sector grows, not only will it increase the average time users spend on Spotify, making it more appealing for advertisers, but as the company increases the number of podcasts on its platform, the amount of royalties paid out to labels as a percentage of revenue will decline.[31]

To address this decline in music revenue—not to mention the royalty-gouging on behalf of legacy record labels, which Spotify handsomely compensates, for now—the company does have the option to cut out the middleman, which it has begun to experiment with through its Spotify for Artists platform. Should it decide to do so, Spotify could effectively replace the labels and become the exclusive distribution arm of an artist. Speculation suggests this could be the company's next big move.[32] Such a move makes sense, given that much of its margins are being handed to the rights holders before they get to the artists themselves.

A Spotify indie label would let the company own a piece of the intellectual property, and avoid having to pay out labels whose distribution reach is waning. It could be good news for artists, the company, and those who make it all possible—the listeners.

EIGHT

Booming Boxes

GREAT COMPANIES are often not the first mover. Instead, as first movers enter a market, iterate, and grow, it is the formidable corporate players who are watching closely from the sidelines—surveying all the mistakes along the way. On a good day, the first mover sets the industry standard, wins over early adopters, and scales successfully. However, oftentimes first movers stick their heads out and learn the hard lessons that subsidize industry development, ultimately paving the way for fast followers to enter the market and grow more cost-effectively.

Ford's Model T was the first mass production automobile, but not the first on the market—that distinction belongs to the Benz Patent Motorcar. Gablinger's low-calorie beer first launched in 1967, but was later trumped by Miller Lite. Netscape dominated the field of web browsers in the 1990s, before losing out to Microsoft's Internet Explorer and, later, Google. The iPod was not the first digital music player (the "MPMan," by Saehan Information Systems in 1997, beat them to it), nor was iPhone the first smartphone (that nod goes to IBM's Simon Personal Communicator in 1992). Facebook was a fast follower to Friendster and Myspace. The list goes on ...

Harry Scherman's Book of the Month Club created the model for subscription-based businesses, but Birchbox helped pioneer the world of subscription boxes as we know it today. When the New York–based cosmetics company launched its beauty box in 2010, the idea of a "subscription box" was novel; but in the few years following Birchbox's emergence it was commerce chaos, with thousands of companies all over the United States spinning up derivatives of the model. Hundreds launched within months of Birchbox's rise, with various categories beyond cosmetics well represented, including vitamins, food, baby products, apparel, video games, personal care, and more.

A *Wired* article in late 2012 captured the momentum of the booming subscription-box space, headlined "From Coffee To Condoms, Now There's A Subscription Service For Everyone." The publication noted several new companies that offered to send boxes of everything from fishing tackle (Mystery Tackle Box), to pantyhose (Hoseanna), to pet food (MyDogBowl), to flowers (H. Bloom), to even a patch of grass for your dog to piss on (Fresh Patch, whose website promises "It's real grass—your dog deserves it").[1] All these companies clamoring for attention in a pivotal year that linked "subscription" to a "monthly box" of goods.

As of 2018, there were about 3,500 subscription-box companies operating in the U.S., in nearly every product category imaginable.[2] Half of those began in the previous twelve months, yet there are plenty from the early wave of box pioneers still battling for market share—including of course, Birchbox, its cosmetics competition, and its main rival/imitator, IPSY.

Birchbox Original

On a sidewalk in New York's Soho neighborhood in July of 2014, Birchbox, a monthly subscription service sending beauty product samples to 800,000 subscribers at the time, opened its first brick-and-mortar store. A display in the front showcased a rotating inventory of top online sellers, alongside a large interactive display which allowed shoppers to input their attributes (hair type, skin color, age, etc.) for additional product recommendations. At a counter at the back, shoppers could put together their own custom boxes filled with samples they handpicked. Downstairs, across from a corner of Birchbox for Men, was a salon where professionals offered manicures, hair styling, and makeup services, as well as free classes for subscribers on techniques like contouring and nail art.

Although the Birchbox store in Soho closed its doors in 2018, the company still has a boutique in Paris and has since partnered with Walgreens to feature a subset of their product line on the legacy pharmacy chain's in-store shelves. While there are conflicting reports as to why the company decided to axe its brick-and-mortar presence in New York, the move seems part and parcel of a strategic shift into profit-first mode after years of growing pains in a subscription niche (cosmetics) that's become increasingly competitive since 2012.

Founded in 2010 by Katia Beauchamp and Hayley Barna, both graduates of Harvard Business School, Birchbox is often credited for kicking off much of the current subscription-box madness. Subscribers get a sample kit of upscale lipsticks, shampoos, and skincare for about $15 bucks a month (prices have increased since 2010). The boxes are curated, to feel "like your friend telling you about the product, the way your friend would teach you," in Beauchamp's words.[3] A typical box might include samples from established brands as well as trendier labels that might be hard to find in a CVS or Lord & Taylor. To entice brands to participate, Birchbox gathers detailed feedback from its customer base by way of surveys, one of several methods that earn members loyalty points they can use as credit toward future purchases. "It's like a huge focus group, if you think about it," said Beauchamp.[4]

If subscribers like a product sample, they can purchase the full-size version directly from the Birchbox website. The two-tier revenue stream provides Birchbox with some impressive firepower:

one channel of recurring revenue through monthly subscriptions, and another from one-off sales of full-sized products. It's the kind of strategy that makes a typical venture firm take notice.

When Birchbox went live in 2010, its innovative model signaled a changing of the guard in the cosmetics industry. While older direct-selling methods used by companies like Mary Kay and Avon still represent a sizeable chunk of the market (with revenues of approximately $3.5 billion and $5.2 billion, respectively), beauty innovators like Birchbox and IPSY continue to chip away at their market share. Since 2011, Avon has seen its revenues decline from over $9 billion to roughly $5 billion today.[5] The house-calling salespeople formerly known as "Avon Ladies" (the brand now calls them "representatives") have complained about lower sales commissions.[6]

In terms of demographics, women aged eighteen to thirty-four now dominate the beauty category, accounting for about half of all buyers, so it's no surprise that salespeople selling cosmetics out of an attaché case aren't doing so great.[7] More than ever before, millennial female shoppers are fueled by a vast network of digital influencers on Facebook, YouTube, and Instagram. And as social influence on the web continues to drive shopping behavior, brands like Birchbox, IPSY, and Sephora are tailoring their offerings accordingly.

The Avon slowdown in the face of digital innovation is a common theme with respect to stories of subscription upstarts: Gillette vis-à-vis the Dollar Shave Club. Blockbuster vis-à-vis Netflix. Most of retail vis-à-vis Amazon. In fact, complacency among legacy brands, rooted in a long history of success, is often the first indicator that they are almost certain to be jostled by new disruptors.

In the case of Avon, versions of innovation efforts included a failed rollout of new software meant to help sales reps move online, and a brutal and tardy redesign of its website in 2014 — the first refresh in over a decade. Meanwhile, nimble rivals like GlossyBox, BoxyCharm, IPSY, and Birchbox are not only generating significant recurring revenue from consumers with a unique business model, and conveying relevance to the key millennial demographic, but also solving relevant problems for brand manufacturers themselves.

Much of the appeal of this sample-box model comes courtesy of its ride-along access to a prospective millennial audience of consumers. Even though Birchbox is often viewed as a competitor of the very brands that participate in the monthly shipments it sends out, its appeal is hard to pass up. The potential benefit to a company like Aveda far outweighs the downsides of being featured in a "Birchbox" and having to share a spot with the likes of Bobbi Brown. As Ellen Greenwald, chief marketing officer of the company that makes Laura Mercier Cosmetics, explains, "People are paying for their samples, so it's a motivated customer."[8]

The IPSY Influence

Birchbox proved that not only was there a strong appetite for beauty products among the next generation, but that consumers would happily subscribe and pay for monthly samples. Rather than push new collections through expensive kiosks and costly advertising campaigns, big brands now had a new, cost-effective way to get in front of potential customers. Birchbox's initial success sparked an explosion of cosmetics copycats, such as GlossyBox and Boxy Charm, which launched within a year of Birchbox. Established retailers also jumped in, with Walmart (in 2014) and Sephora (in 2015) launching their own versions of beauty boxes.

The one copycat that stands out, however, is IPSY. Founded in 2011, its founder, Michelle Phan, had previously built up a loyal following on YouTube with her free makeup tutorials. As her audience increased, Phan spun her influence into IPSY—one of the most successful stories in the subscription-box space to date.

Subscribers, which the company calls "Ipsters," are charged

about $10 a month for what's called a "glam bag" (not a box) of five sample-sized beauty products. Its Birchbox-like feature, called Shopper, lets customers buy full-size products directly from the site. Brands do not pay to appear in the boxes. Instead, they submit products to the company, and hope that Phan and her team choose theirs from among the astonishing 700,000 products that are submitted for consideration each month; if selected, the company provides free inventory in exchange for exposure.[9] By 2015 there were 100,000 new Glam Bag subscribers joining IPSY every month, and by 2018 IPSY had reached a whopping 3 million subscribers.[10]

While the success of Birchbox links back to a vision first sketched at Harvard Business School, IPSY's rise featured a grassroots success story about what it takes to grow a consumer brand in the age of the online influencer. Not only was the company prepared to compete head-on with Birchbox, but Phan planned to use her online sway as the weapon to beat them. As influencer pedigrees go, Phan's numbers are astounding. Her makeup tutorial channel on YouTube has nearly 9 million followers and over 1 billion total views; she has almost 900,000 followers on Twitter, 2 million on Instagram, and over 3 million on Facebook. Those social media accolades have landed Phan on the Forbes 30 Under 30 list, and given her several Teen Choice Award nominations.

The power of influencer marketing on the web cannot be overstated. Data from MuseFind, an influencer marketing platform, shows that 92 percent of consumers trust an influencer more than an advertisement or traditional celebrity endorsement.[11] Influencer clout continues to develop as a viable and trustworthy means to swing the pendulum of buyer behavior. While Birchbox had established a following by offering high-end samples, IPSY understood that its growth trajectory was going to be based on a combination of not only the right business model (which Birchbox had validated early), but the impact of Phan and her engaged following. Simply put, because of Michelle, customers were going to choose IPSY over the alternatives.

U.S. MARKET SHARE OF BIRCHBOX AND IPSY

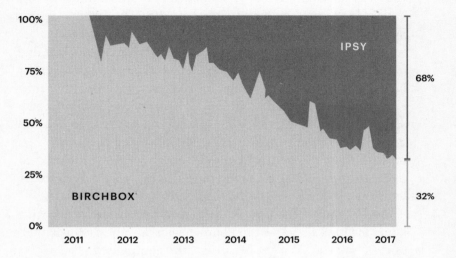

Source: Jason Del Rey, "Birchbox has held acquisition talks with several retailers, including Walmart," Recode, August 9, 2017, https://www.vox.com/2017/8/9/16111176/birchbox-walmart-acquisition-talks-beauty-subscription-retail-online.

How Phan Found Her Fans

Phan's passion for beauty started as a child, when she spent a ton of time in beauty salons. Phan's mother was a nail technician, so tattered beauty magazines and fumes from polish remover were part of her upbringing. In 2005, when she was still a teenager, she began blogging about makeup on a photo-blog site called Xanga under the alias Ricebunny, and cultivated a dedicated following.[12] Here's a sample from an early blog post: "Midterms are over! Wow! I now have a week to just relax and enjoy myself... meaning I will be working on my Skincare's line website and assigned homework during break... there are no vacations in this world of mine. I am an assiduous person."[13]

Though her mom tried to persuade her to pursue a career in medicine, Michelle instead enrolled in art and design at Florida's Ringling College. During her first semester she applied for a job at a Lancôme counter and was rejected, in spite of her evident skill, as too inexperienced—so she launched her own channel on You-Tube, which was then barely a year old. Perhaps to her surprise, her first tutorial was viewed 40,000 times in its first week.

When Phan had to drop out of college after one semester due to a lack of funds, she figured her YouTube videos might help her land a better job than waiting tables. After a year, that first tutorial video had notched 1 million views, and by the fall of 2008 she was averaging 600,000 views a month. As the income from YouTube's partner program grew, Phan decided to move to L.A. to work full-time on her channel.[14] In 2010, she struck a deal to create video tutorials using products by, ironically perhaps, Lancôme. Phan called the deal "delayed gratification."[15]

As karma would have it, her corporate partnership with Lancôme took a backseat to Phan's bigger ambition—the launch of IPSY in 2011. Within five years, the company was valued at half-a-billion dollars.[16] Notwithstanding some iteration along the way, the company's core strategy has remained constant—a commitment to growth via online influencers. In staying true to its roadmap, IPSY has linked Phan's brand to other prominent online vloggers with big followings, such as Bethany Mota, Jessica Harlow, and Andrea Brooks.

The company's strategic turning point came in 2015 when it received $100 million in funding, part of which the company used to fund its Open Studios (OS) initiative, a strategy true to its influencer roots that would grant an all-access pass to thousands of nobodies looking to be the next Michelle Phan. By providing studio space, production, lighting, editing technologies, mobile tools, apps, and mentors to inspire "Ipsters," these budding content creators now had access to all the resources they would need to become the next big cosmetics celebs on the web. Moreover, as IPSY OS highlighted, the program was free of commitments, exclusivities, and fees; the creators themselves would retain 100 percent control of their channels and applicable revenue. For a small group of lucky upcoming stars, IPSY inks a three-year contract that includes a salary and opportunities to work with brands. As you might have guessed, the program was well received, notching over a thousand applicants within an hour of launch.[17]

While acceptance into OS is a lifetime opportunity for individual creators, IPSY benefits from their celebrity, both by having them do tutorials about the products in the Glam Bags and by featuring them in marketing-driven initiatives. Increasing its presence in individual online channels means more revenue and brand exposure for the company. And as wannabes gravitate to the program, Phan's profile becomes more prominent; because everything Open Studios does is rooted in Michelle's origin story, immersing participants get ballooned into the broader excitement of the Phan brand.

In a move to personally reset, Phan decided to leave IPSY in the capable hands of her co-founders, CEO Marcelo Camberos and president Jennifer Goldfarb, in 2017 to focus on a new venture. Yet even without her at the corporate helm, IPSY remains a powerful force in subscription cosmetics—as subscriber count reaches new heights (over 3 million), the website generates over 500 million views a month, alongside the more than 8,000 creators it currently works with.[18]

Birchbox vs. IPSY

Birchbox and IPSY are two very similar companies with two very different strategies: IPSY desires to invest heavily in annual conventions, events, and its influencer ecosphere; while Birchbox takes the more traditional route of international expansion and a brick-and-mortar presence through boutique stores and retail partnerships. In a now-crowded cosmetics market, is there room for both long-term?

While Phan never went to Harvard, she did learn something about the value of scarcity—consider IPSY's Open Studios offering, which conveys an "everyone is welcome" narrative on the website. While it might not seem as obvious, IPSY is indeed "playing Harvard," in that anyone can apply but admission is granted to very few. Couple that with the sheer wattage of Phan's star power on social media, and you have a unique company peddling a complementary strategy true to its founder's origin story.

Although Birchbox's early subscriber base did come from social media, through a proliferation of "unboxing videos" on YouTube, Katia Beauchamp, the company's founder and figurehead, isn't much of an online celebrity. As Birchbox has grown, it has chosen a very different path to IPSY, seemingly tapering online efforts in favor of physical store presence, traditional advertising, acquisitions (it acquired French competitor JolieBox in 2012), and international expansion.

The media loves to write about digital start-ups shifting into the "real world," but practically speaking, it's been a rough ride for Birchbox since its first store opened in 2014. While initially more physical stores were planned for the U.S. market, Birchbox quickly pivoted—laying off a chunk of its employees in 2016 and pausing plans for three more brick-and-mortar stores. On top of the aforementioned challenges, copycat competition had intensified.

Today, the market continues to take shape, and as cosmetics brands fight to stay relevant, many are taking aim at Birchbox specifically. In France, for example, a very relevant market for cosmetics brands, and a place where Birchbox had hoped to grow its global footprint, GlossyBox and MyLittleBox are making more noise. L'Oréal Paris has launched a box of its own, as has Sisley. Back in Birchbox's home market of the United States, brands like Sephora are taking subscription shots as well. In late 2015, Sephora launched Play!, a similarly priced copycat box, and giants like Walmart and Ulta have also launched competitive offerings. Even Macy's has indicated that it's coming to market with a new beauty box in late 2019. And we can't forget Jessica Alba, who's gotten into the game with her company's version, Honest Beauty. Taking a page out of the IPSY playbook, leveraging a celebrity founder can go a long way.

Birchbox deserves much of the credit for an industry shift into sample boxes. There's no question the company's direct-to-customer model had early product-market fit, and a pathway to sustainable growth. But, as competition intensifies, Birchbox's way forward seems murky at best. New entrants, both young and old, amplify the ambiguity of Birchbox's future.

IPSY has stuck to its original blueprint of converting its founder's online followers to revenue-generating subscribers. Yet the results of Birchbox's strategy suggest it's losing the battle. After talks with both Walmart and shopping channel QVC fell through, Birchbox agreed to sell a majority stake in the company to one of its early investors, Viking Global, for a mere $15 million in 2018. Sources say Birchbox's other investors are expected to walk away with nothing.

In a 2018 statement, Beauchamp said, "We are prioritizing product innovation, the evolution of our digital experience, and scaled partnership opportunities."[19]

Barkbox has Bite

Are you a "pet parent"? If so, you are part of the growing number of consumers who consider their pets as members of the family—and spend their money accordingly.

As was the case with Birchbox, another New York–based subscription player has attracted plenty of attention. Founded in 2011, BarkBox, a subscription business targeted to dog lovers, sends canine parents a monthly box filled with toys, treats, and a chew, curated from each month's themed collection. To date, it has received over $80 million in venture funding. Bark quickly expanded its reach in August 2017 through a partnership with Target Corp., which now sells Bark-brand toys and treats in stores and online[20]—this on top of its existing loyal base of over 500,000 paying subscribers.[21]

There are other notable products and services under the Bark & Co. umbrella that are worth mentioning, including BarkPost, a dog-themed content site similar to BuzzFeed's "Cute" section; BarkCam, a photo-sharing app, basically a dog version of Instagram; and BarkBuddy, a "Tinder for dogs" that, according to the website, helps you "find fluffy singles near you." The last one is worthy of a little more explanation—the BarkBuddy app matches humans (not dogs) with dogs up for adoption at shelters across the United States and Canada, with users swiping left or right until the app zeroes in on their perfect pet.

As brand boosting goes, BarkBox has done some other cool things to boost exposure, such as "Open Bark Nights"—comedy shows that customers and employees can bring their dogs to—and BarkPark, a private dog park in Nashville which, at a cost of $19 for a day, $49 for four weeks, or $78 for a season pass, offers, according to its website, "a square block of crisply landscaped green space" and grooming services for dogs—and, for us humans, WiFi, "comfy seating galore," and "inviting modern design." Oh, and humans are allowed to bring booze along with Fido. If alcohol is being consumed, it's hard to imagine this not working out for BarkBox.

Parks and liquor aside, BarkBox has completely cornered the subscription-box pet space—which now consists of BarkBox, at roughly 80 percent market share, and a bunch of nobodies divvying up the crumbs. With revenue expected to hit $250 million in 2018, the next move is likely an IPO.[22] Woof woof!

Bulu Box Crosses the Finish Line

In 2012, Paul and Stephanie Jarrett were inspired to launch subscription upstart Bulu Box at the finish line of the San Francisco half-marathon. The couple had recently moved to the Bay area from New York, and both were shocked at the amount of complimentary products being handed out to racers—in particular, they found it odd how these companies tossing out samples didn't want any customer information in return.

When he did some research into the sample business, Paul noticed plenty of articles online about the up-and-coming subscription player Birchbox, but nothing similar for vitamin brands. As he told me in 2018, "This was that thing [a supplement sample box] that made so much sense to me. I was so surprised I couldn't find what I was after . . . I felt like I was researching poorly."[23]

Paul was intrigued by the subscription-plus-sample model, which offered a new gateway for brands to get samples into the hands of consumers, and a new engine to generate valuable data. Looking specifically at Birchbox as the use case, the cosmetics company was not only growing its subscriber count, it was also amassing mounds of customer information, from email and physical mailing addresses to more nuanced details on buyer preferences.

In addition to being drawn in by the inherent business model, Paul was also encouraged by market trends he stumbled upon in his research. His findings showed a profound timing correlation between two product categories—health supplements and cosmetics—with the former's market entry trailing the latter by only six months. Assuming Birchbox was a "first mover" in makeup subscriptions, Jarrett felt it wouldn't be long before the trend hit the health sector.

Within a couple of hours of launching bulubox.com in June 2012, the site logged more than 200 sign-ups. It took just a few weeks for that number to climb to thousands. The idea continued to gain momentum.

True to the times, Bulu ignored traditional marketing channels like TV, radio, and print, focusing instead on platforms like Bodybuilding.com, Reddit, and Facebook to generate traffic and conversions. Sales grew rapidly to $500,000 in monthly recurring revenue, which resulted in quick rounds of venture capital, and a spot on the Inc. 500 list of fastest-growing private companies. While subscribers can still get their Bulubox, the company has rebranded as Bulu, Inc., having developed a new B2B offering of subscription-box solutions for established brands; their high-profile client list includes Disney, Crayola, and BuzzFeed, among others.

The Honest Company?

Jessica Alba got her big acting break as a teenager, when she was cast as the lead in James Cameron's TV series *Dark Angel*. She has since taken on roles as a hip-hop choreographer, in 2003's *Honey*, as a strong-willed "dancer" in the *Sin City* franchise, and, more recently, as the co-founder and chairperson of The Honest Company, founded by Alba and not-for-profit veteran Christopher Gavigan.

It began with Alba's desire to provide parents with a baby brand they could trust. As with Michael Dubin and Dollar Shave Club (which we'll cover in more detail in the next chapter), Alba's vision grew out of her frustrations as a consumer. When she was pregnant with her first daughter, Alba broke out in hives after washing some baby clothing she had been gifted. When she Googled the ingredients listed on the detergent bottle, she learned many of the "fragrances" were actually toxins.

Surprisingly, maybe, petrochemicals, formaldehydes, and flame retardants are common ingredients in products found in millions of North American homes. The American Food and Drug Administration hasn't updated its cosmetics regulations since 1938 and bans only nine potentially harmful ingredients, compared to other nations that ban up to 1,400 of such chemicals from beauty products.[24]

Concerned by her findings, Alba started hunting for safer alternatives. She soon met Gavigan, an expert on the topic, who was leading a non-profit at the time called Healthy Child Healthy World. With very few companies in the United States producing nontoxic baby products, Gavigan and Alba began crafting a business plan for a start-up whose mission was to provide safe and effective consumer products that were well-designed, reasonably priced, and easy to get.

As things got going, Alba's husband, Cash Warren, introduced her to Brian Lee, a childhood friend of his who had pedigree as an entrepreneur. Lee's first start-up, Legalzoom.com, an online legal documentation service, was ranked among the world's thirty most valuable start-ups by Business Insider in 2011. With reality TV star Kim Kardashian, Lee also founded ShoeDazzle.com in 2009, an early pioneer in fashionable shoes on subscription. Lee, seeing the potential in Alba and Gavigan's plan, joined the team—bringing along Sean Kane from PriceGrabber.com to be the company's president.

After locking down an initial seed investment of $6 million, The Honest Company opened its virtual doors in 2011 with seventeen products, mostly diapers and wipes, all of which were delivered monthly to subscribers' homes. In its first fiscal year, the company notched an impressive $10 million in sales.

While the Honest team intended the company to remain an online seller, it soon began selling certain products in a limited number of boutiques, and then broadened its distribution by moving into Costco. Since 2013, Whole Foods, Nordstrom, buybuy BABY, Destination Maternity, and Target have all been carrying Honest Company products. Today, The Honest Company sells more than 135 products (toothpaste, nipple balm, vitamins, detergent, etc.) on the web and across 4,000-plus retail stores.

By 2015, top-line revenue reached $150 million, attracting some acquisition interest from Unilever. But rapid growth did not come without controversy. In early 2016, a class-action lawsuit accused Honest Co. of selling an ineffective sunblock, and detergents with questionable foaming agents. The company called the investigative reports "false" and "reckless," but was nevertheless forced to reformulate some of its products.[25]

In the wake of the negative press, Unilever broke off acquisition talks, and instead acquired Dollar Shave Club—and Honest rival Seventh Generation.[26] While Alba and her team continue to defend its line, in the face of other civil lawsuits over deceptive labeling and advertising, plans for an IPO have been put on ice.[27] Although revenues have since climbed from $150 million to

$300 million, in the midst of the challenges the company's valuation has fallen from $1.7 billion to an estimated $1 billion.[28]

As with Tesla and its Elon Musk devotees, customers of Honest—moms just like Alba—are loyal to her and her celebrity status. Founders with that kind of following not only bring in dollars, but get a hall pass when controversy strikes (for example, Musk smoking pot with Joe Rogan, claiming we live in a video game, or telling overworked Tesla employees "they will get to see their families a lot when we go bankrupt").[29]

The next chapter of Alba's baby play will be interesting. The declining U.S. birth rate, which fell to a thirty-two-year low in 2018, could be seen as a threat to the long-term fundamentals of the business.[30] However, Honest's rapid revenue growth shows a sizeable appetite for organic diapers, baby products, and other related lines. For time-strapped families with kids, the company's direct-to-customer model is convenient for parents who find store visits to be a hassle. As the company explores expansion, it can rely on the stability of its subscription diaper business— which remains solid. While three-quarters of Honest's revenue is generated online, the majority still comes via the company's $79.95 monthly bundles of diapers and wipes.

The company's partnership with private equity firm L Catterton, which recently injected $200 million, is also a telling advantage.[31] The seasoned team owns stakes in several other wellness and beauty businesses, including Bliss, ELEMIS, and TULA. This experience with mission-based consumer brands, particularly from an operational and network standpoint, is a huge plus. In fact, the partnership with Catterton has already enabled further expansion on a global scale, with Honest inking an exclusive retail distribution partnership with Douglas, the number one beauty retailer in Europe.

Sure, there's always the threat of subscribers choosing to leave Honest for a category substitute; but, assuming L Catterton's advisors push the company to double-down on what's worked so far, I expect that growth will continue until P&G acquires them.

Okay, I'm speculating, but Procter & Gamble Co. was reportedly among several consumer goods manufacturers interested in Honest Co. back in 2016.[32] Maybe they'll come back to the table.

NINE

Dollar Shave Club Disrupts an Industry

THE MEN'S grooming industry is a great case study in understanding the fundamental shift in power—from corporation to consumer—at the center of this book. Gillette and Schick spent about a century pumping out variations of the same products, until Michael Dubin realized that their lack of customer insight was a major opportunity for Dollar Shave Club (and then its East Coast competitor, Harry's) to disrupt the status quo.

Dubin's plan of attack against the long-time incumbents focused on customer pain points. As Dubin put it to *Fortune* magazine, "the beginning of the story is about solving a problem for guys. And the problem that we're solving at the very basic level [is] that razors are really expensive in the store. It's a frustrating experience to go and buy them."[1] Shaving is a simple act, easily accomplished with a standard blade, so why did it have to be an expensive hassle? If a man could get cheap everyday essentials delivered via Amazon, a trip to the local Walgreens to ask a store clerk to unlock a display case—a brutal annoyance—shouldn't be necessary. The solution to men's shaving woes lay in a new value-driven formula, built around the customer, that would remove such headaches.

Behind the scenes of the customer-centric business blueprints were Dubin's first investors: Michael Jones (a former CEO of Myspace) and Dave Fink, two budding venture capitalists who ran a small L.A.-based fund called Science Inc.[2] The firm now has roughly sixty companies in their portfolio, including names like Prize Candle, FameBit, HelloSociety, and the popular underwear subscription company MeUndies. In 2011, however, the shop didn't have much other than a vision to find distinctive direct-to-consumer subscription companies that had brand-building potential and an ability to disrupt.

While Dubin's business plan ticked some of the "investment" boxes, what was compelling about Dollar Shave Club was the founder's vision, sense of humor, and entrepreneurial shrewdness. "What I know is that for me to have successful businesses," Jones told *Inc.* magazine, "I need epic founders and really good ideas."[3] Fink remembers Dubin showing up with a bag of razors and a rough cut of the now-famous YouTube video.

Although not a stand-up comic, as some have speculated, after graduating from Emory University in 2001 and moving to New York to work as an NBC page, Dubin studied improv with the legendary Upright Citizens Brigade for eight years. He credits his improv experience with teaching him how to attract an audience with intelligent humor. "It trains your brain to find what's funny about a situation," he said. "That helps the advertising that we do."[4]

Beyond Dubin's comedic chops, the Science guys also saw the wisdom in the business model. Fink had prior experience with the subscription apparel pioneer Fabletics, and had seen other successful use cases from the likes of The Honest Company, Salesforce, and HubSpot, so he was aware of a subscription play's potential.

With a charismatic founder and a solid model, DSC represented "a thesis we wanted to chase down," Fink told me recently—and they did, cutting Dubin a check for $100,000.[5] While Fink says many of the other start-ups around L.A. wanted the status that a fundraise offered in the form of a fancy office and other perks, "Dubin didn't give a shit about that stuff." Dubin "saw no reason to move out [of Science's offices], because he was getting free rent! He was smart—he'd take advantage of every opportunity possible, knowing the mindshare value Science provided him early on. This guy could have been working out of a garage . . . he was really focused on what mattered. He just wanted to surround himself with the best people possible."[6]

In a sense, Science too was in "start-up" mode, and was willing to operate in unorthodox ways. Where Dubin was lacking, Science filled in the gaps with industry expertise, systems, logistics partners, and even complimentary office space. As Fink explains, "We provided Michael with software engineers, man-hours, rent-free office space, and other additional resources—so, accounting for all that, the actual investment is much higher. That said, Dollar Shave Club paid off in spades."[7] Science's shared resources helped the razor CEO to quickly eliminate missteps, leverage the right forms of social media, and fend off competition—there were about a dozen copycats following DSC's viral video.

Harry's is perhaps the most successful of the imitators that popped up after Dubin and company. Founded by Andy Katz-Mayfield and Jeff Raider of Warby Parker fame, Harry's leapt onto the scene in 2013 with careful design engineering and a bit of philanthropy (a strategy shared with Warby Parker), which helped to position it as a slightly higher-end brand.[8] While Harry's and DSC share similar business models, each brand's positioning has made for a friendly coexistence —Dollar Shave with its fraternity-like following that appreciates value, and Harry's style-oriented appeal to men happy to spend a bit more cash.

AS IS USUAL for massive success stories, auspicious timing was also involved. The early 2000s represented a new broadband-assisted resurgence of online businesses, but many were still forced to invest in costly custom technologies, often hosted on internal servers and infrastructure. The next decade, however, marked an important speed-to-market shift, showcasing how e-commerce start-ups were able to build strong technological foundations without the same restrictive cash outlays.

By 2012, the barriers that historically made entering the e-commerce space costly—such as expensive traditional marketing and custom technology infrastructure—were crumbling, allowing e-commerce as an industry to rapidly evolve. In addition to the likes of Dollar Shave Club, online-first companies such as eyeglass retailer Warby Parker, mattress player Casper, cosmetics noise-makers IPSY and Birchbox, and meal-kit entrant Blue Apron burst onto the scene with similar foundational approaches to building their respective offerings.

While not all of these companies rooted their business models in subscription, each exploited the increasing abundance of open-source or otherwise readily available technology to build momentum. Consider just the simple task of creating a website that could power online transactions. Rather than having to build from scratch, market entrants were launching online stores on platforms like Magento, WooCommerce (Wordpress), and Shopify at a fraction of the cost of their e-commerce predecessors.

At the same time, other solutions to tackle things like automated email, customer service, and D2C logistics provided a unique set of cost-effective tools that completely changed the economics of an online start-up. With newly acquired capabilities to "stack" one solution on top of the next, the agile e-commerce universe was in bloom, giving companies like Warby Parker the ability to launch in a fraction of the time it would have taken ten years beforehand.

And once the infrastructure was in place, attracting customers was not only cost-effective, but had the potential to scale faster than ever before. In 2012, marketing, in the context of direct-to-consumer brands, was inexpensive thanks to buyer-friendly, low-cost CPC (cost per click) and CPM (cost per mille [thousand] impressions) rates on Facebook. Google ads provided another potentially attractive channel for certain brands. Plenty of advertisers capitalized, with companies like Dollar Shave Club, Harry's, and Birchbox leveraging Facebook to acquire millions of customers on the cheap.

The Power of Storytelling

Let's take you out of the reader's seat for just a moment: you are now editor-in-chief at a major news outlet such as the *New York Times*, *Huffington Post*, or the *Globe and Mail* (if you're Canadian, like me). If you wanted to cover the eyewear industry, would you be more likely to publish a piece on Sterling Optical, or on Warby Parker? How about food—would you do a story on Kroger, or Blue Apron? What about mattresses—the American Mattress Company, or Casper? Schick or Harry's? Yellow Cab or Uber?

You get the idea: people love stories about trending companies with a fresh take on an industry. The legacy brand is the fat, weathered jock, while the disruptor is the cool new kid on the block. Unique start-up stories *sell*. Regardless of operational challenges, shallow cash war chests, or temperamental founders drinking too much IPA, the press gravitates toward them—providing a distinct advantage for early-stage companies looking at the media as a viable way to drive consumer awareness.

The narrative coming out of the start-up scene of 2012 combined three interesting elements: the ubiquity of the subscription model; the adept use of technology and social media; and an undeniable, overarching desire to push legacy incumbents off their high horse. As each of the big disruptors scaled up, the mainstream media ran an increasing number of articles talking about the rise of these budding companies, each piece serving as great promotional fodder for their subjects.

This phenomenon isn't new. In the early days of Amazon, Bezos was masterful at storytelling, using the press to spread his

SHAVING MARKET SHARE IN US (2015)

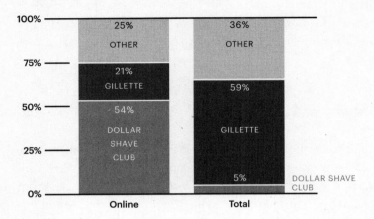

Dollar Shave Club accounted for over half the online razor market the year before it was acquired by Unilever.

Source: "Unilever And Dollar Shave Club: Delivering A Close, Uncomfortable Shave For Procter & Gamble And Others?," Seeking Alpha, July 21, 2016, https://seekingalpha.com/ article/3990306-unilever-dollar-shave-club-delivering-close-uncomfortable-shave-procter-and-gamble-others.

narrative of "the biggest store on Earth" to drive awareness, and ultimately more clicks to his online store. Dubin applied the same approach, using his improv training to write the perfect men's grooming story no journalist could resist. In the months after Dubin's video went viral, articles touting its ingenuity appeared in outlets that included *AdAge*, Business Insider, BuzzFeed, *The Economist*, *Fast Company*, *Forbes* magazine, *Maclean's*, Mashable, TechCrunch, *Time*, and *Wired*.

At first, mainstream observers dismissed DSC as a fly-by-night YouTube company; but, like Amazon, the new shave club quickly silenced naysayers, earning $20 million in revenue in just its second year of operations, and over $60 million the following year. As the company grew, DSC brought in additional capital from the likes of Forerunner Ventures, Pritzker Group, Venrock, and others—raising a total of over $160 million over seven rounds.[9]

By 2015, DSC was selling $152 million worth of razors a year (and had expanded to offer other men's grooming products, including "One Wipe Charlies," a baby wipe for men).[10] At the time, Gillette still controlled about 60 percent of the $3 billion total razor market, but it was a different story online. While e-sales weren't much of thing before DSC, the company had quickly established itself as a $236 million concern for the incumbents.[11] There, DSC suddenly accounted for 54 percent of sales, more than double Gillette's 21 percent.[12]

Unileverage

In 2016, with Dollar Shave Club on track to see $200 million in revenue, the company built on a funny video and $1 razors sold to Unilever for $1 billion, cash. The sale took place about a year after the Dollar Shave Club was valued at $615 million in a $75 million funding round led by Technology Crossover Ventures, according to the *Wall Street Journal*.[13] What started with an exploration of advisory synergies between the two companies ended with Unilever becoming an outright acquirer of the L.A. start-up, with thirty-seven-year-old Dubin remaining as CEO.[14]

The sale remains one of the priciest in the e-commerce space. Unilever's CMO, Keith Weed, told CNBC, "When we bought the Dollar Shave Club, the commentary was 'Unilever goes into shaving'... No, 'Unilever goes into subscription selling,' is what the headline should have been."

Some analysts raised eyebrows at the multiple Unilever paid— five times annual sales. It's not hard to see the upside for Dollar Shave Club from its new affiliation with a ninety-year-old consumer goods giant; but Unilever, too, will get its own fair share of value from the deal. It gains a foothold in the increasingly popular direct-to-consumer market; and it gets access to plenty of data and insight into what resonates with customers—data it can leverage for much of its retail channels. In Unilever's annual report for 2016, the company's president of personal care, Alan Jope, cited "ripping up the rule book and learning new business models" as an important new ideal. Another value driver for Unilever was DSC's personal attention to customer service: it once sent free razors to an unemployed guy to help him look good for interviews. "It's a reminder to all our brands that the people who buy our products should always come first and be the focus of what we do," said Jope.[15]

Unilever also gains access to all the benefits that accompany a subscription model: the power to create loyalty, drive recurring revenue, generate better customer data, and feed all that insight into more effective marketing. DSC already sells other products in addition to razors, including shaving balms and shampoos, so the potential to experiment with product from Unilever's other brands, like Dove and Axe, has incremental revenue potential.

Key performance indicators, such as a company's retention rate, are a great sign of overall consumer satisfaction; by 2017, more than 50 percent of DSC's customers stayed on as subscribers after one year, and 24 percent remained on board by month forty-eight—that's almost one-quarter of its subscribers paying monthly fees for four years.[16]

The ability to create this kind of customer retention in the traditional world of consumer packaged goods (CPG) is unheard of. Creating a consumer-centric brand à la Dollar Shave Club in the age of digital commerce is difficult for most established CPG companies when, as with Unilever, the majority of sales volume has historically come through third-party retailers. Although this kind of retail business model can drive substantial transactions, the relationship with the end-consumer is foggy at best. In other words, brands that sell solely through retailers forego a customer relationship in lieu of a transactional one. Going forward, we will see more established brands selling product via third-party shelves struggle to stay relevant, as consumer expectations increase. Sure, brands can be selective about the channels they choose to sell through. Amazon is always a consumer-centric option for those who want to capture volume and keep the customer happy. Yet, as evidenced by Uniliver's $1 billion snap-up of DSC, there's simply no substitute for building a strong direct-to-consumer brand, built on relationship-driven commerce and disruption of the status quo.

The Importance of Customer Retention

Not surprisingly, churn rates (the proportion of subscribers who leave in a given period) are generally higher for a B2C subscription business than they are for B2B. Individuals, compared to corporations, are more fickle—and run into payment/credit card issues, have a desire to try alternatives, or simply get bored with an offering at a much faster rate than a business does. But reducing churn is imperative across the board—not only to prevent lost revenue, or because the cost of acquiring a new customer is almost always higher than the cost of retaining an existing one, but to boost another metric that directly affects profitability: customer lifetime value (often referred to as LTV). When businesses like DSC can gather valuable data on their subscribers (such as their churn rate), and understand important metrics like customer lifetime value, subsequent decisions related to marketing and customer acquisition are more informed. Contrast this paradigm to a traditional analyst's attempt to predict when Sally might return to the local Walgreens to buy more body soap.

Dollar Shave's subscription success begins with the category itself: men buy razors, and need to change the blades frequently. This consumption and replenishment cycle lends itself perfectly to a subscription model. But to keep customers around for four years, a business needs more than just category fit; a focus on customer service becomes critical. If subscribers sign up but are not taken care of, they cancel quickly, resulting in a rapid increase in subscriber churn. There are countless examples of what great customer service looks like post sign-up, from outbound welcome calls to signed cards mailed on a customer's birthday. In the case of DSC, the company paid close attention to training its customer service reps, not only to satisfy customers who had complaints, but to learn from those who cancelled their subscriptions. Understanding the "why" led to a greater customer retention rate over time.

Finally, Dollar Shave Club's brilliant marketing can't be overlooked as a key success factor. Instead of using traditional media to spread images of male models shaving with needlessly elaborate blades, Dubin took his "everyman" message to YouTube for $4,500. This was not only cost-effective—it's hard to find another example of an ad at this scale with a cost-per-view of less than a fiftieth of a cent—but a highly calculated branding play. Skipping TV, radio, print, and in-store promotion was deliberate, sending a pointed message to its prospective customer base: Dollar Shave Club was a new kind of shaving company, with nothing traditional about it.

As DSC pushed tradition to the sidelines, in 2019 Gillette broke new marketing ground with an ad speaking to the #MeToo movement, as well as one featuring a transgender teen. Though the reception was mostly positive, the first ad sparked a #boycottgillette movement online.

It's hard to make sense of what Gillette was trying to accomplish with these ads. Beyond being controversial, each one seemed like a desperate attempt to be seen as relevant after decades of marketing malaise.

The end result from DSC's budget video was classic word-of-mouth mania about not only its YouTube clip, but the entire brand mission. Telling colleagues about a Gillette ad you saw is unlikely. Certainly, talking about your recent trip to buy some Fusions at CVS isn't interesting. But sharing a link to that hilarious viral video for the razor club you just joined? Well, that's something to talk about.

The Giants Tremble

Gillette should thank Unilever for waking them up. For decades, the 120-year-old company had ruled the men's shaving space unchallenged, enjoying steady sales and profits. When King Camp Gillette founded the company in 1901, "customer experience" wasn't in the zeitgeist of corporate America. The priority was form and function. And, for decades, Gillette stayed in its lane, introducing new handles and blades, never deviating from its product-first perspective to consider changes to its core business. If you look at Schick, the Pepsi to Gillette's Coke, the same patterns emerge. These grooming giants have a deep history of focusing only on product function, oblivious to customer experience.

Function is important, but once your product does what it's supposed to, how many more enhancements make sense? In this particular case, how many blades does a man need? Gillette could have hit the pause button after it released its first three-blade razor in 1998. In 2004 *The Onion* published its legendary fake article by "the CEO and President" of Gillette, headlined "Fuck Everything, We're Doing Five Blades."[17] Apparently, Gillette's product marketing team read the piece, but didn't get the humor memo—the five-bladed Fusion razor came out two years later. In 2018, a Gillette exec told a trade-show audience, "We're debuting a razor with 19 blades and 74 lubrication strips"—before quickly adding, "just kidding."[18] Hey, Gillette exec guy! *The Onion* called— they want their joke back.

Gillette, now under the eye of parent company Procter & Gamble, is a classic example of a legacy brand with zero perspective on what today's customer demands. This "company-first, customer-second" approach is common to frumpy corporations that rely on retailers to manage the customer experience, rather than establishing direct relationships with their end users. Hewlett Packard is another example—it had a great run selling printers below cost, forcing customers into buying the compatible ink cartridges at grossly inflated prices, but when customers caught on and stopped shelling out, HP was forced to revise its model. In response, the company now offers Instant Ink, a subscription service that promises to save customers 50 percent on cartridge replacements.

When Gillette realized its decades-long stranglehold on the razor market was under serious attack, its first counterpunch wasn't an innovation, or even a copycat service, but a lawsuit: in December 2015, Procter & Gamble sued DSC for patent infringement. Dubin was sanguine about the legal hassle, telling CNBC that "at some point the big boys and girls are going to come at you with every weapon in their arsenal. And you know the legal weapon is one of them ... So I don't think that it was a huge surprise." (The suit was settled for undisclosed terms in 2019. P&G also filed several suits against Edgewell Personal Care Co., maker of Schick-brand razors, accusing it of the same.)[19]

In 2017, Gillette launched a DSC replica, Gillette On Demand, a sorry attempt to win back customers who had defected to online leaders DSC and Harry's.[20] The move to develop its own version of a shaving club is just another sign that Gillette is feeling the heat in a changing market, with Dollar Shave and Harry's not only taking swings but landing punches. Copying the innovator isn't a bad thing if you want to stay relevant (especially if the innovation benchmark is set by a bunch of suits pushing patent paper upstream), and despite its obvious conceptual debt to Dubin, Gillette On Demand has provided the company with a decent stake in the new online razor market. But, as some have speculated, if Gillette were a more agile company with fewer layers of crusty management, it might have done a better job of fending off its new rivals. "Frankly, Gillette should have taken out Dollar Shave in year one," says Ali Dibadj, a consumer products analyst at the research and brokerage firm Bernstein.[21]

With Unilever's $1 billion acquisition of DSC, it is evident that an innovative subscription model—in the face of a traditional industry—can equal big money. Upstarts like Dollar Shave and

Harry's get it: the shift in power from corporation to consumer, meaning the customer's voice is now louder than ever; the hyper-growth of online shopping; and the metaphorical megaphone of social media. While resistance seemed to be the initial strategy, Gillette and Schick are now starting to come around. Edgewell Personal Care (Schick's parent company) recently acquired DSC rival Harry's for a reported $1.37 billion in cash and stock, in a move to keep up. The new Gillette On Demand offering, meanwhile, has the company's global VP, John Mang, acknowledging that "guys want to be able to get blades wherever and whenever, and that's one big void we've worked really hard to fill over these past couple years."[22] One thing is clear—selling razors "direct" isn't just a gimmick; it's indicative of a burgeoning consumer-centric subscription-based economy that's going mainstream.

TEN

Food, the Final E-Commerce Frontier

THE CURRENT technological revolution is progressing at a dizzying pace, forcing countless industries to undergo complete overhauls. Traditional newspapers have watched circulation and advertising numbers plummet as real-time social feeds like Twitter, Facebook, and LinkedIn become the default news outlets for many. Financial advisors are feeling the heat in the wake of robo-advisors like WealthFront, Ellevest, and Wealthsimple, all of which offer consumers robust portfolio management at annual fees of less than 0.5 percent on account balances. Ride-sharing services like Uber and Lyft are pushing taxi companies to the sidelines. Traditional television is exiting the scene as Netflix, Apple TV, and Amazon own more of our entertainment dollars.

Until recently, technological innovation in food and grocery has lagged behind these categories. In fact, most of us still get in our own cars, shopping list in hand, to travel to and from the grocery store each week. If you think about it, it's kind of shocking that we STILL do this. However, sweeping changes to the world of

SHARE OF TOTAL SALES THAT ARE ONLINE

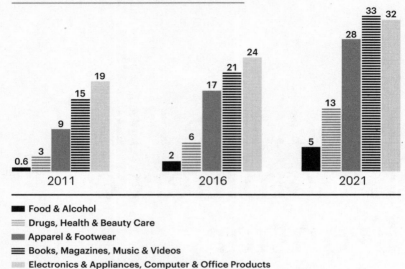

Groceries have lagged behind other categories in building online sales.

Source: Felix Richter, "Groceries Trail Other Categories in Transition to Online," Statista, July 25, 2018, https://www.statista.com/chart/14852/share-of-online-sales-by-product-category/.

food and grocery are happening—and fast. Meal-kit subscription boxes like HelloFresh and Blue Apron, grocery delivery companies like Instacart, and, of course, Amazon are providing new alternatives to the ways we meal-plan, shop, cook, and consume.

One big change in recent years contributing to faster innovation in the food industry is the growing demand for organic products. As a result, the supply side has evolved and a new list of organic players has not only flooded the market, but led to intense competition. Initially, only Whole Foods, Trader Joe's, and Sprouts Farmers Market were satisfying the demand. However, legacy chains like Walmart, Costco, and Kroger have now all gotten into the action, responding to the increasing consumer desire for healthier options at affordable prices. In fact, the category as a whole (pun intended) is no longer led by Whole Foods—instead, the new front-runner is Costco.

A second, and perhaps more important shift, is the rise of online grocery sales. Going back to my comment about our traditional shopping-cart behavior, the industry has to date been among the least affected by e-commerce, with only 2 percent of food and beverage sales in the U.S. being made online in 2018— but online sales are expected to grow about 20 percent each year and nearly double by 2025, as millennials and Gen Z use technology to find more efficient ways to shop.[1] The same online consumer who's buying stuff on Amazon and using Uber to get to work is quickly adopting direct-delivery options like Blue Apron and Instacart (among others) for all their grocery needs.

There are lots of reasons to like the long-term prospects of the newcomers to the food scene, but their success will depend to a significant degree on what Amazon does. Although Amazon has historically been thought of as an online marketplace for just about everything other than food, the behemoth has been in the food game since 2007, and its recent acquisition of Whole Foods is a sign it's about to up the ante.

Fresh Competition

While Amazon is taking up plenty of media room when it comes to the next wave of food tech, credit for much of the recent innovation goes well beyond Bezos. Subscription-backed meal kits, for instance, have made small fortunes on their creative delivery models. Blue Apron, HelloFresh, and Plated, pioneers and leaders in the space, send millions of boxes directly to households each month, containing chef-designed recipes, along with all the necessary ingredients—allowing customers to eat well without having to meal-plan, portion, or grocery shop. While exact subscription counts are hazy, all three have surpassed half a million subscribers.

The meal-kit business model is said to have originated in Sweden, with either Middagsfrid (Swedish for "dinnertime bliss") in 2007, or Linas Matkasse in 2008 being the first to market. As meal kits spread to several Northern European countries, a range of new entrants emerged, including the current U.S. market leader, HelloFresh, out of Berlin. And while still considered novel, the meal-kit industry is expected to reach $10 billion in the United States by 2020.[2]

Blue Apron and Plated, the first U.S.-based meal kits to make a real market splash, were both founded by Harvard Business School students. Matt Salzberg of Blue Apron and Nick Taranto and Josh Hix of Plated all attended the prestigious school in 2008, and after stints elsewhere (including Silicon Valley for Salzberg, and the Marine Corps, of all things, for Taranto) Salzberg launched Blue Apron with Ilia Papas in 2012, and Taranto and Hix reconnected to launch Plated the same year.

Both companies started operations with nearly identical business models, offering chef-recommended recipes along with the required ingredients for a single meal, sent automatically a few times each week, depending on the customer's chosen subscription plan.

Blue Apron, its name a nod to aspiring chefs around the world, initially packaged and shipped everything from a commercial kitchen in Long Island, New York. Salzberg says the origins of Blue Apron were a love of food coupled with frustration at the effort involved: "We liked trying new ingredients, new recipes, new techniques, but we found it really inaccessible to cook at home. It was expensive, it was time-consuming and it was difficult to find recipes that we trusted."[3] The first set of recipes was sent to Salzberg's friends, the perfect beta test for meals that could have been a total flop. Luckily, the kits were a hit and the ball was in motion. As serendipity would have it, they raised their first big round, $3 million, from Salzberg's former employer, Bessemer Venture Partners (you'll recall they were also early investors in Shopify). By 2015 the company was valued at $3 billion, and in 2017 raised another $200 million through its IPO.

Plated got some PR rocket fuel shortly after its launch from a 2014 appearance on the TV show "Shark Tank," where the guys struck a deal with billionaire Mark Cuban. The deal later fell apart during due diligence, but the appearance led to more business than Plated had seen in its two years of existence.[4] Taranto and Hix had soon raised a total of $55 million, before Plated's big sale in 2017 to U.S.-based grocery giant Albertsons for $300 million.

HelloFresh, originally founded in Berlin, spread across Europe and into the United States. By 2014, HelloFresh was delivering one million meals per month in markets across the globe. Founders Dominik Richter, Thomas Griesel, and Jessica Nilsson decided to go public in 2017, with an IPO on the Frankfurt Stock Exchange—then valued at €1.7 billion, twice the valuation of Blue Apron at the time. As of 2018, the company controlled roughly 36 percent of the market, edging past rival Blue Apron's 35 percent.[5]

WHILE MEAL-KIT companies like Blue Apron and Plated compete for global market share, carving out a smaller niche in food subscriptions can also have a profitable upside. Oatbox, a Canadian company delivering healthy breakfast options, launched onto the scene after Marc-Antoine Bovet and his co-founders noticed a surge of subscription companies with names like Blue Apron, Dollar Shave Club, and Birchbox gaining popularity. Among other things, the guys noticed a gap in the meal-kit market—while several companies provided lunches and dinners, nobody offered breakfast, "the most important meal of the day, and the most neglected," Bovet says.[6]

The breakfast industry itself is fascinating. For decades, old-school brands like General Mills, Kellogg's, and Post have held a firm grip on sales of cereal through grocery retail. Anecdotally, customers have kept to their morning ritual of Cheerios and 2 percent milk. But as consumers focus on healthy eating and a slimmer waistline, sales of cereals are declining at the expense of whole-grain organics and a myriad of low-carb options.

Breakfast has also been the most hurried meal of the day, a good reason why hand-held foods like protein bars are booming. If quick isn't an option, consumers will often skip breakfast entirely. Before starting Oatbox, Bovet recalls constantly missing his first meal. "I didn't feel great when I missed breakfast. I wanted to make something tasty... there was a big hole in the market."[7]

Aside from the protein craze, healthy snack bars are exploding. Lärabar, from General Mills, has a fruit-and-greens bar that is "vegan-friendly," with one-quarter cup of kale per bar. SaladShots Snack Bar offers the "goodness of a salad" with the "convenience of a bar." Flavors like Choco Balsamic are formulated with greens and superfoods. Then there are bars called "That's it."—made of healthy ingredients like black beans, carrots, and kale. The self-improvement claims of various "brain boosting" ingredients are the focal point of bars like Zone Perfect's Revitalize for Mental Focus, which uses green tea extract for an energy boost and choline to support brain health. The IQ BAR "Brain + Body" bar is fortified with medium-chain triglycerides to improve cognitive performance. The list goes on.

The recent market adoption of healthy snacks has helped subscription specialty food companies find a niche as well. UrthBox focuses on non-GMO, organic, and all-natural snacks. Keto Krate is a subscription box for those on a ketogenic diet; all snacks have five grams of carbs or less. The company delivers eight-plus keto-friendly products every month.

Since launching in 2008 in the U.K., leading subscription snack company Graze has expanded its product line to over 200 snack combinations through snack subscription boxes, an online shop, and selected retailers. Since its U.S. debut in 2013, the company has sold over $150 million worth of snacks in that market alone, and continues to expand its European presence. Over 5,000 people have signed up for Graze in Ireland; next on the list are Sweden, Germany, and the Netherlands.[8] In a bid to continue its wave of niche consumer brand acquisitions, Unilever swallowed up Graze in early 2019. Unilever has a good track record of nurturing smaller food brands; in 2001, it acquired Ben & Jerry's ice cream and it succeeded in expanding the brand globally.

Back to Canada, where Oatbox's trajectory has been impressive. Since launching in 2014, the company has quickly grown its customer base, and now delivers hundreds of thousands of breakfast boxes each month.[9] In mid-2017, Oatbox closed a seed round and plans to use the funds to support accelerated growth in the breakfast market.[10] The company has also introduced new breakfast bars, oatmeal, coffee, and teas to its product mix to boost both average order size and operating margins.

Yet, despite the pace of growth, Oatbox still focuses heavily on customer service, answering inquiries wherever consumers choose to interact with the brand, be it via email, Facebook, live chat, or Instagram. Satisfaction rates have paid dividends in the form of reduced churn: although Bovet chooses not to share exact figures, Oatbox cancellations are low, and customer lifetime values remain high, between nine and twelve months per subscriber. That's a healthy range for a food company in the subscription space.

In the wake of the changing consumer preferences that Oatbox and others have capitalized on, the strategy for legacy brands has been to swallow up the best of the bunch rather than innovate themselves. We saw this with Unilever's recent purchase of Graze. In September of 2018, Hershey's purchased the Pirate's Booty line of snacks from B&G Foods for $420 million. In 2016, General Mills acquired Epic Provisions, a category-creating meat-snacks company and maker of EPIC Bars, EPIC Bites, and EPIC Hunt and Harvest Mix. General Mills is the same company that famously acquired Lärabar back in 2008, kicking off a frenzy in new snack/energy bar start-ups. Kellogg's recently purchased Chicago Bar Company, maker of RXBAR, for $600 million. Kellogg Company CEO Steve Cahillane remarked, "With its strong millennial consumption and diversified channel presence including e-commerce, RXBAR is perfectly positioned to perform well against future food trends."

THE MERGING of upstart disruptors and legacy chains is giving birth to a new wave of omni-channel (a type of retail that integrates the different methods of shopping available to consumers) food options—and competition is heating up. The Albertsons' acquisition of Plated means that Taranto and Hix's meal-kit offering will now be available both in-store and online. Kroger's swallowing of Chicago-based meal-kit provider Home Chef, for $700 million, means the company's own program, Prep+Pared, will likely consolidate with Home Chef. Blue Apron recently inked a deal to sell its kits in Costco locations. And there are other challenges ahead for meal-kit companies, which suggest more potential M&A activity in the near future.

The leading meal-kit companies have done well to move the adoption needle, but the path forward is uncertain. Challenges in quality control, lead times, customer retention, and good old-fashioned competition plague the business fundamentals of these companies today.

When it comes to food quality, picking the freshest tomato or cucumber becomes essential, as one little bruise can ruin the entire experience. Ian Brooks, the CEO of HelloFresh Canada, told me that "customers are pretty patient; they'll wait an extra day for their box. But, if you ship a red pepper with a black spot on it, the customer will mark your brand down hard." [11] While certain markets differ, such as Australia, where HelloFresh ships in the cold supply chain all the way to the customer door (without ice packs), markets like Canada are not quite as sophisticated logistically.

Canada is a huge market geographically, and aspects of the meal-kit business model differ drastically depending which area you're in. With an expansive 3,400-mile-wide delivery area, direct delivery is a value-add for busy families in both urban and rural markets, but a logistical nightmare for companies wanting to reach them. This puts additional pressure on delivery times and food quality consistency. As customers increasingly get comfortable with next-day delivery courtesy of Amazon and Instacart, HelloFresh's four-day average is a major problem.

And no matter what country you're in, there's the apparent environmental impact, which continues to be a big debate.

Brooks, an experienced operations and procurement consultant from McKinsey and Co. who joined HelloFresh in 2015, was attracted to the company not just because subscription meal kits were on the rise, but because the senior leadership team was committed to reducing food waste. There are environmental benefits to meal kits—in the U.S. and Canada, as much as 40 percent of food bought in the grocery store goes to waste, but with meal kits that number drops to 1 percent.[12]

On the flip side, though, some consumers argue that the kits produce a pretty big packaging footprint. While most meal kits use either reusable, recyclable, or compostable packaging, there is still a bit of a gap between what's possible and what's practical. Some meal-kit services are attempting to take on the burden. Blue Apron, for instance, allows its subscribers to return a few weeks' worth of packaging to be recycled for free, and Sun Basket, a San Francisco-based outfit started in 2014, recently launched a new 100 percent recyclable or compostable packaging system. In response to the consumer critique, Plated co-founder Josh Hix says the food we buy in grocery stores has just as much packaging as a typical meal kit; it's just that "we don't see it." [13] Another potential consideration is the carbon emissions caused by all the vehicles needed to deliver direct to the customer.

Beyond the packaging, meal-kit delivery times, food errors, and generally high price points, customer retention remains a challenge for most of the big players. Nearly 90 percent of HelloFresh's American clients had stopped using the service one year later, and Blue Apron also faces similar challenges in hanging on to customers. To counter the attrition, companies like Blue Apron have to rely heavily on acquisition, using platforms like Facebook to sign up more customers at a faster pace than the rate at which they're losing them. And recent estimates suggest CAC (customer acquisition cost) is going up in the meal-kit space. HelloFresh, for instance, is spending as much as $389 per U.S. customer—and CAC numbers are expected to climb, as increased competition means a proverbial bidding war for traffic on Facebook, the critical auction channel most are using to acquire consumers.[14]

THESE CHALLENGES are taking a toll, and meal-kit brands now face an uphill battle. Blue Apron's trajectory has been especially rocky since its IPO—shares began trading just two weeks after Amazon announced its acquisition of Whole Foods, and as a result the company was forced to lower its share price estimates to $10 to $11 from the $15 to 17 range.[15] In its first quarterly earnings report, Blue Apron lost $31.6 million, and saw its customer base drop by 9 percent. In the wake of revising its forecasts downward, the company blamed costs associated with automating its warehouses, where it had been experiencing errors and delays.[16] The company has been hemorrhaging customers of late—by the end of 2018, subscribers were down to 557,000, about half what it had at the time of its IPO.[17]

Blue Apron, while innovative, has really struggled at nailing logistics and properly retaining customers once they're on board, two critical aspects of its business operations. Recent attempts to label itself a technology company (to support the claim, it touts its sophisticated inventory software, which manages a large footprint of fulfillment centers) certainly won't provide a solid win-back strategy it can present to shareholders.[18]

However, Blue Apron should get credit for its incredible branding and innovative core offering. In a way, Blue Apron has played the role of American meal-kit trailblazer. Moreover, the meals are delicious, and for many of its subscribers, the kits provide a true value-add. The technology infrastructure the company touts as its core competence is effective at managing work flows.

But, ultimately, the technology's core function is to support a human-powered operation: thousands of men and women chopping veggies, placing ingredients in baggies, and packing boxes. Keeping customers happy month after month hinges on those very same people not screwing things up—a daunting task when software cannot, at least as of 2019, replace or automate the role.

It looks like investors agree. As of September 2018, Blue Apron's stock price had closed trading at $1.87, way down from its IPO price of $10. And it could get worse—fulfillment struggles are superficial in comparison to what lies ahead: Amazon, the competition, and death by customer attrition.

Amazon Brings Home the Bacon

When Amazon snapped up Whole Foods for $13.7 billion in 2017, the news sent shock waves through the grocery sector and retail landscape. Walmart still controls the biggest share of brick-and-mortar U.S. food and grocery business by far, with about 14.5 percent of all revenue in the sector, followed by Kroger at 7.2 percent, Whole Foods at 1.2 percent, and Amazon with a minuscule 0.2 percent share (though they are the category leader in online groceries, with an 18 percent market share).[19] But the assumption is that the organics takeover signals that Bezos plans to dominate the category in the not-so-distant future.

The deal sparked all kinds of speculation into what strategy Amazon has in store. The move might be part of a broader logistics plan to get closer to the urban-household fridge. Although Amazon's new brick-and-mortar footprint is small for now— Whole Foods has approximately 450 locations across North America whereas Kroger, for example, has almost 2,800—those Whole Foods locations are primarily positioned in urban centers, close to both current customers and potential customers with high disposable income. Proximity to the well-educated, and well-off, is an attractive plus for Amazon, whose fulfillment centers are mostly rural.

The acquisition might also mean a bigger data science play, as Amazon ropes in the countless customer records from its new organics entity and feeds them into other parts of the company flywheel, such as Amazon Fresh, Amazon Go, Subscribe and Save, and Prime Pantry.

Amazon has done well to create these ancillary food offerings, which each address a specific pain point. Amazon Fresh is great for those who don't want to go anywhere but still want their groceries. The same-day home delivery service, which launched in 2007, has quietly expanded beyond its home base in Seattle, and now operates in most U.S. cities, as well as in international markets like London, Berlin, and Tokyo. Amazon Go—the cashierless stores where shoppers grab what they want and skip the checkout line altogether—is tailored to those who still want to shop and pick groceries, but hate the hassles of lines, checkouts, and payments. Subscribe and Save provides that perfect convenient option for those who want their basics sent to them regularly without thinking about it—consumers can sign up to have their favorite consumables (as well as many non-food items, like household cleaners, diapers, etc.) delivered regularly, at a preselected cadence, for a discount. And more recently, there is Amazon's add-on subscription service, called Prime Pantry. Prime members pay an extra $5 a month for the ability to shop for non-perishable household items in "everyday package sizes" (one box of cereal, a box of Oreos, etc.) and have orders of over $10 shipped for free. Each of these offerings is sure to be part of Amazon's bigger plans for food supremacy.

Less obvious, perhaps, are the company's plans for leveraging Alexa, its virtual assistant, who will complement Amazon's last-mile advantage. As Amazon uses its logistics and big data advantages to take over the fridge, Alexa could soon be the medium by which consumers request everything they need. ("Alexa, I'm running out of milk. Order more.")

We've seen Bezos's knack for understanding customer behavior and significant paradigm shifts before. His $13.7 billion bet on food signals his view that grocery is shifting, and Amazon is slated to capitalize as progressives ditch cars and shopping carts for technology-led efficiencies. Investor sentiment concurs—news of the Whole Foods acquisition prompted shares of a large group of rival grocers, including Walmart, Kroger, and Costco, to quickly sink by between 13 and 6 percent, while Whole Foods shares shot up nearly 30 percent.[20] Investors look to be betting on Amazon to climb to the "top of the food chain."

Instacart Delivers

As Amazon throws its weight around in the grocery space, a close relative, Instacart, is making a name of its own. Instacart launched its grocery delivery service in 2012, around the same time as Blue Apron got into the meal-kit game. Users of Instacart simply pick the groceries they want through a smartphone app; its part-time workforce does the shopping and delivery, saving users the hassle of physically going to a grocery store. The company collects delivery fees from customers, related fees from grocery partners, and advertising income from brands like Coca-Cola, Unilever, P&G, and others.

By 2017, the online grocery market had reached a "tipping point," according to Instacart founder and CEO Apoorva Mehta, where selling groceries online went from being a neat novelty to a necessary offering for grocery retailers. Instacart had soon partnered with seven of the top eight North American grocers, and received $200 million of Series E funding, which valued the company at about $4.2 billion.[21] By March of 2019, Instacart was delivering to over 108 million households across the U.S. and Canada, and had partnered with over 300 local, regional, and national retailers.[22]

It may sound like a rapid rise, but Instacart was Mehta's twentieth start-up. He grew up in Canada, studied electrical engineering at the University of Waterloo in Ontario, then worked for a variety of technology companies, such as Qualcomm and BlackBerry. Eventually he moved to Seattle to be a supply-chain engineer at Amazon, where he developed fulfillment systems to get packages from Amazon warehouses to customer doors—some early foreshadowing of what was to come. The two years at Amazon improved Mehta's tech expertise and taught him how to tackle various logistics challenges, but something was still amiss.

After departing Amazon, Mehta played around with plenty of start-up ideas, including a social network for lawyers. "I knew nothing about these topics," he says, "but I liked putting myself in a position where I had to learn about an industry and try to solve problems they may or may not have had."[23] He landed on the idea of Instacart by thinking about the problems he experienced in his day-to-day life—like buying groceries every week without a car. In a move to scratch his own itch, Mehta coded the first iteration of the platform himself, and did the grocery shopping on the app's first test run.

The core idea of ordering groceries online and having them delivered wasn't new. In fact, the business model was wrapped around one of the most storied failures to come out of the dot-com bust—Webvan.

Webvan's idea to ship groceries directly to customers had technology bulls excited, but now the company is nothing more than a notorious cautionary tale from the dot-com bubble, carefully studied by business schools and venture investors alike. Founded by Louis Borders of Borders bookstores in 1996, the company raised a total of $394 million in venture funding from names like Sequoia, Benchmark Capital, and Goldman Sachs, before raising another $375 million from its IPO in November of 1999—despite reporting revenue of only $395,000 and losses of more than $50 million. As the company expanded, led by an executive team without any previous experience in the supermarket industry, things quickly got out of hand. Webvan proceeded to lose a total of $800 million before going bankrupt in 2001.

Mick Mountz, one of the company's former senior executives (and another Harvard Business School grad), re-emerged out of the Webvan ashes in 2003. After studying the colossal failure, Mountz concluded that the company's downfall wasn't due to market timing, lack of funding, or a poor strategic vision, but an inflexibility of systems to support the high cost of fulfillment. Spotting an opportunity, Mountz launched Kiva Systems, a new order-fulfillment system using mobile robots for warehouse automation—in essence, a better way to pick, pack, and ship orders of stuff.

Kiva got a tepid reception from potential investors in its home city of Palo Alto, California, so Mountz cleverly moved the start-up to Massachusetts the following year. He soon landed investors, and Kiva quickly captured some big-name clients, including Staples, which installed a Kiva system at a Pennsylvania distribution center in 2006 and a second system in Colorado in 2007, as well as Office Depot, Crate and Barrel, and Saks Fifth Avenue. In 2012, Kiva was acquired by Amazon for $775 million. At the time it was Amazon's second-largest acquisition ever, topped only by Zappos, which the company bought in 2009 for $1.2 billion.[24] Post-acquisition, Jeff Bezos recruited four former Webvan executives into the new Kiva/Amazon, including Mountz, who would stay on as CEO.[25]

Mountz and his Webvan colleagues were tasked by Bezos with studying the archives of Webvan (again) in preparation for a more prudent rollout of "Webvan II"—this time called Amazon Fresh, which expanded beyond a few Seattle neighborhoods for the first time in 2013.[26] Kiva Systems is now known as Amazon Robotics, the system that powers most of Amazon Fresh's fulfillment operations.

IN THE years between Webvan's bankruptcy and the rise of Webvan-inspired imitators Amazon Fresh and Instacart, grocery delivery was made more feasible by new technologies—especially smartphones, which could do things like process transactions and hire individuals to perform tasks. And there were plenty of use cases to back up the model, with apps like Uber and TaskRabbit sitting in the middle of supply and demand.

As Instacart grew, it established deeper relationships with grocers, giving them access to its growing user base in exchange for a listing fee. One of the most important of such partnerships was with Whole Foods—Instacart's first big national partner, which it inked a deal with in 2014. Under the agreement, Instacart got its own cashiers and staging areas at the upscale organic retailer's stores. In 2016, the relationship deepened, with Whole Foods securing an equity stake in Instacart and signing a five-year contract to make Instacart the exclusive delivery provider for most of its merchandise.

Things looked pretty good for Instacart, until the Amazon news broke in June of 2017. Whole Foods, arguably Instacart's most important partner and the source of 10 percent of its revenue, had become a subsidiary of its biggest rival overnight. "Every major grocery retailer in the country was calling us," Mehta says. "It really was like a thermonuclear bomb against the entire grocery industry." He assembled his 300 staff and told them the deal meant a war. "When we look back, that may have been a turning point for Instacart," he says.[27] Unsurprisingly, in late 2018, Whole Foods and Instacart announced that the two parties would dissolve their partnership. About 350 Instacart shoppers who did the picking at Whole Foods stores on behalf of app users lost their jobs.

Since the Amazon deal, Instacart has reinforced, and in some ways, redefined its value proposition. Its fastest-growing markets, like Chattanooga, Tennessee, are not places where Whole Foods dominates, so there's room to deepen penetration in these areas. Moreover, to fend off Amazon, Instacart has some additional short-term plays. First, it can deepen its relationships with existing partners, like Kroger and Costco, which still command a major share of the U.S. market. In this context, Instacart has carved out a new role as something of an Amazon hedge, emerging "as a sort of savior to traditional grocery retail," according to one observer.[28] In addition to serving as a key strategic partner to eight of the largest grocers in the U.S., it has added several prominent regional chains, like Aldi's, H-E-B, Albertsons, Publix, Kroger, and Wegmans, to its arsenal. Costco, too, announced that it was deepening its partnership with Instacart.

Second, the company can continue to focus on food quality and technology. Food-wise, Instacart relies on its personal shopper network, which has the critical task of picking the freshest avocado of the bunch. On the tech side, Instacart is investing in different aspects of its offerings, including voice-ordering. Recently, Instacart acquired Toronto delivery start-up Unata to help develop its voice-ordering and coupon-circulation technology. Launched in 2011, Unata specializes in e-flyers, digital loyalty programs, and digital coupons for grocers. The company recently launched voice-ordering capabilities, allowing people to make orders or build grocery lists through devices like Google Home. "Unata and Instacart have long shared a vision of innovating the grocery industry and building the online grocery shopping experience of the future," said Chris Bryson, Unata's CEO.[29]

INSTACART DESERVES kudos for nailing food delivery, a historically difficult business problem to solve. As a result, the company has gone on to raise a ton of well-deserved capital, to the tune of about $1 billion, much of which will be used to continue to expand. With more than 500,000 customers and approximately $2 billion in revenue as of 2018, the company that started as a big-city service has spread to smaller regional markets. Engagement is also improving—the average Instacart shopper spends about $95 an order, twice a month; Instacart Express customers, who pay $149 a year for free deliveries (a Prime-like subscription strategy), order twice as often, spending about $5,000 a year.[30]

Beyond expansion, Instacart is investing in smart innovation. The company recently filed a patent that reveals plans to release a mobile self-checkout system to bypass in-store checkouts. The mobile app would ostensibly let concierge shoppers fulfill orders without having to stand in line, all in the interest of making delivery faster and more efficient.[31]

Then there's the growing portfolio of grocery partners, all of which are terrified of what Amazon might do next. Since Amazon has upped the food ante, legacy grocers are staring at a future where automation and direct delivery are critical for business survival. As a result, Instacart still represents the most viable option for those retailers not wanting to tinker with the daunting task of handling last-mile delivery themselves.

But as retailers outsource last-mile delivery to Instacart, what isn't clear is whether or not these partnerships will deepen or wither. Instacart's partner chains being forced to bring delivery back in-house is a realistic possibility if consumers demand a more streamlined experience from their grocer of choice. In the case of Amazon, customers get the one-stop-shop experience via Amazon Prime Now and Amazon Fresh delivery (including from Whole Foods stores), which is both price-competitive and efficient.

Amazon is not the only worry, of course. In Arkansas, Walmart U.S. (as of 2018, Walmart Canada has been using Instacart as its strategic partner) is attempting to play ball, offering home delivery for $9.95 on a $30 minimum order. While the service can't yet guarantee one- and two-hour fulfillment, as Instacart can in some areas, its low prices and international reach make the retailer a possible threat. Target, too, is getting into direct delivery through its recent acquisition of Instacart rival Shipt.

Nevertheless, market fundamentals look good for Instacart. There is still room to grow, since only about 7 percent of Americans buy groceries online. The $850 billion market's shift to web-only is certain to accelerate. And, since Americans generally fill their grocery bag with food from more than one retailer, Instacart's brand-agnostic offering is well-positioned. Yes, certain questions hang in the balance, including whether Instacart will decide to replace its personal shoppers with robots; whether it will be forced to build costly fulfillment facilities despite its anti-Webvan, asset-light approach; or whether it will be strongarmed by Amazon. Time will tell.

Food 3.0

Despite the differences between subscription-based meal kits like Blue Apron, Amazon's suite of grocery offerings, and grocery delivery solutions like Instacart, a few overarching themes have propelled all these companies to the forefront of innovation—convenience, efficiency, and trust. Notwithstanding the challenges that lie ahead, each of these brands, along with tech trailblazers outside the food industry, have created value propositions that hit on all three.

What makes Amazon tick is not its product mix. There are plenty of comparable retailers selling the same stuff—Alibaba, Walmart, and eBay, to name a few. Yet only Amazon peddles one-day shipping for Prime members. With a third of the United States subscribing to Prime as of 2019 (and climbing), Bezos has shown the power of selling convenience and efficiency. As people become more comfortable shopping on Amazon and liaising with its customer service team, trust in Amazon is also rising.

Food innovators got the memo. Instacart's differentiators are now more than just best-in-class logistics—speed, quality, and trust are now key. Its secondary value-add is selection—the more grocery partner options Instacart has in its network, the better the customer experience.

Meal kits have done some amazing things to remove the hassles of meal planning and grocery shopping, which appeals to customers wanting convenience and efficiency; but the sector faces more dire challenges. With direct delivery on the rise, from grocery stores as well as on-demand restaurant delivery services, the landscape is changing fast. Legacy chains can take advantage by plugging into Instacart, while restaurants can fire the local delivery guy and use DoorDash or Uber Eats instead. As direct delivery becomes ubiquitous, the meal-kit moat looks weak in the face of change. While at one point the offering was strong on both convenience and efficiency, other direct entrants have raised the bar. The newly defined value differentiator now defaults to the pre-portioning of ingredients, the removal of meal planning for busy families, and the reduction of food waste (which is still a question mark for some environmentalists). Is that enough to justify what its subscribers are paying? Considering the high attrition plaguing these companies, it doesn't look like it.

WITH AMAZON's distribution system and new presence in brick-and-mortar organics, the company still remains the most viable threat to just about every player in the food space. Expect Amazon and the competition to increasingly leverage technology to transition consumers from physical to online stores, supported by a more robust supply chain. The rapid pace of innovation means direct delivery will be better, faster, and more efficient over time—both for Amazon, and those who intend to compete.

Then there's the trend toward more personalization. As each company in the sector generates more data on the consumer, subsequent offerings will individualize. Bezos has the advantage here too, with a new list of Whole Foods customers to add to the mountains of data already on hand. As of mid-2018, the number of Prime members alone, over 100 million, is increasing at a rate of 40 percent per annum. Hey, I noticed you bought some Lärabars last month. Would you like us to send you a second box of their newest flavor alongside your next shipment?

The growth of Amazon's Prime subscribers, combined with the company's buying power and access to cheap capital, adds an important final layer to think about—a likely shift into a deflationary (lowering of food prices) food environment at the hands of Bezos, where high-quality food, typically reserved for the upmarket consumer, becomes more easily accessible and affordable for the masses. This fundamental economic swing, which is yet to manifest, is sure to benefit Amazon, as well as its loyal consumers—yet hurt just about everyone else in the industry.

ELEVEN

A Fashion Industry Refit

RETAIL IS IN the midst of a paradigm shift as consumers move online for everything from diapers to dresses. Plenty of traditional players are struggling or shutting down stores as a result of changing consumer habits. Payless ShoeSource filed for Chapter 11 bankruptcy protection and announced it was closing all 2,100 of its U.S. stores, while Gymboree is getting rid of 800 locations. A number of other retailers, including The Gap, have hinted that store closures are coming. The *Washington Post* has called it a "retail apocalypse," with more than 15,000 store closures since 2017.[1] Amid all this carnage, there is a new wave of retail beneficiaries, many of which we will explore in this chapter.

Amazon, of course, continues to dominate web commerce, but select consumer brands have narrowed in on unique offerings to compete, and thrive. Stitch Fix (the "Netflix of Fashion") and some of its competitors have used a different strategy to carve out market share in the world of fashion. In an industry that you'd think would require a healthy brick-and-mortar presence—after all, you can't try on a JPEG of a pair of jeans, no matter how many different angles and zoom features you get—there are

CHANGE IN CLOTHING PRICES VS. ALL GOODS, 1995–2014

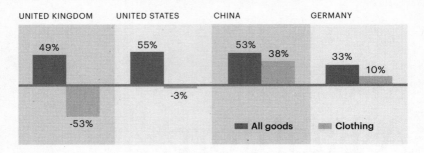

Clothing has become more affordable in many countries since the 1990s.

Source: Nathalie Remy, Eveline Speelman, and Steven Swartz, "Style That's Sustainable: A New Fast-Fashion Formula," McKinsey & Company, October 2016, https://www.mckinsey.com/business-functions/sustainability/our-insights/style-thats-sustainable-a-new-fast-fashion-formula.

a healthy number of online fashion providers, including, among others, Nordstrom's Trunk Club, Indochino, and fashion lender Rent the Runway, with creative business models. Each uses components of subscription to lock in loyalty and recurring revenue. While Trunk Club has struggled since its sale to Nordstrom in 2014, Stitch Fix has paved the way for what the next phase of fashion retail will look like. Rooted in personalization, founder Katrina Lake's company has crafted a unique combination of highly curated fashion and data science to get women (and now men) what they want out of an outfit, without ever stepping foot in a store.

Get Your Stitch Fix

When it comes to aspiring entrepreneurs conjuring up ideas for innovative businesses, it seems they spike the founder water at Harvard Business School. Stitch Fix, created by Katrina Lake and Erin Morrison Flynn, has quickly become one of the most popular e-commerce quasi-subscription services in the United

States—in fact, some suggest Stitch Fix may be the most innovative and cash-efficient e-commerce retailer in the modern digital era. The company has redefined what makes an apparel business work in today's changing retail environment.

Stitch Fix began in 2012 by targeting fashion-conscious women who loved looking great but hated going anywhere to shop. New customers to the website fill out a form detailing their style preferences, clothing needs, and price points. Algorithms then churn out a set of potential choices, which one of the company's stylists tailors to the individual customer before shipping five items direct, for a $20 fee. Anything a customer doesn't want can be returned free of charge. Should a customer keep any of the items, the $20 styling fee is applied toward the purchase—and customers who keep all five items receive a 25 percent discount. The brands included in a customer "fix" vary, but typically include items from trendy names like Citizens of Humanity, Scotch & Soda, and Barbour.

While Stitch Fix shies away from calling itself a true subscription company, customers can opt for subsequent boxes to be delivered automatically at a frequency of their choice. The setup is a bit outside the norm for subscription business models, but the automated shipping option provides the company with smoother revenue patterns over time as more and more customers toggle the sub-commerce option. And, while exact subscription numbers are hazy, repeat business is a strong point; Stitch Fix says that of its 2.19 million active clients, 86 percent were repeat buyers in 2017.[2]

Stitch Fix is not the first company to try out a personal shopping service on the web; in 2009, Trunk Club sensed a demand for "assisted commerce," and began offering curated apparel to men. The Chicago-based company sold to Nordstrom for $350 million in 2014—although Nordstrom has struggled to make Trunk Club a continued success as a result of a few important factors. Nordstrom expanded Trunk Club's store presence, opening several brick-and-mortar "clubhouses" where customers could shop in person; however, performance fell short. As you might recall, Birchbox experienced similar struggles when it, too, got away from its D2C roots with physical stores in the U.S., later shutting down its Soho location to shave costs while simultaneously scrapping plans for more locations. Systems integration woes also limited Trunk Club's progress post-merger. It finally fully integrated its distribution systems with Nordstrom's nearly three years later, suggesting that synergies related to fulfillment and merchandising weren't cohesive early on. Finally, Nordstrom's pricing strategy isn't customer-friendly. The upscale retailer has tried to cut costs at Trunk Club by adding a $25 fee to items shipped for home try-on, credited toward any purchases made, a service that used to be free. This company-first, customer-second strategy has ostensibly caused more cancellations and an increase in churn. Nordstrom co-president Erik Nordstrom acknowledged in 2016 that the company needed to be "more accurate" in responding to customer needs, later adding that Trunk Club had taken a $197 million write-down.[3]

The challenges at Trunk Club do serve as a cautionary tale, but Lake's company has not only learned from those mistakes but shown no signs of slowing down. After a somewhat rocky start following its IPO in November 2017, the company's stock price has nearly doubled on the back of more than 3 million active clients and an algorithmically driven styling process.[4] Stitch Fix has consistently operated with positive EBITDA (earnings before interest, tax, depreciation, and amortization) numbers, gross profit in the 45 percent range, and an upward trend in revenue since inception. In 2019 alone, the company is on track to bring in nearly $1.6 billion in revenue, surpassing estimates for both Yelp and Zynga—and its own expectations.[5] The company became the tenth largest online fashion retailer in the U.S. in 2018—all this with plenty of cash still on the balance sheet.

KATRINA LAKE was only thirty-four years old when she led Stitch Fix's public offering, and was the only woman to lead a tech IPO that year. In March 2019, she received the "Pitch Prize"—named after Franklin "Pitch" Johnson, one of the first venture capitalists in Silicon Valley—in recognition of her many accomplishments as an entrepreneur and business leader. Lake follows an esteemed list of Pitch Prize honorees, including Reid Hoffman of Linked-In, Marissa Mayer of Google and Yahoo, and Ben Silbermann of Pinterest. But there's another reason to admire Lake as a leader, beyond her business success.

In June 2017, Justin Caldbeck, the co-founder of VC firm Binary Capital, resigned after six women shared stories of his inappropriate sexual behavior. It then came to light that in 2013, when Caldbeck was at Lightspeed Venture Partners—an early investor in Stitch Fix—Lake complained to the firm that Caldbeck had sexually harassed her, and asked that he be removed from his observer role on the Stitch Fix board of directors. The firm did comply with her request, but continued to employ him, and asked Lake to sign a non-disparagement agreement—effectively forcing her to choose between speaking publicly about Caldbeck's behavior, or securing critical early investment in her company. She signed the agreement.[6]

While the NDAs have ensured that both Lake and Lightspeed have kept mum on the issue, Lake has since spoken publicly—and rather heroically—about the treatment of women in the venture capital landscape. In an appearance on NPR's podcast "How I Built This," Guy Raz asked about the Lightspeed episode. Lake addressed the broader issue of overt sexualized treatment of female founders, pointing a finger directly at prominent venture capitalist Chris Sacca. As Lake described it, while Sacca was addressing an audience of thousands from a conference stage, he touted his unconventional style of working with entrepreneurs, where those seeking funding would not only visit his home (rather than an office), but chat in his hot tub, drink beer, and hang out. A pregnant Lake, sitting in the audience, was appalled by Sacca's address. She said to Raz, "I was pregnant at the time. There was no way I was going to go to some guy's home I've never met, let alone get in a bikini. Moreover, since I am pregnant, I can't go in a hot tub or drink beer… I guess I'll never be in his pipeline."[7]

SEVERAL FACTORS, beyond the strength of Katrina Lake's leadership, contribute to the success of Stitch Fix's strategy, which is almost anti-Amazon-like. Rather than a growth-at-all-costs mindset, Stitch Fix has focused on unit economics since the outset, operating with core capabilities such as data, personalization, and premium customer service to drive profits. The company also nailed business fundamentals, like product-market fit, as well as key aspects of its operations infrastructure such as fulfillment and customer service. Stitch Fix's killer moat, however, is a combination of a subscription-style model and hyper-sophisticated data science. Like Netflix, the success of Stitch Fix's unique play suggests that when it comes to clothing (rather than content), personalized shopping informed by a relentless focus on data trumps Amazon's one-size-fits-all offering (Prime Wardrobe).

The driver of Stitch Fix's data bus is Eric Colson, the company's chief algorithms officer, and a former VP of data science and engineering at, you guessed it, Netflix, where he was largely responsible for building the streaming giant's recommendation engine. At Stitch Fix, Colson has added areas like recommendations, human computation, resource management, inventory management, algorithmic fashion design, and others.

How serious is the company about data? Stitch Fix provides a full "Algorithms Tour" of "how data science is woven into the fabric of Stitch Fix" at every stage of a purchase, from assigning a customer to a warehouse or human stylist, to predicting items they will like, to managing inventory. If this kind of thing tickles your fancy, you can geek out here: https://algorithms-tour.stitch-fix.com/.

For us normal folk, let me highlight a few pertinent examples of what's going on internally. Broadly speaking, Stitch Fix learns about (and tracks) client preferences, both individually and as a whole. With client feedback on things like fit, brand preference, and purchase history, the company is able to constantly improve its understanding of customer-style patterns. Doing so makes subsequent modeling, and personalization, more accurate and effective.

The clothing items a customer will receive are initially chosen by algorithm scores and machine learning before they touch the hands of one of the company's stylists. When a new customer signs up they fill out a "Style Profile" to describe their clothing preferences. But the company knows there can be a gap between stated and unstated preferences, and to complicate matters even further, it's not always easy to describe a style in words. So, to address the obvious challenge of forming an accurate picture of someone's personal style preferences, Stitch Fix uses machine learning to do things like pull photos of clothing that customers like (e.g., from Pinterest, Facebook, and Instagram), while simultaneously searching for visually similar items in stock. Algorithms then select a range of style options to present to the 3,000+ internal Stitch Fix expert stylists, who ultimately hand-select what fills a customer's box. The human stylists are intelligently matched to each and every Stitch Fix customer. Knowing not every stylist will be a good fit for each new client, the company uses algorithms to determine which of the available stylists is best suited to each customer who has requested a shipment. Once there's a match, and a curated assortment of items is finalized, the first Stitch Fix box is packed and shipped out.

It's a complex process with many moving parts. And, as the company points out on the Algorithm Tour web page, the first shipment is just the beginning:

> She opens the box, is hopefully delighted, keeps what she wants and sends back the rest, and then *tells us what she thinks about each article of clothing*. There is a symbiotic relationship between her and Stitch Fix, and she gives us very insightful feedback that we use not only to better serve her next time, but also to better serve other clients as well.

After that initial customer shipment, the company uses machine learning tools to anticipate client needs, model future demand (a key piece for buying future inventory), build inventory depletion models to manage what's in stock, develop analytics to improve upon what stylists suggest to their client base, and more.

More than seventy-five data scientists employed by Stitch Fix have helped it become a technological pioneer in online fashion, and its robust execution has left Stitch Fix in a league of its own— although competition is certain to intensify from both upstarts and larger brands who smell profit in the pool.

Gentleman's Box Unpacks Profit

As Stitch Fix was hitting its stride, Chris George, an e-com-merce entrepreneur from Michigan, was approached by a friend, John Haji, with a business idea. Echoing one of Trunk Club's core assumptions when the company got started in 2009, Haji believed that plenty of guys were style-conscious; they just didn't like to shop. So he began to work out an idea to sell merchandise to fashion-minded men.

Initially, George was lukewarm to the idea, but as he dug into business trends he became captivated by the explosion of online subscription-box companies. Notwithstanding the early success of Trunk Club and Stitch Fix, it was primarily George's research into trending men's Google searches that piqued his interest in launching a business with Haji. The sheer number of Google searches for "men's hairstyle" and "men's fashion acces-sories" was the turning point, recalls George.[8] The more he read about names like Birchbox (which hadn't yet launched "Birchbox Man"), Harry's, and Trunk Club, the more George—who told me in an interview that he shops from his basement—believed that Haji had spotted a real opportunity to target men looking to up their style game.[9]

With confidence in their business vision, Chris George, John Haji, and a third partner, Paul Chambers, launched Gentleman's

Box in November 2014. At first, they shipped only to the U.S., but soon expanded to Canada (after Ryan Kesler, a hockey player then with the NHL's Vancouver Canucks, posted about GB on his Twitter account) and within a few months were shipping to Mexico, the United Kingdom, Australia, and New Zealand. Some five years later, the Royal Oak, Michigan–based company has amassed tens of thousands of subscribers in over thirty-five countries, who receive curated boxes of stylish accessories like socks, ties, and cuff links. Gentleman's Box runs on fuel from its Instagram influencers, fans on Facebook, and quality affiliate traffic from sites like mysubscriptionaddiction.com.

Perhaps the most important milestone in the company's short lifespan was landing a deal with *GQ* magazine in their first year. Despite not yet having a subscriber base, the partners promised they could get *GQ* 1,000 subscribers in six months (an admittedly arbitrary number, recalls George).[10] Today, subscribers to Gentleman's Box automatically receive a *GQ* subscription as part of signing up.

Gentleman's Box has kept a rather low profile, ensuring its existing customers are happy before prioritizing new-customer acquisition. This heavy focus on retention has proven to be a driver of continuous profit from loyal customers. Whether someone is attempting to cancel as a result of price point, or because of what George calls "product fatigue," GB's live agents do what they can to satisfy each subscriber and keep them on board.

While Gentleman's Box shares obvious similarities with Dollar Shave Club—most notably, the business model and target market—George believes that what distinguishes his company from Michael Dubin's is George's continuous drive toward *profitable* growth, an approach to scaling up that involves a more prudent stewarding of the business, rather than chasing runaway growth. When asked about the Unilever acquisition of the razor start-up, George points to DSC's lack of profitability at the time of sale, and says parties that show an interest in acquiring Gentleman's Box (the company's ultimate goal is to sell) must show an appreciation for the same profit-first mindset of its founders.

Fabletics's Communication Problem

A lesson in the perils of growth without solid fundamentals can be found in the story of Fabletics, a brand fronted by co-founder Kate Hudson, which kicked off in 2013 selling subscription boxes of fitness apparel for women (and later men). The company was conceived by Adam Goldenberg and Don Ressler, co-CEOs of owner JustFab Inc., the parent company to both JustFab and ShoeDazzle.

Fabletics has done a decent job competing with the Lululemons of the fashion world, but it has also drawn its fair share of criticism from both consumers and watchdog groups. The company has faced numerous complaints from customers claiming the monthly subscriptions are too hard to cancel. In general, high complaint counts related to subscriptions suggest a broader and more systemic customer service problem.

When Shawn Gold was asked to join JustFab Inc. as CMO in 2016, he did some digging on the company's reputation and described what he found in a Medium post:

> I Googled JustFab Inc. and its brands: ShoeDazzle, FabKids, JustFab and Fabletics. What I found was a little disheartening: on page one of the results, some news reports were focusing on [disgruntled customers], highlighting over 1000 customer complaints to the Better Business Bureau. The company had settled a 2013 investigation with the county of Santa Clara, California for $1.8 million, and several stories insinuated that JustFab's customers were being tricked into becoming members. The implication was that the company was, to put it bluntly, sleazy and dishonest.[11]

Some of those stories went beyond "insinuating": the now-defunct Gawker once called JustFab "the biggest scam in online fashion," and an investigative piece in 2015 found over 1,400 Better Business Bureau complaints and 234 Federal Trade Commission complaints about Just Fab.[12] While on the surface the optics don't look good, to be fair, things weren't as bad as they seemed. The number of complaints represent only a small percentage of the total number of Fabletics's customers.

The more important question is: What to make of the $1.8 million Santa Clara settlement? The settlement arose from claims that the company used misleading tactics, resulting in customers who thought they were making a one-off purchase being signed up for subscription services that would automatically bill their credit card each month unless they declined that shipment within the first five days.

The issue boils down to a Columbia House–like communication problem of disclosure, and a subpar customer service operation. Fabletics is just one example of a company experiencing a problem common to subscription players who don't prioritize these pillars of customer service. As a rule of thumb, it's safe to assume the average customer doesn't read detailed terms and conditions, so Fabletics and others suffering from spiking complaints and cancellations can cool the fire simply by making billing plans, return policies, and cancellation terms clear and conspicuous. In other words, the yoga pants don't need to be transparent, but the terms of service do.

Since 2016, the Fabletics team has stabilized complaint levels through 24/7 service and customer-enabled cancellations via the web—a smart move to cede control from the company and place it back in the hands of the consumer. However, expect the athleisure subscription company's future to be very unsettled as plenty of other subscription options, from Lululemon, SweatStyle, Sweaty Betty, Ellie, Adidas, and Under Armour, place additional pressure on Hudson and co.

Green the Runway

As things get competitive in the world of activewear in a box, Rent the Runway, yet another subscription business launched by Harvard grads, is doing something different. Founded in 2009 by Jennifer Hyman and Jennifer Fleiss, RTR (as the kids call it) rents out clothes, handbags, jewelry, and accessories to subscribers. The company is known to be a pioneer in the space, the first to sell the idea of renting a wardrobe vs. buying one. The business model has garnered significant investor attention, with RTR having raised over $500 million in funding thus far. Moreover, the company has served 9 million customers to date, complementing its recent valuation of approximately $1 billion.

When Rent the Runway first launched, it offered formal dresses that women could rent for weddings and other events. As the company expanded, so did its product suite, with nearly three-quarters of its 9 million clients now able to rent work attire, casual wear, and more. For $99 a month, its "unlimited" plan allows subscribers to rent four items at a time, from over 450 brands, either through the website or at recently opened storefront locations in New York City, Washington, D.C., Chicago, San Francisco, and Los Angeles. The price includes cleaning and insurance for minor damages.

And cleaning is taken very seriously. In fact, the company's dry-cleaning warehouse—160,000 square feet—is the world's biggest, and processes over 2,000 items per hour. The art of dry cleaning is key to the company's continued success, as clothes must be cleaned and shipped as fast as possible to make the logistics work. If a piece of clothing has been worn but isn't stained, it goes into a washing machine selected to extend its lifespan. But if it comes back with visible spots, it goes to a "spotter," a stain-removal technician who draws on expert knowledge of fibres, materials, and chemicals to determine how best to treat it. It's such an important role that, Hyman has said, "the hardest position to recruit has not been engineers, it has been spotters."[13] In fact, Rent the Runway offers a program to employees who want to learn spotting as a trade, which is one of the most lucrative roles in the warehouse, at roughly $30 an hour. (The program takes almost two years to complete, if you're thinking about a career change!)

The specialized behind-the-scenes operations support the

many benefits of renting clothes, such as a rotating wardrobe, access to trendy upscale designer items, a smarter and smaller closet—and, perhaps most important, a reduced environmental footprint. With disposable fashion now on environmentalists' radar, innovators like RTR are making their mission more about sustainability than tackling high-priced designer blouses.

New Pantone colors, new styles, and new trends—not to mention the human desire to consume—all contribute to sustainability issues surrounding the industry; fast-fashion brands like Zara, H&M, and others bear some responsibility for enabling a wasteful cycle whereby consumers are perpetually buying new clothes and tossing out what's no longer "on trend." Cotton, which accounts for about 30 percent of all textile fibre consumption, is usually grown using a lot of water, pesticides, and fertilizer. Since the countries with the largest fabric- and apparel-making industries rely mainly on fossil fuels for energy production, making one kilogram of fabric generates an average of twenty-three kilograms of greenhouse gases.[14]

With sustainability as a goal, Hyman, RTR's co-founder and chief executive, once claimed she wanted to put Zara and H&M, the giants of discount disposable fashion retail, out of business. That's a tall order. But what does seem plausible is Hyman and company leading the next wave of conscious consumers who choose to buy the idea of renting style versus owning it.

With the fast-fashion industry generating massive carbon emissions, chemical runoff, and landfill gluts, other companies, like Gwynnie Bee and Le Tote, are popping up and helping to change the culture of consumption.

Gwynnie Bee, founded by its current CEO Christine Hunsicker, rents women's fashion to the plus-sized market. Originally run out of Hunsicker's New York City apartment, Gwynnie Bee now operates from offices in the U.S. and India, with roughly 350 employees helping ship millions of boxes annually to its growing customer base. The company's new division, Caastle—the name references "clothing as a service"—is now providing a full-suite-logistics back-end, including cleaning, returns, packing, shipping, and more, for legacy retailers such as Ann Taylor and New York & Company.[15]

Then there's Le Tote. The San Francisco–based company, founded in 2012, has garnered significant traction and staying power. Le Tote follows the same rental model as RTR (though with a purchase option), and includes a line of maternity wear. Subscribers can opt to receive a monthly curated "tote" or shop the thousands of items on the site, which include brands like Nike, Free People Movement, Kenneth Cole, French Connection, and Kate Spade. Monthly plans cost $79 ($89 for maternity), and customers can buy the items they want to keep—at a noticeable discount to mainstream retail.

As North American consumers become increasingly concerned with sustainability, and as global demand for clothing increases over the coming decade as millions of people in developing countries enter the middle class and spend more on apparel, rental options look poised to expand even further.

Prime Your Wardrobe

As the world of fashion innovates around broad themes like subscription, sustainability, and rental, let's acknowledge the elephant in the room. Where does Amazon fit into all this, and how are brands like Stitch Fix and Rent the Runway faring with one of the world's largest companies as a competitor?

Prime Wardrobe is Amazon's not-so-loud answer to the increasingly popular personalized shopping service trend that Stitch Fix and others have brought to the forefront. After a beta launch in 2017, accessible by invitation only, Amazon rolled out Prime Wardrobe to the broader market in June 2018. The service allows Prime members to order items like shoes, clothing, or accessories for no up-front charge, and decide within a week what to keep and what to return. Amazon's hassle-free logistics are quick and painless for customers, and items on offer include brands outside its private label line such as Under Armour, Adidas, Kate Spade, Tommy Hilfiger, Levi's, and others. Shipping is free, of course, and customers are only charged for the items they keep—a plus for the budget-conscious shopper who resents e-tailers charging at checkout before items get to the doorstep.

There are, however, key differences between Amazon's model and that of Stitch Fix and the broader lot of innovators. First, Prime Wardrobe is a do-it-yourself offering targeted at the everyday online shopper. Unlike Stitch Fix and Trunk Club, for example, Prime Wardrobe has no personal stylists on hand helping to eliminate choice fatigue; instead, members fill their own box with their own choices.

Second, Amazon Wardrobe removes more purchase friction than a traditional e-commerce apparel experience, since customers aren't being charged initially—which makes it easier to justify shopping for the clothes one does in fact end up purchasing. And kudos to Bezos for helping to limit buyer's remorse with a flexible seven-day "try before you buy" policy. Yet even this core value proposition doesn't seem to be enough of a differentiator for Amazon long-term.

Flexible return policies are now table stakes for most omnichannel retailers. And, while online shoppers disagree on the acceptable timing of a credit card charge—for example, at time of sale vs. a week later—it's not clear whether the Prime Wardrobe option provides a compelling alternative to an apparel e-tailer with a liberal thirty-day return policy.

Amazon isn't trying to put a pin in the rental wardrobe balloon just yet, so Rent the Runway and Gwynnie Bee are safe for now. But it's hard to see how Prime Wardrobe might take reasonable market share from Stitch Fix, Trunk Club, and Le Tote, who make their mark with personalized curation—an ostensibly no-choice model driven by stylists who do the work for customers who crave ultimate convenience—freedom from browsing and choosing.

Stitch Fix has established this noticeable competitive advantage over not only Prime Wardrobe, but other apparel retailers attempting to compete. While subscription is a driver for just about any clothing retailer wanting to capture customer loyalty, fashion is highly personal—and therefore not an easy business model to execute. In the fall of 2018, roughly a year after Gap Inc. launched its initial subscription box, babyGap Outfit Box, the retailer stopped the program. During its fourteen-month pilot in baby clothes, Gap had also introduced a pajama box and an outfit box for kids with its Old Navy brand, neither of which is active now.

The Gap's attempted foray into subscription apparel provides some key lessons on why fashion brands fail in sub-commerce. First, category fit. Although apparel can work for subscription, it's not as predictable as other categories that feature consistent consume-and-replenish cycles—like personal care or beauty. Second, since (as mentioned) fashion is personal, the importance of curation, selection, and data science makes it difficult for most legacy brick-and-mortar retailers to merchandise effectively, minimize returns, and compete with companies that rely heavily on superior data to scale successfully (i.e., Stitch Fix, Rent the Runway, Le Tote). In other words, your typical Gap women's apparel buyer doesn't necessarily make a good e-subscription merchandiser. Third, the competition. When Walmart signaled that it was moving aggressively into kids' subscription boxes, with already established successes in direct-to-customer beauty, grooming, and baby boxes, Gap had its work cut out for it. Last, The Gap lacked some key capabilities. Rather than attempt to build out its business line with a strategic partner (as Walmart has done with Brandshare, which manages and executes just about every step in the box process), it opted to try and do so in-house. Yikes.

Contrast The Gap's shortcomings with what makes Stitch Fix tick: direct-to-customer savvy driven by personalization, curation, data, and brand awareness, all of which work in concert to attract its niche group of shoppers, who want high fashion, month after month, without hassle. And, as each monthly box is shipped, its receiver's evolving style profile means Stitch Fix, through the power of its algorithms, gets even better at what it does.

While Stitch Fix, Rent the Runway, Le Tote, and others in their category stand to not only survive but thrive in the face of Amazon's fashion play, legacy retailers catering to the mass market—Amazon's actual target—will see more of their market share erode.

TWELVE

Bricks and Bytes—Online Hits the Streets

WE'VE DISCUSSED a number of success stories in this book so far, and if we go down the list, most built their loyal consumer base by going direct to customer. Whether we're talking about product companies like Dollar Shave Club or novel services like Spotify, they were able to generate hundreds of millions, and sometimes billions, in revenue without ever opening a physical space. And though that might be the new normal as we enter the next chapter of digital commerce, there's been an interesting pivot by online-first consumer brands into traditional omni-channel, adding an offline presence to their core e-commerce model in order to reach new heights.

Warby Parker, widely considered a first-mover category disruptor in eyewear, was initially all about avoiding high-priced glasses by eliminating the overhead incurred by physical stores. Warby's lean start-up model, where consumers could buy cool frames for less by shopping online, made perfect sense. Then, in 2013, in the wake of Warby Parker's rise to darling of online retail,

E-COMMERCE VS. MALL STORE SALES IN THE US

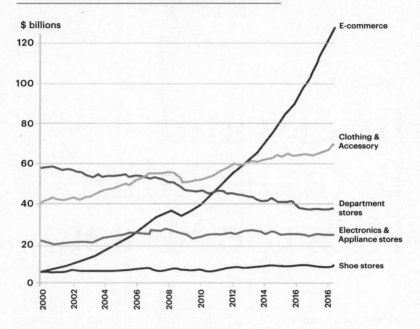

As e-commerce continues to grow rapidly, sales at most brick-and-mortar retailers, especially mall stores, remain stagnant.

Source: Wolf Richter, "E-Commerce Does it Again: The Stores that Got Pummeled," Wolf Street, August 17, 2018, https://wolfstreet.com/2018/08/17/despite-strong-retail-sales-brick-mortar-meltdown-pummels-these-stores-the-most-e-commerce/.

the company switched gears, announcing its first flagship store location, in New York City. Their store count has since grown to roughly 100 locations across North America, with thirty more planned for the latter half of 2019.

Warby's successful move from online to omni-channel has prompted others to mimic the strategy. Most online-to-offline copycats typically believe that selling online has a proverbial revenue ceiling, and, in turn, that brick-and-mortar expansion offers a way to break through the glass, letting the next wave of new customers discover, engage, and purchase in-store (and/or online).

Some are using physical stores as inventory-free showrooms. Warby Parker shoppers, for example, try on products in-store before ordering their final selection, which is later shipped direct, off the website. Indochino, another online-first brand and a leader in made-to-measure menswear, created its store showroom concept around an appointment-based experience. Customers go online to book a timeslot with one of the company's "style guides," who then takes measurements and selects customization options, all in person, before the order is processed online. As with Warby Parker's glasses, the suit is then shipped direct—in this case, approximately four weeks later.

Other online-first businesses have partnered with established legacy retailers to build a real-life presence in order to soften overhead costs. Casper, a New-York-based mattress brand that began testing its physical presence with pop-up trailers in select cities, has since partnered with Target, Nordstrom, and the Hudson's Bay Company (in Canada) to make their products available for in-store purchase. Their Canadian-based counterpart Endy did the same, announcing similar partnerships with other showroom retailers across Canada. In 2018, Birchbox announced a partnership with Walgreens that saw Birchbox showcase products in several Walgreens locations. Walgreens now owns a minority stake in the cosmetics company.

Opinion is divided on whether brands with an online-first growth story should be taking their businesses to storefronts. The bulls argue that, notwithstanding retail brick-and-mortar's decline and the high cost of things like build-out and monthly rent, companies like Warby Parker and Indochino do have a business case—namely, that $3 trillion out of $3.4 trillion, or almost 90 percent, of retail sales in the U.S. are still courtesy of brick-and-mortar. Moreover, e-commerce predictions suggest that global online sales will still only account for 17.5 percent of total global retail by 2021 (up from nearly 14 percent in 2018).[1]

And while that sounds good on the surface, the bull case misses a key point: stores suck a ton of cash from a growing upstart, and unless you've got a nice war chest to risk—or a firmly entrenched partner to piggyback on—a move into stores is inherently dangerous.

Bonobos, another online-to-offline player in apparel, which owned its own factories, was saddled with challenges once it began to use venture funding to launch its personalized-fit Guideshops—and in the end, the company sold to Walmart in 2017, in what looked like a desperate move to cover cash lost from its physical expansion and to return capital to its venture investors. As mentioned, Birchbox, too, had to shut its doors in New York and scale back additional store plans as a result of financial challenges, opting instead to partner with Walgreens.

This isn't to say that digital-native brands should steer clear of physical stores. The strategy can work well for specific categories, like eyeglasses, or swimwear, where people have a hard time determining fit via a website. Since glasses are personal and pricey, there is a cohort of people who simply prefer to try 'em on in person. Rather than alienating that potential customer base, it's prudent to consider a physical store. Cleverly, Warby didn't sign an expensive lease when it first started to test things out. In fact, in 2012, the company used a classic yellow school bus as a mobile storefront, for a cross-country retail tour it called the Warby Parker Class Trip—kind of like the Peterman Reality Tour (if you didn't catch the Seinfeld reference, move on). The bus rolled through different American cities, showcasing Warby's $95 frames to thousands of curious shoppers. When the tour was well received, Warby knew the next iteration might resemble something more permanent.

Companies like Amazon and Shopify, which maintain plenty of cash on the balance sheet, have a much easier time experimenting with in-store experiences. Amazon has done so since 2015, the year it opened a half-dozen bookstores, a score of campus locations, and a grocery store without cashiers (Amazon Go). Shopify recently opened its first physical space in Los Angeles, called ROW DTLA, described on the website as "a destination for current and aspiring business owners to learn, experiment, and build with Shopify." These initiatives are digestible if store failure is nothing but a rounding error. As you might recall from the Amazon chapter, Prime's 100,000 individual customers spend about $1,400 a year across the Bezos ecosystem. Amazon can afford to meet customers on Mars if that's where they're shopping.

WeWork—Building Community

It's hard to talk about budding subscription players and online/offline hybrids without mentioning a nine-year-old company that, at one point in 2019, was on the verge of a $50 billion valuation. WeWork, the SoftBank-backed community workspace company started by two visionary founders in 2010, now occupies more Manhattan office space than any other company, renting 5.3 million square feet in Manhattan, and knocking the previous title holder, JPMorgan Chase, off its throne.[1]

WeWork, the hottest brand in coworking, has spread like a virus. In 2017 alone, the company opened ninety buildings across the globe. As of Spring 2019, WeWork locations numbered over 600. The company has attracted over 260,000 monthly paying members since inception—and the demand is increasing. Occupancy rates rose to 84 percent across all establishments in 2018, up from 78 percent occupancy one year prior. In certain cities, WeWork is close to 100 percent occupancy, with prospective members waiting for vacancies.

WeWork, rooted in a subscription membership model birthed by founders Adam Neumann and Miguel McKelvey, has nearly perfected what a community co-working space should be: festive, trendy, aspirational, and community-oriented. Both men seem to have come by the vision honestly—McKelvey grew up in a hippie commune in Eugene, Oregon, and Neumann spent his early years in Israel living on a kibbutz.

The two met in the mid-2000s in New York City, when McKelvey was working as a junior draftsman at an architectural firm. His coworker was roommates with Neumann, who had moved to

New York (after serving in the Israeli Defence Forces) to tinker with a couple of start-ups selling baby clothes. Neumann and McKelvey soon found themselves working across the hall from one another in Brooklyn. Often the guys would chat about how the building they both worked out of could make more efficient use of its space. What started as casual conversation soon amounted to a mini-pitch to their Brooklyn landlord.

In a bid to lease out one of the unused floors, Neumann floated the idea of letting he and McKelvey do a full office makeover, and lease out the newly finished area as shared offices. Although the initial conversation didn't bear fruit, subsequent follow-ups resulted in the landlord agreeing to try the concept out on another property he owned across the street. The pair drafted floor plans and a brand vision for what they called Green Desk, an environmentally conscious shared workplace, and came back with a formal proposal. The landlord accepted, and a new business partnership was in motion. The initial Green Desk pilot was profitable, quickly growing to 350-plus members in the one location, but when it became clear the landlord was working his own agenda, Neumann and McKelvey crafted a deal to sell Green Desk to him, and each walked away with a few million.[2]

The cash from the deal provided an opportunity to recreate the Green Desk vision using a different brand name and location, this time calling it WeWork. The first location bearing the moniker opened at 154 Grand Street, in New York's Soho neighbourhood, in April 2011. The location was at full occupancy within a couple of months.

After several years of continuous growth, Neumann found himself in a position to meet with Masayoshi Son, Japan's wealthiest man and CEO of the SoftBank Group. Although SoftBank has invested over $10 billion in WeWork, the company, which announced plans to go public in early 2019 as The We Company, has since delayed its IPO (as of September 2019) as a result of tepid investor interest, plunging valuations, and questions about its leadership.[3]

When the company's s-1 (the form that companies must file to the U.S. Securities and Exchange Commission before an IPO) became public in August 2019, it prompted intense scrutiny of its finances—and of the odd behavior of Neumann, whose prolific pot smoking and aspirations to the prime ministership of Israel were detailed in the *Wall Street Journal*.[4] Neumann stepped down as CEO in September 2019, reportedly at the insistence of SoftBank.[5]

WEWORK'S FUNDAMENTAL business model isn't unique. In fact, the idea to create shared space for profit was brought to the mainstream in 1989, when Mark Dixon launched Regus, a company that offered tenants community office space complete with maintenance, staff, and a flexible lease term. When Regus went public in October of 2000, it was valued at £1.5 billion and was considered the first large-scale shared office space pioneer. But, like many first movers, Regus fell into unforeseen business ditches. Namely, the first big dot-com bubble burst, which saw many tenants vacate Regus offices around the world in favor of more affordable options like home-based set-ups and coffee shops. Having inked long-term leases with landlords, the firm was left holding the bag with too few tenants to cover the gap. After a near collapse, Regus re-emerged from bankruptcy and remains a formidable player today. However, new entrants, like WeWork, have surfaced with competing offerings.

WeWork's MO, much like that of Regus, is to sign long-term leases, renovate, and then rent out desks and closed-door offices to members on a per-month basis—taking enough margin along the way. On the consumer side, the no-lease, subscription-based model provides WeWork members with a low-risk option to get access to state-of-the-art office space for as low as $500 a month.

Critics of WeWork's business model suggest the company could face a similar fate to that of Regus. In many respects, the flag-raising is warranted. At the beginning of 2019, WeWork had about $34 billion of lease obligations, was nowhere near profitable, and was shown to be losing about $2 billion a year.[6] Despite the sobering financials, bulls, on the other hand, argue that the company has also examined how Regus got burned, and has crafted a strategy to mitigate its risk.

In the event of a weakened economy sparking a member exodus, WeWork has hedged, somewhat. Rather than holding each property under WeWork's main corporate entity, the company has spread things around, using corporate shelters, which it calls "special-purpose entities," to isolate the parent company from a possible blow-up. More important, the firm is inking lease deals that split profits 50/50, where incumbent landlords pay for the build-out and share in the revenue. WeWork is also adding buildings to its asset list, setting up a new division called ARK that purchases buildings outright and leases them back to WeWork.[7]

Yet the most important source of stability may be the firm's evolving, diverse profile of paying members. Initially, 95 percent of WeWork occupants were start-ups (the segment most likely to fail in business), but the pie is now sliced three ways—only a third can be called start-ups, while the balance is equally split between small-to-medium-sized businesses and corporate-enterprise-level clients like Shopify, Microsoft, HSBC, Samsung, Lyft, and Facebook, which WeWork claims save about $18,000 a head when they move into a WeWork office.[8] The big-firm movement into "We Space" means a more stable set of tenants to help weather any volatility in start-up entrances and exits.

Meanwhile, Regus is doing its best to stay relevant through its core brand, as well as its other co-working outfits like Spaces. IWG, the parent home to both companies, touts its Regus banner as having both more locations (about 3,000) and members (over 2 million) than WeWork—yet the publicly traded company is valued at "only" $4 billion, prompting plenty of analysts to both question Regus's future and WeWork's valuation—which, using comparable metrics, should be closer to $3 billion.[9] In other words, investors who've been willing to put money into WeWork at a $40 billion valuation have to believe that each of the company's members is worth about $156,250 and that, by comparison,

Regus's members are worth roughly $11,000—leading some skeptics, including Scott Galloway of NYU's Stern School of Business, to call WeWork "the most overvalued company in the world."[10]

Unlike IWG, WeWork doesn't believe it is a real estate company. So, if WeWork isn't a real estate play, what is it? The company used the word "technology" 123 times in their S-1. While hundreds of pages of documentation laid out some of the company highlights, SEC requirements forced WeWork to disclose a more sobering tale: that of a real estate company mired in mounting financial losses that were hidden behind the veil of a sexy start-up story.

Beyond the unit economics, WeWork does have a profound understanding of its core customer, which has helped the brand to nail its value proposition. Progressive millennials, one of its targets, are socially conscious, environmentally responsible, and hate the idea of commitments, contracts, and lock-ins—which explains their contempt for leases peddled by commercial landlords, and their love of the less restrictive, more community-based WeWork offering. As for Gen X, another big WeWork consumer cohort, a recent study claimed that 67 percent of Gen X leaders are effective in "hyper-collaboration," and value the freedom to innovate and the flexibility to manage their work/life balance.[11] As such, WeWork's coworking spaces, which appear to break down metaphysical and metaphorical walls, are a natural fit.

Nevertheless, parts of the ongoing WeWork narrative feel a lot like that of Amazon, where growth and vision trump conventional metrics like profits.

The halting of WeWork's public offering is not just about mounting financial losses and an unconventional CEO. It indicates that broader investor sentiment towards such venture darlings is shifting; they're starting to be seen as not just less attractive, but outright dangerous investments.

As of late October 2019, WeWork had given up control of the company to SoftBank, who said it would inject more than $5 billion in capital, at an $8 billion valuation—a fraction of the

$47 billion price tag it had assigned WeWork in its last round of financing. SoftBank will also pay Neumann $1 billion for his shares in the company and extend him $500 million in credit to help him repay a loan from J.P. Morgan, on top of a $185 million consulting fee.[12] In plain terms, the deal means SoftBank has invested more in WeWork than the company is worth (as of October 2019), and given Neumann an allowance to retire off the grid and escape the carnage he's left behind.

Conclusion

DOLLAR SHAVE CLUB has come a long way since its 2012 video. Under the new stewardship of Unilever, DSC is still growing, despite competition from Harry's, Gillette, and others. In 2018, DSC hit 4 million subscribers, and it has expanded its product offering beyond razors to offer toothpaste, hair gel, body wash, shave butters, and more. Harry's, DSC's closest competitor, has experienced a similar life cycle: in 2019, it sold to Edgewell Personal Care, owner of Schick and Wilkinson brands, for $1.37 billion.

Both are classic examples of disruption: long-established incumbents in a traditional industry are pushed aside by value-driven innovators who tackle customer frustrations and pain points, rather than focusing on unnecessary product enhancements. Dollar Shave was bolstered by incredibly creative marketing and storytelling, which fueled the first innings of organic sign-ups, free press, and revenue. But, ultimately, the long-standing success of Dollar Shave Club—and other direct-to-customer subscription commerce companies that followed—was a result of a firm commitment to building loyalty through a superior customer experience.

As of mid-2019, the surge of subscription-based businesses has continued, among start-ups and established brands alike—and the trend isn't slowing. Strong performance has prompted established brands, such as Nike, Banana Republic, and Bloomingdale's, to create new subscription offerings. Sephora's Play!, and Walmart's Beauty, Kids, and Grooming boxes, are growing. Macy's has also indicated that it's coming to market with a new beauty box in late 2019. Recent estimates point to about 3,500 subscription-box companies operating in the U.S. alone.[1] On the SaaS side, Gartner predicts that by 2020, all new enterprise software companies and 80 percent of existing providers will have shifted to subscription-based models. Most of the prominent software players, including Microsoft, HubSpot, and Salesforce, are already there.

Finding the right subscription category fit is a good first step in assessing whether or not a business has subscription potential. Personal care, pet food, and vitamins, to name a few, are perfectly conducive to subscriptions. As we've seen with Harry's and Dollar Shave Club, razors, for instance, are lightweight, easily packaged, and purchased frequently. This consumption and replenishment cycle fits neatly into the model.

Crossing over into other popular subscription categories, we see similar themes. Products like coffee (e.g., Blue Bottle), diapers (e.g., Honest Company), and snacks (e.g., Graze) make for great offerings. Beauty products, too, are generally lightweight, novel, and frequently purchased—and, as a result, we see companies like IPSY, Birchbox, GlossyBox, and BoxyCharm taking advantage.

Yet not all product categories fit the mold. Companies selling shoes, watches, or handbags, for example, will have a hard time coming up with a compelling subscription offering. Fashion apparel, while successful in certain instances, is also difficult to execute because of the importance of data science and personalized merchandising. Some clothing companies, like The Gap, that have attempted subscription apparel offerings have faltered in the absence of these important capabilities.

The success of companies like Stitch Fix, which have built their business around data and personalization, reveals another important generalization here—subscription businesses gather data on their customers at a much faster pace than a more traditional business model. The continuity component of subscriptions means consistent touchpoints with the consumer. Data from those touchpoints compounds, and can then be used to optimize subsequent offerings. Stitch Fix has nailed this data optimization game. Dollar Shave Club is now aiming to adhere to customer needs and up the shopping experience by offering product trial kits, a fun-sized combo of grooming goods. IPSY and Birchbox are leveraging data from their sample boxes to optimize subsequent shipments so they're more in tune with consumer preferences.

While customer acquisition is crucial, arbitrage opportunities exist for brands savvy enough to focus equally hard on customer retention. Robust customer service teams that catch potential subscription cancellations before they happen, thereby retaining a subscriber for an extra month or more, stand to improve both lifetime value and churn; we've seen firsthand, through upstarts like Oatbox and Gentlemen's Box and giants like Amazon and Salesforce, how this type of customer-centric rigor can lead to massive retention.

As the number of subscription businesses tick upward in 2020 and beyond, not all new entrants will be winners. Common pitfalls like lack of category fit, market timing, and competition will plague many who introduce new offerings. But perhaps the biggest chunk of the failures will come from those whose customer-service infrastructure cannot match what the new online customer demands. While we see customer acquisition as an important part of any scaling business, subscription demands a more intense focus on the customer once they sign up (in other words, on customer retention). Columbia House and Fabletics missed the memo, and more recently, so did Starbucks Coffee—which, in 2015, launched its fresh-delivery subscription, giving online customers access to its line of premium small-lot coffees, only to pull the program two years later. Customer complaint levels played a role in the decision to abandon subscription, and e-commerce in general. While the coffee giant's in-store experience is still second to none, the company couldn't replicate it online.

Despite the beauty of subscription models, there are challenges to navigate. The importance of Facebook to direct-to-consumer brands cannot be overstated. As competition increases, companies will battle for eyeballs on Facebook and Instagram, where the bulk of ad dollars are being spent. The ever-changing marketing landscape means higher customer acquisition costs are inevitable, putting even more pressure on the cash flows of upstarts. Companies like Hubble Contacts, a budding subscription contact-lens company out of New York City, has already begun spreading funds across other sources like podcasts, direct mail, Pinterest, Snap, and Google to hedge against the increasing CPC and CPM rates on the social media platform. Notwithstanding the diversification efforts, Jesse Horwitz, the company's co-founder, told me his team still relies heavily on Facebook, above all, for customer acquisition.[2]

The Importance of Loyalty

The success of Prime has prompted many established brands to rethink the structure of their existing loyalty programs, revisiting and revamping them along the way. While points-based loyalty programs still seem to be ubiquitous, moving forward, loyalty programs will look a lot more Prime-like, rooted in VIP-style subscriptions.

With more than 500,000 customers and approximately $2 billion in revenue as of 2018, Instacart is building loyalty and engagement via its fee-4-VIP subscription-based Instacart Express program. And, the numbers look promising—the average Instacart shopper spends about $95 an order, twice a month (roughly $2,300 a year); Instacart Express customers, on the other hand, who pay $99 a year for free deliveries (a Prime-like strategy), order twice as often, and spend about $5,000 a year.[3]

GNC revamped its old Gold Card Rewards program, launching myGNC PRO Access in early 2017. For $39.99 per year, PRO Access members receive benefits like free shipping, quarterly member-only sales days, monthly customized PRO boxes (which contain samples, coupons, and new products that are tailored to their lifestyles and goals), and more. PRO members purchase twice as often and spend significantly more than regular non-PRO customers. Bed Bath & Beyond has a similar loyalty program called BEYOND+, which also runs $39.99 a year. It offers members 20 percent off purchases along with free shipping, and other benefits such as 50 percent off decor design services, exclusive offers, and member-only shopping events. While BB&B continues to struggle, the one bright spot is the revamped loyalty program—BEYOND+ members shop 2.5 times more than the retailer's average customer and generate four times more revenue. Restoration Hardware's RH Member program, at $100 a year, gives members 25 percent off and other perks like interior design consultation. As of Spring 2018, RH CEO Gary Friedman reported that 95 percent of Restoration Hardware's business is driven by its nearly 400,000 members, saying, "We can confidently declare our move from a promotional to membership model a success. Membership has enhanced our brand, streamlined our operations, and vastly improved the customer experience."[4] Other brands that have moved in this subscription direction include Overstock.com, Barnes & Noble, AMC Theatres, and Chinese e-commerce giant Alibaba—whose 88 VIP program functions as a super-subscription that extends benefits to a wide array of services beyond its core e-commerce platforms.

Points-based loyalty was long in vogue, from Air Miles to Amex. But the next chapter of loyalty will be driven by fee-4-VIP subscription programs as brands chase higher customer lifetime value, order frequency, loyalty, and engagement. Why? Paid subscriptions provide brands with a more predictable source of recurring revenue, which can be used to subsidize more loyalty program benefits like free shipping, coupons, and exclusive events. In turn, customers receive more value, and thus become more engaged, use the programs more frequently, and ultimately spend more money. From Prime to Instacart to GNC, the numbers back it up.

Points-based loyalty programs simply don't see the same customer engagement. The average breakage rate (number of points not spent divided by number of points issued) for points-based loyalty programs is a whopping 80 percent, a key indicator that while customers are collecting points, they are not redeeming them and may not see them as valuable.[5] While free points-based programs sound good on the surface, long redemption times, poor awareness and understanding of the benefits, and overall lack of usage (high breakage) means we are about to see the death of points programs.

Shopping Gets Smart

As we head toward a new phase of consumerism propelled by the burgeoning subscription-based economy, progressive strategists and thought leaders are imagining a future in which the business model provides a fully automated shopping experience. A future where the majority of consumer goods are purchased by subscribing, selecting a frequency of delivery, and checking out is not far away. The combination of smart technology, predictive data, and sophisticated software can determine what goods are delivered when and to which household.

Global Market Insights estimates the market for smart speakers is roughly $4.5 billion. That number is expected to leap to $30 billion by 2024. As a result, companies are betting big on voice, pouring a ton of money into the category. Estimates suggest Apple, Google, Facebook, and Microsoft are spending roughly 10 percent of their annual research budgets on voice recognition technology.[6] This isn't going to be a cute fad. We're headed into a world where voice recognition becomes the most common way to interact with the internet.

U.S. HOUSEHOLDS WITH SMART SPEAKERS

Q1 2017	7%
Q4 2020	75%

Gartner predicts that soon three-quarters of homes will have smart speakers like Amazon Alexa or Google Home.

Source: Bret Kinsella, "Gartner Predicts 75% of US Households will Have Smart Speakers by 2020," Voicebot.ai, April 14, 2017, https://voicebot.ai/2017/04/14/gartner-predicts-75-us-households-will-smart-speakers-2020/.

Consider Amazon's big bet on AI and smart tech. Although not the first to invent voice recognition—Apple's Siri and Google's Assistant predated Alexa by a few years—Amazon, which holds 42 percent of the global market for connected smart speakers, is likely to dominate the smart home devices market. When Echo was introduced in November of 2014, at first the technology seemed like a cool nice-to-have. But, some 47 million-plus sold later, Echo, in combination with Alexa voice recognition, makes this combination of AI and voice a likely mainstay in household kitchens, bedrooms, and bathrooms in the next five years. Google's combo of Google Home powered by Google Assistant won't be far behind.

Amazon is about to make shopping incredibly convenient. Sure, it has the goal of getting you hooked on Prime. But having Alexa in your kitchen and bathroom means a quick shout-out to the virtual assistant when you're out of milk or toothpaste. A confirmation from Alexa, and your carton of 2 percent and tube of Colgate will be delivered next day—oh, and Alexa will ask if you'd like to automate recurring deliveries of both via Subscribe and Save for a discount. As a treasure trove of data rolls in on how Amazon shoppers use Alexa, Bezos and company get to make the software even more useful. The better Alexa becomes at understanding what you want, the more effective it gets at making suggestions as to how Amazon can get it to you, be it a case of Coke, a new pair of jeans, or a new book. A future with AI in combination with subscription is inching closer, thanks to Amazon's ability to ship anything, anywhere in just a couple of days. Mix in a little Alexa, and we're headed for a new era of automated "shopping" experiences.

Great digital companies are sprouting up everywhere, building new consumer offerings that are compelling and extraordinary. We've covered many of them in this book. Successful companies in the next phase of consumerism will be those who do a great job of providing superior customer experiences and service, while focusing on building intimate customer relationships. The rest will let transaction- and customer-acquisition greed seep in, like most fledgling retailers who haven't gotten the message. We're entering the next wave of commerce—where customer relationships trump transactions. See you on the other side.

Acknowledgments

TO MY WIFE ERIKA—who has stood by me and supported me through every idea and endeavor I have ever had. I love you.

To my three children, Loah, Hudson, and Ezra. My greatest sources of joy. Hopefully, one day you will forgive Daddy for not writing a children's book. I am so proud of each of you and always will be.

To the amazing entrepreneurs I've outlined in this book. Your vision and creativity has given me the foundation on which to put pen to paper.

A special thank you to Figure 1 Publishing, and my editor-in-chief, Michael Leyne, who helped me to not only craft something I'm proud of, but to celebrate the milestones along the way.

Notes

INTRODUCTION

1 Diana Ransom, "How Dollar Shave Club Rode a Viral Video to Sales Success," *Inc.*, July/August 2015, https://www.inc.com/magazine/201507/diana-ransom/ how-youtube-crashed-our-website.html.

2 John Patrick Pullen, "How a Dollar Shave Club's Ad Went Viral," *Entrepreneur*, October 13, 2012, https://www.entrepreneur.com/article/224282.

3 "Dollar Shave Club Video: The Script," Think Tall Films, March 21, 2013, https://thinktallfilms.tumblr.com/post/45910213723/ dollar-shave-club-video-the-script.

4 Kris Frieswick, "The Serious Guy Behind Dollar Shave Club's Crazy Viral Videos," *Inc.*, April 2016, https://www.inc.com/magazine/201604/ kris-frieswick/dollar-shave-club-michael-dubin.html.

5 Kiel Porter and Alex Barinka, "TPG-Backed Makeup Startup Ipsy is Considering a Sale or IPO," *Bloomberg*, August 31, 2018, https://www.bloomberg.com/news/articles/2018-08-31/ tpg-backed-makeup-startup-ipsy-is-said-to-consider-sale-ipo.

6 Molly Fleming, "Dollar Shave Club Shifts Business Model as Subscription Growth Slows," *Marketing Week*, October 18, 2018, https://www.marketingweek.com/2018/10/18/ dollar-shave-club-changes-business-model-as-subscriber-growth-slows/.

7 Stephen Shankland, "Adobe Kills Creative Suite, Goes Subscription-Only," *CNET Magazine*, May 6, 2013, https://www.cnet.com/news/adobe-kills-creative-suite-goes-subscription-only/; Rob Walker, "How Adobe Got Its Customers Hooked on Subscriptions," *Bloomberg*, June 8, 2017, https://www.bloomberg.com/news/articles/2017-06-08/ how-adobe-got-its-customers-hooked-on-subscriptions.

8 Craig Hanson, "Why We're (Still) Underestimating the Impact of the Subscription Movement," *Next World Insights* (blog), Next World Capital,

July 16, 2018, https://insights.nextworldcap.com/why-were-still-underestimating-the-impact-of-the-subscription-movement-286a63665021.

9   Tony Chen, Ken Fenyo, Sylvia Yang, and Jessica Zhang, "Thinking Inside the Subscription Box: New Research on E-commerce Consumers," McKinsey & Company, February 2018, https://www.mckinsey.com/industries/high-tech/our-insights/thinking-inside-the-subscription-box-new-research-on-ecommerce-consumers.

10   Erika Malzberg, "The Subscription Economy Index Update: Fall 2018," Zuora, September 19, 2018, https://www.zuora.com/2018/09/19/the-subscription-economy-index-update-fall-2018/.

11   "Push My Buttons: Experiments in Automated Consumption," *The Economist*, Oct. 22, 2016, https://www.economist.com/business/2016/10/22/push-my-buttons.

1. WHY SUBSCRIPTION WORKS

1   Kevin Kelly, "1,000 True Fans," *The Technium* (blog), last modified December 6, 2016, https://kk.org/thetechnium/1000-true-fans/.

2   Kelly, "1,000 True Fans."

3   Ibid.

4   Ibid.

5   Kevin Kelly, "The Reality of Depending on True Fans," *The Technium* (blog), April 21, 2008, https://kk.org/thetechnium/the-reality-of/.

6   Thomas Barrabi, "Retail Apocalypse: These Big Retailers Closing Stores, Filing for Bankruptcy," *Fox Business*, January 4, 2018, https://www.foxbusiness.com/features/retail-apocalypse-22-big-retailers-closing-stores.

7   Lauren Debter, "Toys 'R' Us Files for Bankruptcy, But Will Keep Stores Open," *Forbes*, September 19, 2017, https://www.forbes.com/sites/laurengensler/2017/09/19/toys-r-us-bankruptcy/.

8   R. "Ray" Wang, "Research Summary: Sneak Peeks from Constellation's Futurist Framework and 2014 Outlook on Digital Disruption," *Constellation Research* (blog), February 18, 2014, https://www.constellationr.com/blog-news/research-summary-sneak-peeks-constellations-futurist-framework-and-2014-outlook-digital.

9   Bo Burlingham, "Subscription Services: The Perfect Business Model?," *Inc.*, May 22, 2014, https://www.inc.com/bo-burlingham/why-john-warrillow-is-all-about-subscription-services.html.

10   Erin Bury, "Need Recurring Revenue? Think Subscription Boxes," February 3, 2014, https://business.financialpost.com/entrepreneur/fp-startups/need-recurring-revenue-think-subscription-boxes.

11   Patrick Sisson, "9 Facts about Amazon's Unprecedented Warehouse Empire," *Curbed*, November 19, 2018, https://www.curbed.com/2017/11/21/16686150/black-friday-2018-amazon-warehouse-fulfillment.

2. THE ORIGINS OF SUBSCRIPTION

1 Molly St. Louis, "9 Companies that Nailed the Whole 'Surprise and Delight' Thing," *Inc.*, August 28, 2017, https://www.inc.com/molly-reynolds/9-companies-that-nailed-the-whole-surprise-and-del.html.

2 Janey Thornton, "Profile: Harry Scherman & the 'Book of the Month' Club," *BookBarn* (blog), January 26, 2018, https://bookbarnbbi.wordpress.com/2018/01/26/profile-harry-scherman-the-book-of-the-month-club/.

3 "Book-of-the-Month Club, Inc.," Company-Histories.com, accessed January 7, 2019, http://www.company-histories.com/BookoftheMonth-Club-Inc-Company-History.html.

4 Meeghan Smolinsky, "A New Reading Experience: Book of the Month Club," Pennsylvania Center for the Book, Fall 2010, https://pabook.libraries.psu.edu/literary-cultural-heritage-map-pa/feature-articles/new-reading-experience-book-month-club.

5 Heather A. Haveman, "Antebellum Literary Culture and the Evolution of American Magazines," *Poetics* 32, no. 1 (February 2004): 11, https://www.researchgate.net/publication/222571293_Antebellum_literary_culture_and_the_evolution_of_American_magazines.

6 "Playboy's Circulation Worldwide from 1960 to 2015 (in millions)," Statista, accessed January 7, 2019, https://www.statista.com/statistics/485332/playboy-circulation-worldwide/.

7 "Our History," PlayboyEnterprises.com, accessed January 7, 2019, http://www.playboyenterprises.com/about/history/.

8 Jennifer Gould Keil, "Playboy's Exclusive New NYC Club All About 'Millennial Luxury,'" *NYPost*, June 4, 2018, https://nypost.com/2018/06/04/playboys-exclusive-new-nyc-club-all-about-millennial-luxury/.

9 Will Kenton, "Breakage," Investopedia, February 7, 2018, https://www.investopedia.com/terms/b/breakage.asp#ixzz5Mwz6GTOE.

10 Rebecca Lake, "23 Gym Membership Statistics That Will Astound You," CreditDonkey, December 29, 2014, https://www.creditdonkey.com/gym-membership-statistics.html.

11 Ana Swanson, "What Your New Gym Doesn't Want You to Know," *Washington Post*, January 5, 2016, https://www.washingtonpost.com/news/wonk/wp/2016/01/05/what-your-new-gym-doesnt-want-you-to-know/.

12 "Our Houses," Soho House, accessed January 8, 2019, https://www.sohohouse.com/houses.

13 Chris Kirkham and Erich Schwartzel, "Exclusive Soho House Wants More Members—Lots of Them," the *Wall Street Journal*, May 12, 2018, https://www.wsj.com/articles/exclusive-soho-house-wants-more-memberslots-of-them-1526130743.

14 Kirkham and Schwartzel, "Exclusive Soho House Wants More Members."

15 Robert Palmer, "The 50s: A Decade of Music that Changed the World," *Rolling Stone*, April 19, 1990, https://www.rollingstone.com/music/music-features/the-50s-a-decade-of-music-that-changed-the-world-229924/.

16 "Columbia House Company History," Funding Universe, accessed January 9, 2019, http://www.fundinguniverse.com/company-histories/columbia-house-company-history/.

17 "CRC Music Factory—Columbia Record Club," Voices of East Anglia, accessed January 9, 2019, http://www.voicesofeastanglia.com/2013/02/crc-music-factory-columbia-record-club.html

18 "Columbia House Company History," Funding Universe.

19 Tom Corrigan, "Fat Lady Sings for Columbia House," the *Wall Street Journal*, August 10, 2015, https://www.wsj.com/articles/columbia-house-owner-files-for-bankruptcy-1439233090.

20 Laura Wagner, "'8 CDs for a Penny' Company Files for Bankruptcy," *The Two-Way*, NPR, August 11, 2015, https://www.npr.org/sections/thetwo-way/2015/08/11/431547925/8-cds-for-a-penny-company-files-for-bankruptcy.

21 Stacy Weckesser, "Negative Option Billing is the Shady Marketing Practice You're Probably Already Falling for," Bluewater Credit, accessed January 9, 2019, http://bluewatercredit.com/negative-option-billing-shady-marketing-practice-youre-probably-already-falling/.

22 "Government Regulation," AdAge Encyclopedia, *AdAge*, Sept. 15, 2003, https://adage.com/article/adage-encyclopedia/government-regulation/98679/.

23 Ethan Trex, "It's a Steal! How Columbia House Made Money Giving Away Music," Mental Floss, June 21, 2011, http://mentalfloss.com/article/28036/its-steal-how-columbia-house-made-money-giving-away-music.

24 D'Arcy Jenish and Warren Caragata, "Rogers Cable Apologizes," *The Canadian Encyclopedia*, March 11, 2014, https://www.thecanadianencyclopedia.ca/en/article/rogers-cable-apologizes.

25 Trex, "It's a Steal!"

26 Daniel Kreps, "Columbia House Files for Bankruptcy, Blames Streaming," *Rolling Stone*, August 11, 2015, https://www.rollingstone.com/music/music-news/columbia-house-files-for-bankruptcy-blames-streaming-62345/.

3. AMAZON PIONEERS CUSTOMER CENTRICITY

1 David Streitfeld, "Amazon Hits $1,000,000,000,000 in Value, Following Apple," the *New York Times*, September 4, 2018, https://www.nytimes.com/2018/09/04/technology/amazon-stock-price-1-trillion-value.html; Ryan Vlastelica, "Amazon Becomes Most Valuable Company, Inching Past Microsoft," *Bloomberg*, January 7, 2019, https://www.bloomberg.com/news/articles/2019-01-07/amazon-becomes-most-valuable-company-inching-past-microsoft.

2   Quora, "I Worked with Jeff Bezos, and These are the Traits that Helped Make Him the World's Richest Man," *Inc.*, November 27, 2017, https://www.inc.com/quora/i-worked-with-jeff-bezos-these-are-traits-that-helped-make-him-worlds-richest-man.html.

3   Marissa Laliberte, "You'll Never Guess What Amazon Was Almost Called—and Why They Had to Change the Name," *Reader's Digest*, accessed January 14, 2019, https://www.rd.com/culture/amazons-name-origin/.

4   Avery Hartmans, "15 Fascinating Facts You Probably Didn't Know About Amazon," *Business Insider*, Aug. 23, 2018, http://www.businessinsider.com/jeff-bezos-amazon-history-facts-2017-4.

5   Caroline Cakebread, "Amazon Launched 22 Years Ago this Week—Here's What Shopping on Amazon was Like Back in 1995," *Business Insider*, July 20, 2017, http://www.businessinsider.com/amazon-opened-22-years-ago-see-the-business-evolve-2017-7#2004-a-full-department-store-and-a-search-engine-of-its-own-4.

6   Alex Wilhelm, "A Look Back in IPO: Amazon's 1997 Move," TechCrunch, December 11, 2017, https://techcrunch.com/2017/06/28/a-look-back-at-amazons-1997-ipo/.

7   Brad Stone, *The Everything Store: Jeff Bezos and the Age of Amazon* (New York: Little, Brown, 2013), 163.

8   Taylor Soper, "Full Text: In Annual Shareholder Letter, Jeff Bezos Explains Why it Will Never be Day 2 at Amazon," GeekWire, April 12, 2017, https://www.geekwire.com/2017/full-text-annual-letter-amazon-ceo-jeff-bezos-explains-avoid-becoming-day-2-company/.

9   Jim Edwards, "One of the Kings of the '90s Dot-com Bubble now Faces 20 Years in Prison," *Business Insider*, December 6, 2016, https://www.businessinsider.com/where-are-the-kings-of-the-1990s-dot-com-bubble-bust-2016-12.

10 Timothy B. Lee, "The Little-known Deal that Saved Amazon from the Dot-com Crash," Vox.com, April 5, 2017, https://www.vox.com/new-money/2017/4/5/15190650/amazon-jeff-bezos-richest.

11 Todd Spangler, "Amazon Has More Than 100 Million Prime Subscribers, Jeff Bezos Discloses," *Variety*, April 18, 2018, https://variety.com/2018/digital/news/amazon-prime-100-million-subscribers-jeff-bezos-1202757832/; Jason Del Rey, "What Amazon Prime's 100 Million Milestone Doesn't Show: The Battle to Keep Growing in the U.S.," April 19, 2018, Recode, https://www.recode.net/2018/4/19/17256410/amazon-prime-100-million-members-us-penetration-low-income-households-jeff-bezos.

12 Eugene Kim, "Bezos to Shareholders: It's 'Irresponsible' Not to be Part of Amazon Prime," *Business Insider*, May 17, 2016, https://www.businessinsider.com/amazon-ceo-jeff-bezos-says-its-irresponsible-not-to-be-part-of-prime-2016-5.

13 Louis Columbus, "10 Charts That Will Change Your Perspective of Amazon Prime's Growth," *Forbes*, May 4, 2018, https://www.forbes.com/sites/louiscolumbus/2018/03/04/10-charts-that-will-change-your-perspective-of-amazon-primes-growth/; Michael R. Levin and Joshua N. Lowitz, "Amazon Prime Members Stay Members," Consumer Intelligence Research Partners, LLC, June 1, 2016, http://files.ctctcdn.com/150f9af2201/8768026b-925d-4733-b357-375db7411f66.pdf.

14 Columbus, "10 Charts."

15 Trefis Team, "Netflix And Amazon: Competitors Or Complementary," *Forbes*, June 1, 2017, https://www.forbes.com/sites/greatspeculations/2017/06/01/netflix-and-amazon-competitors-or-complementary/#2eaeb46a56cc.

16 Columbus, "10 Charts."

17 Jordan Novet, "Amazon's Cloud is Big Enough to be the Fifth-largest Business Software Company in the World," CNBC, February 3, 2018, https://www.cnbc.com/2018/02/03/aws-is-the-fifth-biggest-business-software-company-in-the-world.html.

18 Silicon Review Team, "Vmware Aims to Expand Services to Azure and Google," *The Silicon Review*, June 2, 2018,

19 Alison Griswold, "Amazon Web Services Brought in More Money than McDonald's in 2018," Quartz, February 1, 2019 https://qz.com/1539546/amazon-web-services-brought-in-more-money-than-mcdonalds-in-2018/.

20 Stephanie Condon, "In 2018, AWS Delivered Most of Amazon's Operating Income," ZDNet, January 31, 2019, https://www.zdnet.com/article/in-2018-aws-delivered-most-of-amazons-operating-income/.

21 Jordan Novet, "Amazon says AWS Revenue Jumped 46 Percent in Third Quarter," CNBC, October 25, 2018, https://www.cnbc.com/2018/10/25/aws-q3-results.html.

22 Alex Hern, "Amazon Web Services: The Secret to the Online Retailer's Future Success," *The Guardian*, February 2, 2017, https://www.theguardian.com/technology/2017/feb/02/amazon-web-services-the-secret-to-the-online-retailers-future-success.

23 Ron Miller, "How AWS Came to Be," TechCrunch, July 2, 2016, https://techcrunch.com/2016/07/02/andy-jassys-brief-history-of-the-genesis-of-aws/.

24 Miller, "How AWS Came to Be."

25 Hern, "Amazon Web Services."

26 Ibid.

27 Benjamin Wootton, "Who's Using Amazon Web Services?," Contino, January 26, 2017, https://www.contino.io/insights/whos-using-aws.

28 Parker Harris, "Salesforce Selects Amazon Web Services as Preferred Public Cloud Infrastructure Provider," Blog, Salesforce, May 25, 2016, https://www.salesforce.com/blog/2016/05/salesforce-aws-public-cloud-infrastructure.html.

29 "Salesforce Announces Service Cloud Einstein and Amazon Connect Integration," press release, Salesforce, March 28, 2017, https://www.salesforce.com/company/news-press/press-releases/2017/03/170328-3/.

30 Barb Darrow, "Marc Benioff Touts Amazon as Salesforce's New Best Friend," *Fortune*, May 19, 2017, http://fortune.com/2017/05/19/salesforce-amazon-benioff/.

31 "It Make [sic] Sense for Amazon to Build its Second HQ Near Washington," *The Economist*, March 8, 2018, https://www.economist.com/united-states/2018/03/08/it-make-sense-for-amazon-to-build-its-second-hq-near-washington.

32 Larry Dignan, "Alexa for Business Likely to Win in Smart Office, Leverage AWS, Echo, Developers and Consumers," ZDNet, January 19, 2018, https://www.zdnet.com/article/alexa-for-business-likely-to-win-in-smart-office-leverage-aws-echo-developers-and-consumers/.

33 Ibid.

34 "Learn More About How AWS is Working to Achieve Its Goal of 100% Renewable Energy Usage for our Global Infrastructure Footprint," Amazon Web Services, accessed January 18, 2019, https://aws.amazon.com/about-aws/sustainability/sustainability-timeline/.

35 John Furrier, "How Andy Jassy Plans to Keep Amazon Web Services On Top of the Cloud," November 27, 2017, https://www.forbes.com/sites/siliconangle/2017/11/27/exclusive-how-andy-jassy-plans-to-keep-amazon-web-services-on-top-of-the-cloud/.

36 Larry Dignan, "Alibaba Cloud Hits Annual Revenue Run Rate Tops $4.4 billion, ZDnet.com, May 15, 2019, https://www.zdnet.com/article/alibaba-cloud-hits-annual-revenue-run-rate-tops-4-4-billion/.

37 Hari Kannan and Christopher Thomas, "Public Cloud in China: Big Challenges, Big Upside," McKinsey&Company, July 2018, https://www.mckinsey.com/industries/high-tech/our-insights/public-cloud-in-china-big-challenges-big-upside.

38 "Chinese Tech Companies Plan to Steal American Cloud Firms' Thunder," *The Economist*, January 18, 2018, https://www.economist.com/business/2018/01/18/chinese-tech-companies-plan-to-steal-american-cloud-firms-thunder.

39 Kannan and Thomas, "Public Cloud in China."

40 "Chinese Tech Companies Plan to Steal American Cloud Firms' Thunder," *The Economist*.

4. NETFLIX CHILLS TV

1   "Can Netflix Please Investors and Still Avoid the Techlash?" *The Economist*, June 28, 2018, https://www.economist.com/leaders/2018/06/28/can-netflix-please-investors-and-still-avoid-the-techlash.

2 "Netflix is Moving Television Beyond Time-slots and National Markets," *The Economist*, June 30, 2018, https://www.economist.com/briefing/2018/06/30/netflix-is-moving-television-beyond-time-slots-and-national-markets.

3 Ibid.

4 Seth Fiegerman, "Netflix Adds 9 Million Paying Subscribers, But Stock Falls," CNN Business, January 17, 2019, https://www.cnn.com/2019/01/17/media/netflix-earnings-q4/index.html; "Number of Netflix Streaming Subscribers in the United States from 3rd Quarter 2011 to 4th Quarter 2018 (in millions)," Statista, accessed January 21, 2019, https://www.statista.com/statistics/250937/quarterly-number-of-netflix-streaming-subscribers-in-the-us/.

5 Scott Galloway and Mark Mahaney, "Mark Mahaney on the Future of Netflix," October 26, 2016, in *A Conversation with Scott Galloway*, podcast, L2 Inc, https://www.l2inc.com/daily-insights/the-future-of-netflix-with-mark-mahaney.

6 Aline Van Duyn, "DVD Rentals Pass Their Screen Test," *Financial Times*, October 4, 2005.

7 Brian Barrett, Jason Parham, Brian Raftery, Peter Rubin, and Angela Watercutter, "Netflix is Turning 20—But Its Birthday Doesn't Matter," *Wired*, August 29, 2017, https://www.wired.com/story/netflix-20th-anniversary/.

8 Willy Shih, Stephen Kaufman, and David Spinola, "Netflix," Harvard Business School, April 27, 2009, https://slideblast.com/netflix_59509ad11723dd456abc3b8a.html.

9 Greg Sandoval, "Blockbuster Laughed at Netflix Partnership Offer," *CNET Magazine*, December 12, 2010, https://www.cnet.com/news/blockbuster-laughed-at-netflix-partnership-offer/.

10 Shih et al., "Netflix."

11 Netflix Media Center, "NETFLIX.com Transforms DVD Business Eliminating Late Fees and Due Dates From Movie Rentals," press release, December 16, 1999, https://media.netflix.com/en/press-releases/netflixcom-transforms-dvd-business-eliminating-late-fees-and-due-dates-from-movie-rentals-migration-1.

12 Sandoval, "Blockbuster Laughed."

13 Shih et al., "Netflix."

14 Ibid.

15 Greg Satell, "A Look Back at Why Blockbuster Really Failed and Why It Didn't Have To," *Forbes*, September 5, 2014, https://www.forbes.com/sites/gregsatell/2014/09/05/a-look-back-at-why-blockbuster-really-failed-and-why-it-didnt-have-to/.

16 Ibid.

17 Marc Graser, "Epic Fail: How Blockbuster Could Have Owned Netflix," November 12, 2013, https://variety.com/2013/biz/news/epic-fail-how-blockbuster-could-have-owned-netflix-1200823443/.

18 Reed Hastings, quoted in Matt Preuss, "Netflix IPO: A Lesson in Investor Relations from Reed Hastings," Founders Forward (blog), Visible, May 25, 2018, https://visible.vc/blog/netflix-ipo/.

19 Matthew Ball, "Netflix Isn't Being Reckless, It's Just Playing a Game No One Else Dares (Netflix Misunderstandings, Pt. 3)," July 8, 2018, REDEF, https://redef.com/original/5b400a2779328f4711d5675e.

20 Ball, "Netflix Isn't Being Reckless"; Christine Wang, "Netflix Says Its Cash Burn Will Peak This Year, Then Go Down," CNBC, January 17, 2019, https://www.cnbc.com/2019/01/17/netflix-says-its-cash-burn-will-peak-this-year-then-go-down.html.

21 Ibid.

22 Liane Yvkoff, "You Might Be Waiting a While for 'Full Self-Driving Approval' To Stream Netflix in a Moving Tesla," Forbes, July 29, 2019, https://www.forbes.com/sites/lianeyvkoff/2019/07/29/you-might-be-waiting-a-while-for-full-self-driving-approval-to-stream-netflix-in-a-moving-tesla/.

23 Matthew Ball, "Netflix is a Product & Technology Company (Netflix Misunderstandings, Pt. 2)," REDEF, May 12, 2018, https://redef.com/original/5aef99591e5d473edfd9a4c5.

24 Ball, "Netflix Is a Product & Technology Company."

25 Ibid.

26 Josef Adalian, "Inside the Binge Factory," Vulture, June 2018, https://www.vulture.com/2018/06/how-netflix-swallowed-tv-industry.html.

27 Ball, "Netflix Isn't Being Reckless."

28 Anna Hecht and Shawn M. Carter, "Disney vs Netflix: Here's Which Stock Would Have Made You Richer if You Invested $1,000 10 Years Ago," CNBC Make It, April 24, 2019, https://www.cnbc.com/2019/04/24/would-investing-1000-dollars-in-disney-or-netflix-have-made-you-richer.html.

29 Nathaniel Lee and Sara Silverstein, "Scott Galloway: Netflix Could Be the Next $300 Billion Company," Business Insider, April 24, 2017, https://www.businessinsider.com/scott-galloway-netflix-next-300-billion-company-2017-4.

30 "Netflix is Moving Television Beyond Time-Slots and National Markets," The Economist, June 30, 2018, https://www.economist.com/briefing/2018/06/30/netflix-is-moving-television-beyond-time-slots-and-national-markets.

5. FROM SALES TO SALESFORCE

1 Marc Benioff and Carlye Adler, Behind the Cloud: The Untold Story of How Salesforce.com Went From Idea to Billion-Dollar Company—and Revolutionized an Industry (San Francisco: Jossey-Bass, 2009), 255.

2 "Advertising Revenue of Google from 2001 to 2018 (in billions of U.S. dollars)," Statista, accessed June 11, 2019, https://www.statista.com/statistics/266249/advertising-revenue-of-google/; "Digital Ad Spending 2019," eMarketer, March 28, 2019, https://www.emarketer.

com/content/global-digital-ad-spending-2019; "Facebook's advertising revenue worldwide from 2009 to 2018 (in million U.S. dollars)," Statista, accessed June 11, 2019, https://www.statista.com/statistics/271258/facebooks-advertising-revenue-worldwide/.

3 "A Brief History of Customer Relationship Management," CRM Switch, September 12, 2013, https://www.crmswitch.com/crm-industry/crm-industry-history/.

4 "Gartner Says CRM Became the Largest Software Market in 2017 and Will Be the Fastest Growing Software Market in 2018," Gartner, press release, April 10, 2018, https://www.gartner.com/en/newsroom/press-releases/2018-04-10-gartner-says-crm-became-the-largest-software-market-in-2017-and-will-be-the-fastest-growing-software-market-in-2018; Laurence Goasduff, "Cloud to Represent 75% of Total Spend on CRM in 2019," Gartner, April 4, 2019, https://www.gartner.com/smarterwithgartner/cloud-to-represent-75-of-total-spend-on-crm-in-2019/.

5 Ron Miller, "Salesforce Keeps Revenue Pedal to the Metal with Another Mammoth Quarter," TechCrunch, May 30,2018, https://techcrunch.com/2018/05/30/salesforce-keeps-revenue-pedal-to-the-metal-with-another-mammoth-quarter/.

6 Carlye Adler, "The Fresh Prince of Software," *CNN Money*, March 1, 2003, https://money.cnn.com/magazines/fsb/fsb_archive/2003/03/01/338759/index.htm.

7 Benioff and Adler, *Behind the Cloud*, 1–2.

8 Ibid., 3.

9 Marc Benioff, "How to Create Alignment Within Your Company in Order to Succeed," Salesforce Blog, April 8, 2013, https://www.salesforce.com/blog/2013/04/how-to-create-alignment-within-your-company.html.

10 Bill Gross, "The Single Biggest Reason Why Start-ups Succeed," filmed March 2015 in Vancouver, BC, TED video, 6:41, https://www.ted.com/talks/bill_gross_the_single_biggest_reason_why_startups_succeed.

11 Benioff and Adler, *Behind the Cloud*, 3.

12 Ibid., 5–6.

13 Ibid., 20–21.

14 Ibid., 13.

15 Ibid., 37.

16 Jason Compton, "Salesforce.com IPO Raises $110 Million," Destination CRM, June 23, 2004, https://www.destinationcrm.com/Articles/CRM-News/Daily-News/Salesforce.com-IPO-Raises-$110-Million-44252.aspx.

17 Matt Weinberger, "The Rise of Marc Benioff, the Bombastic Salesforce CEO Who's Buying Up Time Magazine for $190 Million," *Business Insider*, September 17, 2018, www.businessinsider.com/the-rise-of-salesforce-ceo-marc-benioff-2016-3.

18 "Masterful Salesmanship Has Pushed Salesforce to Ever-Greater Heights," *The Economist*, January 4, 2018, https://www.economist.com/business/2018/01/04/masterful-salesmanship-has-pushed-salesforce-to-ever-greater-heights.

19 Ibid.

20 Ibid.

21 "2. Salesforce," 100 Best Companies, *Fortune*, accessed June 12, 2019, http://fortune.com/best-companies/salesforce/.

22 Benioff and Adler, *Behind the Cloud*, 244–45.

23 Ibid., 139.

24 Benioff and Adler, *Behind the Cloud*, 153; and "Philanthropic Programs," Salesforce.org, accessed June 12, 2019, https://www.salesforce.org/philanthropic-programs/.

25 Benioff and Adler, *Behind the Cloud*, 168.

26 Bob Evans, "Why Cloud Customer Success is New Top Priority for Salesforce, Microsoft, Workday, SAP And Oracle," *Forbes*, May 25, 2018, https://www.forbes.com/sites/bobevans1/2018/05/25/why-cloud-customer-success-is-new-top-priority-for-salesforce-microsoft-workday-sap-and-oracle/.

27 Diana Edmundson, "7 Reasons Salesforce Essentials is Perfect for Your Small Business," Salesforce UK blog, July 20, 2018, https://www.salesforce.com/uk/blog/2018/07/7-reasons-salesforce-essentials-is-perfect-for-your-small-busine.html.

28 Salesforce Ventures website, accessed September 24, 2019, https://www.salesforce.com/company/ventures/portfolio/.

29 "Salesforce Ventures Introduces $100 Million Canada Trailblazer Fund," Salesforce, press release, May 3, 2018, https://www.salesforce.com/company/news-press/press-releases/2018/05/180503/.

30 Benioff and Adler, *Behind the Cloud*, 258.

31 Nick Turner, Gerry Smith, and Nico Grant, "Salesforce's Benioff to Buy Time Magazine, Boosting Influence," *Bloomberg*, Sept. 16, 2018, https://www.bloomberg.com/news/articles/2018-09-17/salesforce-s-benioff-to-buy-time-magazine-boosting-influence.

32 Ari Levy, "Salesforce's Marc Benioff Unplugged for Two Weeks, and Had a Revelation That Could Change the Tech Industry," CNBC, January 5, 2019, https://www.cnbc.com/2018/12/30/salesforce-marc-benioff-talks-tech-ethics-time-magazine-and-vacation.html.

33 Victor Antonio, "How AI is Changing Sales," *Harvard Business Review*, July 30, 2018, https://hbr.org/2018/07/how-ai-is-changing-sales; and "PowerDialler for Salesforce," Salesforce Appexchange, accessed June 11, 2019, https://appexchange.salesforce.com/appxListingDetail?listingId=a0N300000016ay4EAA/.

34 Antonio, "How AI is Changing Sales."

6. SHOPIFY YOUR BUSINESS

1   Kim Bhasin, "How Those Color-Block Bikinis Took Over the Beach," *Bloomberg*, August 17, 2015, https://www.bloomberg.com/news/articles/2015-08-17/how-those-color-block-bikinis-took-over-the-beach.

2   "Shopify Announces Fourth-Quarter and Full Year 2018 Financial Results," Shopify, press release, February 12, 2019, https://investors.shopify.com/Investor-News-Details/2019/Shopify-Announces-Fourth-Quarter-and-Full-Year-2018-Financial-Results/default.aspx.

3   James Bagnall, "Shopify to Triple Size of Ottawa Headquarters," *Ottawa Citizen*, updated March 20, 2017, https://ottawacitizen.com/business/local-business/shopify-to-triple-size-of-ottawa-headquarters.

4   Tobi Lütke, "The Apprentice Programmer," Tobi Lütke (blog), March 3, 2013, https://tobi.lutke.com/blogs/news/11280301-the-apprentice-programmer.

5   Trevor Cole, "Our Canadian CEO of the Year You've Probably Never Heard of," the *Globe and Mail, Report on Business Magazine*, November 27, 2014, https://www.theglobeandmail.com/report-on-business/rob-magazine/meet-our-ceo-of-the-year/article21734931/.

6   Lütke, "The Apprentice Programmer."

7   Ibid.

8   Ibid.

9   Nassim Nicholas Taleb, *Antifragile: Things that Gain from Disorder* (New York: Random House, 2014), 90.

10 Abigail Hess, "Here's How Much the Average Student Loan Borrower Owes When They Graduate," CNBC, February 15, 2018, https://www.cnbc.com/2018/02/15/heres-how-much-the-average-student-loan-borrower-owes-when-they-graduate.html.

11 Adam Levinter and Carl Rodrigues, "36: Basement to $1 Billion, with SOTI's Carl Rodrigues," November 2, 2018, in *E2: Entrepreneurs Exposed*, hosted by Adam Levinter, podcast, http://entrepreneursexposed.libsyn.com/36-basement-to-1-billion-with-sotis-carl-rodrigues.

12 Tobias Lütke, "How did Shopify Get Started?," Quora, answered May 20, 2011, https://www.quora.com/How-did-Shopify-get-started.

13 "How Shopify Grew From a Snowboard Shop to a $10B Commerce Ecosystem," Product Habits, accessed June 14, 2019, https://producthabits.com/shopify-grew-snowboard-shop-10b-commerce-ecosystem/.

14 Cole, "Our Canadian CEO of the Year," *Report on Business Magazine*.

15 "Shopify API Platform and App Store Launched," PRweb, June 2, 2009, https://www.prweb.com/releases/shopify_app_store/shopify_api/prweb2488884.htm.

16 Dayna Winter, "Celebrating 8 Years of Ecommerce: 14 Shopify Stores Launched in Our First Year," Shopify (blog), May 30, 2014, https://www.shopify.ca/blog/14314785-celebrating-8-years-of-ecommerce-14-shopify-stores-launched-in-our-first-year.

17 Cole, "Our Canadian CEO of the Year."

18 Darrell Etherington, "Shopify Debuts Fully Integrated Credit Card Payment
    Processing for Its E-Commerce Platform, TechCrunch, https://techcrunch.
    com/2013/08/12/shopify-debuts-fully-integrated-credit-card-payment-
    processing-for-its-e-commerce-platform/.

19 "Shopify—Funding Rounds," Crunchbase, accessed June 14, 2019,
    https://www.crunchbase.com/organization/shopify/funding_rounds/
    funding_rounds_list#section-funding-rounds.

20 Daniel Sparks, "10 Stocks That are Crushing the Market in
    2018, The Motley Fool, July 16, 2018, https://www.fool.com/
    slideshow/10-stocks-are-crushing-market-2018/.

21 "The Hottest Stock on the NYSE is . . . A Completely Illegal Get-Rich-Quick
    Scheme (with a Good Software Platform)," Citron Research, October 4, 2017,
    https://citronresearch.com/citron-exposes-the-dark-side-of-shopify/.

22 "Shopify PS Ratio (TTM," YCharts, accessed August 9, 2019, https://ycharts.
    com/companies/SHOP/ps_ratio.

23 Stephanie Bedard-Chateauneuf, "Shopify Inc. is Targeting Market Share Before
    Profit," The Motley Fool, February 20, 2018, https://www.fool.ca/2018/02/20/
    shopify-inc-is-targeting-market-share-before-profit/.

24 Sajjad Shahid, "Top Ecommerce Platforms Market Share in 2018,
    Cloudways, December 19, 2018, https://www.cloudways.com/blog/
    top-ecommerce-platforms/.

25 "Shopify Welcomes LA to Our First-Ever Physical Entrepreneur
    Space," Shopify, October 11, 2018, https://news.shopify.com/
    shopify-welcomes-la-to-our-first-ever-physical-merchant-space.

26 "Shopify to Open First Bricks-and-Mortar Service Location
    This Year," the Globe and Mail, Report on Business Magazine,
    May 8, 2018, https://www.theglobeandmail.com/business/
    article-shopify-to-open-first-brick-and-mortar-service-location-this-year/.

27 Canadian Press, "Ontario Chooses Shopify to Run Online Cannabis
    Sales," CBC, February 12, 2018, https://www.cbc.ca/news/canada/ottawa/
    ontario-shopify-marijuana-online-shopping-1.4531228.

28 Mark Rendell, "Shopify to Run B.C.'S Online Cannabis Sales, Financial
    Post, June 22, 2018, https://business.financialpost.com/cannabis/
    shopify-to-run-b-c-s-online-cannabis-sales.

7. THE SPOTIFY SOUNDTRACK

1   Mark Gurman and Debby Wu, "Apple to Unveil High-End
    AirPods, Over-Ear Headphones For 2019," Bloomberg, June 25,
    2018, https://www.bloomberg.com/news/articles/2018-06-25/
    apple-is-said-to-amplify-its-audio-device-strategy-in-2019.

2   Felix Richter, "Streaming Drives Global Music Industry Resurgence," Statista, April 3, 2019, https://www.statista.com/chart/4713/ global-recorded-music-industry-revenues/.

3   Tom Ball and Eric Auchard, "Music Streaming Revenues Surge and Investors Like the Beat," Reuters, April 24, 2018, https://www.reuters.com/article/us-music-sales/music-streaming-revenues-surge-and-investors-like-the-beat-idUSKBN1HV1KL.

4   Amy Watson, "Spotify's Revenue Worldwide from 2013 to 2018 (in million euros)," Statista, February 11, 2019, https://www.statista.com/ statistics/813713/spotify-revenue/.

5   Spotify Hits 108M Paying Users and 232M Overall, but Its Average Revenue Per User Declines, Manish Singh, July 31, 2019, https://techcrunch. com/2019/07/31/spotify-108-million/.

6   Jordan Ritter interview by Brian McCullough, "The Napster Story With Jordan Ritter," April 16, 2017, in *Internet History Podcast*, http://www. internethistorypodcast.com/2017/04/the-napster-story-with-jordan-ritter/.

7   "The Choir was Singing, but Not in Tune, As Napster's CEO Stepped Up Before The Senate Judiciary Committee In Washington," ZDNet, July 12, 2000, "https://www.zdnet.com/article/the-testimony-of-napster-ceo-hank-barry/."

8   "The Choir Was Singing."

9   Tyler Jenke, "Bootleggers are Holding Rare Radiohead Material for a $150k Ransom," Tone Deaf, June 5, 2019, https://tonedeaf.thebrag.com/ radiohead-rare-150k-ransom/.

10 Steven Bertoni, "Sean Parker: Agent of Disruption," *Forbes*, September 21, 2011, https://www.forbes.com/sites/stevenbertoni/2011/09/21/ sean-parker-agent-of-disruption/.

11 Wikipedia, "Sean Parker," accessed September 24, 2019, https://en.wikipedia.org/wiki/Sean_Parker#Plaxo.

12 Ibid.

13 Scribd.com, "Sean Parker's Email to Spotify's Daniel Ek," August 25, 2009, https://www.scribd.com/doc/67465758/Sean-Parker-s-Email-to-Spotify-s-Daniel-Ek.

14 Sean Parker, email message to Daniel Ek and Shakil Khan, August 25, 2009, https://www.scribd.com/doc/67465758/Sean-Parker-s-Email-to-Spotify-s-Daniel-Ek.

15 Alexia Tsotsis, "Live from Facebook's 2011 F8 Conference [Video]," TechCrunch, September 22, 2011, https://techcrunch.com/2011/09/22/ live-from-facebooks-2011-f8-conference-video/.

16 Ibid.

17 Marc Hogan, "The Record Industry Expects a Windfall. Where Will the Money Go?" Pitchfork, May 30, 2019, https://pitchfork.com/features/article/ the-record-industry-expects-a-windfall-where-will-the-money-go/.

18   Daniel Sanchez, "Apple Music, Not Spotify, Ranks as the Most Popular
     Music Streaming Service," Digital Music News, March 29, 2018, https://www.
     digitalmusicnews.com/2018/03/29/verto-analytics-study-apple-music-spotify/.

19   Steve Knopper, "As Spotify Prepares to Go Public, Music Industry Divided on
     Royalties," *Rolling Stone*, March 7, 2018, https://www.rollingstone.com/
     music/music-news/as-spotify-prepares-to-go-public-music-industry-
     divided-on-royalties-118197/.

20   Ibid.

21   Ibid.

22   From phone conversation with Daniel Goldenberg, September 23, 2019.

23   Ibid.

24   Ibid.

25   Lisa Marie Segarra, "Taylor Swift's Spotify Songs Made an Insane Amount of
     Money in a Week," *Fortune*, June 23, 2017, http://fortune.com/2017/06/23/
     taylor-swift-spotify-songs-money/.

26   Knopper, "Spotify Prepares to Go Public."

27   Amazon.com, Amazon Music, accessed September 24, 2019,
     https://www.amazon.com/gp/dmusic/promotions/AmazonMusicUnlimited.

28   "Spotify Ad Campaign Turns Mirror on Music Lovers with 'Weird 2016' Stats,"
     Newstalk, November 29, 2016, https://www.newstalk.com/business/spotifys-
     new-ad-campaign-throws-up-plenty-of-weird-2016-listening-stats-562620.

29   Tim Ingham, "Profits, Payments and Podcasts: 5 Takeaways from Spotify's Q3
     Earnings Call," Music Business Worldwide, November 5, 2018,
     https://www.musicbusinessworldwide.com/profits-payments-and-podcasts-5-
     takeaways-from-spotifys-q3-earnings-call/; Jon Porter, "Spotify is First to 100
     million Paid Subscribers," The Verge, April 29, 2019, https://www.theverge.
     com/2019/4/29/18522297/spotify-100-million-users-apple-music-podcasting-
     free-users-advertising-voice-speakers.

30   Tim Ingham, "Spotify Can't Keep Losing More Than $1 Billion
     a Year. Can Podcasts Rescue Its Business Model?" *Rolling Stone*,
     November 2, 2018, https://www.rollingstone.com/music/music-news/
     can-podcasts-rescue-spotify-business-model-749970/.

31   Ingham, "Profits, Payments and Podcasts."

32   Kabir Sehgal, "Spotify and Apple Music Should Become Record Labels So
     Musicians Can Make a Fair Living," CNBC, January 26, 2018, https://www.
     cnbc.com/2018/01/26/how-spotify-apple-music-can-pay-musicians-more-
     commentary.html; "Having Rescued Recorded Music, Spotify May Upend the
     Industry Again," *The Economist*, January 11, 2018, https://www.economist.com/
     news/business/21734488-its-clout-streaming-could-allow-it-sign-new-artists-
     itself-challenging-major-record.

8. BOOMING BOXES

1   Sarah Mitroff, "From Coffee to Condoms, Now There's a Subscription Service for Everyone," *Wired*, November 21, 2012, https://www.wired.com/2012/11/subscription-services-2012/.

2   Andria Cheng, "The Subscription Box Industry is Getting More Crowded Than Ever," *Forbes*, May 30, 2018, https://www.forbes.com/sites/andriacheng/2018/05/30/the-subscription-box-industry-is-getting-more-crowded-than-ever/.

3   Deborah L. Cohen, "Makeup Startup Thinks Inside the Box," Reuters, November 17, 2010, https://www.reuters.com/article/us-column-cohen-birchbox-idUSTRE6AG3B620101117.

4   Cohen, "Makeup Startup."

5   "Total Revenue of Avon Products Inc. Worldwide from 2011 to 2018 (in billion U.S. dollars)," Statista, accessed June 17, 2019, https://www.statista.com/statistics/670869/avon-inc-global-revenue/.

6   Chavie Lieber, "The Uncertain Fate of Avon in a Digital Beauty World," Racked, April 30, 2015, https://www.racked.com/2015/4/30/8515985/avon-digital-business.

7   Alison McCarthy, "Millennials Dominate US Beauty Market," eMarketer, December 14, 2016, https://www.emarketer.com/Article/Millennials-Dominate-US-Beauty-Market/1014857.

8   Cohen, "Makeup Startup."

9   Geoff Weiss, "How Ipsy, Michelle Phan's Million-Member Sampling Service, Is Giving Birchbox a Run for Its Money," *Entrepreneur*, March 31, 2015, https://www.entrepreneur.com/article/244536.

10 Weiss, "Michelle Phan's Million-Member Sampling Service"; Sarah Perez, "Ipsy's New Subscription Delivers Full-Size Beauty Products, Not Samples," TechCrunch, August 27, 2018, https://techcrunch.com/2018/08/27/ipsys-new-subscription-delivers-full-size-beauty-products-not-samples/.

11 Deborah Weinswig, "Influencers are the New Brands," *Forbes*, October 5, 2016, https://www.forbes.com/sites/deborahweinswig/2016/10/05/influencers-are-the-new-brands/.

12 "Michelle Phan Biography," Biography, accessed June 18, 2019, https://www.biography.com/personality/michelle-phan.

13 Michelle Phan, "Midterms Are Over!," Ricebunny's Xanga site, March 7, 2009, available at https://web.archive.org/web/20090328182810/http:/ricebunny.xanga.com/.

14 "Michelle Phan Biography."

15 Weiss, "Michelle Phan's Million-Member Sampling Service."

16 Natalie Robehmed, "How Michelle Phan Built a $500 Million Company," *Forbes*, October 5, 2015, https://www.forbes.com/sites/natalierobehmed/2015/10/05/how-michelle-phan-built-a-500-million-company/.

17 Jamie Cuccinelli, "Michelle Phan Launches Ipsy Open Studios, a Free Studio Space & Mentorship Program to Help Kick Start Your Career," *Bustle*, June 9 2015, https://www.bustle.com/articles/89095-michelle-phan-launches-ipsy-open-studios-a-free-studio-space-mentorship-program-to-help-kick.

18 "Yield Growth Announces Sales and Marketing Alliance with ipsy, the World's Largest Beauty Subscription Service," Yield Growth Corp, press release, April 30, 2019, https://www.globenewswire.com/news-release/2019/04/30/1812266/0/en/Yield-Growth-Announces-Sales-and-Marketing-Alliance-with-ipsy-the-World-s-Largest-Beauty-Subscription-Service.html.

19 Elizabeth Segran, "Here's Why Nobody Wants to Buy Birchbox, Even After VCs Spent $90M," *Fast Company*, https://www.fastcompany.com/40567670/heres-why-nobody-wants-to-buy-birchbox-even-after-vcs-spent-90m.

20 Digitalcommerce360.com, "Bark: The Makers of BarkBox," accessed September 24, 2019, https://www.digitalcommerce360.com/2018/02/06/case-study-barkboxs-path-150-million-sales-profitability/.

21 Cara Salpini, "The bite in BarkBox's retail gameplan," April 3, 2018, https://www.retaildive.com/news/the-bite-in-barkboxs-retail-gameplan/517974/.

22 "When is the BarkBox IPO Date?," Money Morning, February 14, 2018, https://moneymorning.com/2018/02/14/when-is-the-barkbox-ipo-date.

23 Adam Levinter and Paul Jarrett, "24: Scaling Through Subscription, with BuluBox Founder & CEO, Paul Jarrett," June 26, 2018, *E2: Entrepreneurs Exposed*, hosted by Adam Levinter, podcast, https://entrepreneursexposed.libsyn.com/24-scaling-through-subscription-with-bulubox-founder-ceo-paul-jarrett.

24 Alyssa Katzenelson and Scott Faber, "On Cosmetics Safety, U.S. Trails More Than 40 Nations," Environmental Working Group, March 20, 2019, https://www.ewg.org/news-and-analysis/2019/03/cosmetics-safety-us-trails-more-40-nations.

25 Derek Blasberg, "How Jessica Alba Built a Billion-Dollar Business Empire," *Vanity Fair*, November 2015, https://www.vanityfair.com/style/2015/11/jessica-alba-honest-company-business-empire.

26 Jason Del Rey, "Jessica Alba's Honest Company is Replacing Its CEO After a Sale to Unilever Fell Through," Recode, March 16, 2017, https://www.vox.com/2017/3/16/14951098/new-honest-company-ceo-change-nick-vlahos.

27 Jordan Valinsky, "Jessica Alba's Honest Co. Just Got a $200 Million Lifeline," CNN Money, June 6, 2018, https://money.cnn.com/2018/06/06/news/companies/honest-company-funding/index.html; "How Jessica Alba Built the $1 Billion Honest Company," July 19, 2018, http://www.thefashionlaw.com/home/from-the-big-screen-to-a-billion-dollar-brand-how-jessica-alba-built-the-honest-co.

28 Valinksy, "Jessica Alba's Honest Co."

29 Mark Matousek, "Elon Musk Set Off Weeks of Confusion and Controversy One Year Ago Today by Tweeting that He Was Thinking of Taking Tesla Private— These Are 37 Of His Wildest Quotes," *Business Insider*, August 7, 2019, https://www.businessinsider.com/elon-musk-shocking-quotes-tweets-2018-10.

30 Bill Chappell, "U.S. Births Fell To A 32-year Low In 2018; CDC Says Birthrate is in Record Slump," NPR, May 15, 2019, https://www.npr.org/2019/05/15/723518379/u-s-births-fell-to-a-32-year-low-in-2018-cdc-says-birthrate-is-at-record-level.

31 Ed Hammond and Melissa Mittelman, "Jessica Alba's Honest Co. Gets Investment from L Catterton," *Bloomberg*, June 6, 2018, https://www.bloomberg.com/news/articles/2018-06-06/jessica-alba-s-honest-co-gets-investment-from-l-catterton.

32 Jason Del Rey, "Jessica Alba's Honest Company Has Been in Talks to Sell to a Big Consumer Product Giant," Vox, September 9, 2016, https://www.vox.com/2016/9/9/12858866/honest-company-acquisition-sale-procter-gamble-unilever.

9. DOLLAR SHAVE CLUB DISRUPTS AN INDUSTRY

1   Adam Lashinsky, "How Dollar Shave Club Got Started," *Fortune*, March 10, 2015, http://fortune.com/2015/03/10/dollar-shave-club-founding/.

2   Salvador Rodriguez, "Meet Science, the L.A. 'Startup Studio' Behind Dollar Shave Club and Google's Latest Acquisition," Inc., October 16, 2013, https://www.inc.com/salvador-rodriguez/science-famebit-los-angeles.html.

3   Ibid.

4   Frieswick, "The Serious Guy."

5   Dave Fink, interview by the author, April 27, 2018.

6   Ibid.

7   Ibid.

8   Steven Bertoni, "Razor Wars: Harry's Raises $75 Million to Fight Gillette and Dollar Shave Club," *Forbes*, July 7, 2015, https://www.forbes.com/sites/stevenbertoni/2015/07/07/razor-wars-harrys-raises-75-million-to-fight-gillette-and-dollar-shave-club/.

9   Crunchbase, "Dollar Shave Club > Funding Rounds," CrunchBase, accessed June 19, 2019, https://www.crunchbase.com/organization/dollar-shave-club/funding_rounds/funding_rounds_list#section-funding-rounds.

10 "Unilever buys Dollar Shave Club, Co-Founder Michael Dubin to Remain CEO," CNBC, July 20, 2016, https://www.cnbc.com/2016/07/20/unilever-buys-dollar-shave-club-co-founder-michael-dubin-to-remain-ceo.html.

11 Serena Ng and Paul Ziobro, "Razor Sales Move Online, Away from Gillette," the *Wall Street Journal*, June 23, 2015, https://www.wsj.com/articles/SB12147335600370333763904581058081668712042.

12 Phil Wahba, "Gillette Says It's Fighting Back in the Shaving Club Wars," *Fortune*, October 23, 2015, http://fortune.com/2015/10/23/gillette-shaving-club-wars/.

13 *The Wall Street Journal*, "Unilever Buys Dollar Shave Club, Sharon Terlep, July 20, 2016, https://www.wsj.com/articles/unilever-buys-dollar-shave-club-1468987836.

14 Mike Isaac, "Dollar Shave Club Sells to Unilever for $1 Billion," the *New York Times*, July 20, 2016, https://www.nytimes.com/2016/07/20/business/dealbook/unilever-dollar-shave-club.html.

15 Lucy Handley, "Michael Dubin: Shaving America," CNBC, updated April 11, 2019, https://www.cnbc.com/2017/06/21/michael-dubin-shaving-america.html.

16 Nikhil Basu Trivedi, "The Secret Behind Dollar Shave Club's Billion Dollar Success in One Graph," Medium, May 30, 2017, https://medium.com/@nbt/the-secret-behind-dollar-shave-clubs-billion-dollar-success-in-one-graph-f02fba883635.

17 James M. Kilts, "Fuck Everything, We're Doing Five Blades," *The Onion*, February 18, 2004, https://www.theonion.com/fuck-everything-were-doing-five-blades-1819584036.

18 Kaitlyn Tiffany, "The Absurd Quest to Make the "Best" Razor," Vox, December 11, 2018, https://www.vox.com/the-goods/2018/12/11/18134456/best-razor-gillette-harrys-dollar-shave-club.

19 Barrett J. Brunsman, "P&G Settles Lawsuit with Unilever's Dollar Shave Club," *Cincinnati Business Courier*, March 29, 2019, https://www.bizjournals.com/cincinnati/news/2019/03/29/p-g-settles-lawsuit-with-unilever-s-dollar-shave.html; Barrett J. Brunsman, "Former P&G Executive Named CEO of Rival," *Cincinnati Business Courier*, February 7, 2019, https://www.bizjournals.com/cincinnati/news/2019/02/07/former-p-g-executive-named-ceo-of-rival.html.

20 Tracy Maple, "Gillette Wants a Slice of the Online Razor Club Business," Digital Commerce 360, July 16, 2015, https://www.digitalcommerce360.com/2015/07/16/gillette-wants-slice-online-razor-club-business/.

21 Jeff Harder, "The Razor Wars Have Begun and Somebody's Going to Get Hurt," *Globe Magazine*, June 21, 2017, https://www.bostonglobe.com/magazine/2017/06/21/the-razor-wars-have-begun-and-somebody-going-get-hurt/WbNBloosk1BgiHFzdkp16M/story.html.

22 Ibid.

10. FOOD, THE FINAL E-COMMERCE FRONTIER

1   Andrew Lipsman, "Grocery Ecommerce 2019: Online Food and Beverage Sales Reach Inflection Point, eMarketer, April 8, 2019, https://www.emarketer.com/content/grocery-ecommerce-2019.

2   "Direct-to-Door Meal Kit Service Market Revenue Worldwide on 2015 and 2020 (in billion U.S. dollars)," Statista, February 22, 2016, https://www.statista.com/statistics/655037/global-direct-to-door-meal-kit-service-market-revenue/.

3   Alyson Shontell, "How Blue Apron Became a $2 Billion Startup in 3 Years," *Inc.*, October 20, 2015, https://www.inc.com/business-insider/how-blue-arpon-became-a-2-billion-dollar-startup.html.

4   Catherine Clifford, "How 2 Young Guys Went From The Brink Of Bankruptcy To Selling Their 'Shark Tank' Business for $300 million," CNBC, September 22, 2017, https://www.cnbc.com/2017/09/22/how-shark-tank-business-plated-sold-to-albertsons-for-300-million.html.

5   Rani Molla, "HelloFresh is Now Bigger Than Blue Apron in the U.S.," Recode, March 26, 2018, https://www.vox.com/2018/3/26/17165030/hellofresh-blue-apron-meal-kit-delivery-marketshare-acquisition-organic-green-chef.

6   Paul Delean, "Healthy Options are a Package Deal At Oatbox and Yumibox," *Montreal Gazette*, November 14, 2016, https://montrealgazette.com/business/healthy-options-are-a-package-deal-at-oatbox-and-yumibox.

7   Tom Vierhile, "2018 Cereal Trends: Morning Maneuvers," March 12, 2018, Prepared Foods, https://www.preparedfoods.com/articles/121018-cereal-trends-morning-maneuvers?v=preview.

8   Hugh Williams, "N26 Valued at USD$3.5bn; Graze Continues European Expansion," DTC Daily, July 22, 2019, https://www.dtcdaily.com/2019/07/n26-valued-at-usd3-5bn/.

9   Kirk Falconer, "Healthy Breakfast Provider Oatbox Closes $1.55 mln Seed Round," PEHUB Network, June 14, 2017, https://www.pehub.com/canada/2017/06/3457680/.

10 "Oatbox Raises C$1.55MM in Seed Funding to Accelerate Growth in Breakfast Industry," Newswire, press release, June 14, 2017, https://www.newswire.ca/news-releases/oatboxtm-raises-c155mm-in-seed-funding-to-accelerate-growth-in-breakfast-industry-628378283.html.

11 Ian Brooks, interview by the author, May 8, 2018.

12 Sam Nickerson, "Concerned About Food Waste? Study Finds Meal Kits May Be Greener than Grocery Shopping," EcoWatch, April 26, 2019, https://www.ecowatch.com/meal-kits-environmental-impact-2635612047.html.

13 Adam Levinter and Josh Hix, "45: The Rise of Meal Kits, w/ Plated Co-Founder Josh Hix," March 7, 2019, in *E2: Entrepreneurs Exposed*, hosted by Adam Levinter, podcast, http://entrepreneursexposed.libsyn.com/45-the-rise-of-meal-kits-w-plated-co-founder-josh-hix.

14 Adam Levy, "Should You Invest in Meal Kits?" The Motley Fool, July 7, 2018, https://www.fool.com/investing/2018/07/07/should-you-invest-in-meal-kits.aspx.

15 Lauren Hirsch and Angela Moon, "Meal-Kit Maker Blue Apron Goes Public, Demand Underwhelms as Amazon Looms," Reuters, June 28, 2017, https://www.reuters.com/article/us-blueapron-ipo/meal-kit-maker-blue-apron-goes-public-demand-underwhelms-as-amazon-looms-iduskbn19J1c5.

16 Jing Cao and Alex Barinka, "How Blue Apron Wooed Then Disappointed Wall Street," Bloomberg, December 6, 2017, https://www.bloomberg.com/news/articles/2017-12-06/how-blue-apron-wooed-then-disappointed-wall-street.

17 Suman Bhattacharyya, "Blue Apron is Hemorrhaging Subscribers As It ExpandsRetail Partnerships Strategy," Digiday UK, January 31, 2019, https://digiday.com/retail/blue-apron-hemorrhaging-subscribers-expands-retail-partnerships-strategy/.

18 "Upstart Meal-Kit Companies May Need a New Recipe for Growth," *The Economist*, https://www.economist.com/business/2018/04/14/upstart-meal-kit-companies-may-need-a-new-recipe-for-growth.

19 Lauren Thomas, "Don't Worry, Wal-Mart; Amazon Buying Whole Foods is Just a 'Drop in the Bucket,'" CNBC, June 21, 2017, https://www.cnbc.com/2017/06/21/dont-worry-wal-mart-amazon-buying-whole-foods-is-just-a-drop-in-the-bucket.html.

20 Sarah Whitten, "Whole Foods Stock Rockets 28% on $13.7 Billion Amazon Takeover Deal," CNBC, June 16, 2017, https://www.cnbc.com/2017/06/16/amazon-is-buying-whole-foods-in-a-deal-valued-at-13-point-7-billion.html.

21 Apoorva Mehta, "Tipping Point," Instacart News, February 11, 2018, https://news.instacart.com/tipping-point-1a9b6335f905.

22 "Cheers! Instacart Expands Alcohol Delivery Experience for Customers Across the U.S.," Instacart News, March 12, 2019, https://news.instacart.com/cheers-instacart-expands-alcohol-delivery-experience-for-customers-across-the-u-s-13641a1d7567.

23 Tracey Lien, "Apoorva Mehta Had 20 Failed Start-Ups Before Instacart," *South Florida Sun-Sentinel*, January 27, 2017, https://www.sun-sentinel.com/la-fi-himi-apoorva-mehta-20170105-story.html.

24 Kyle Alspach, "8 Things You Might Not Know About Kiva Systems," March 19, 2012, https://www.bizjournals.com/boston/blog/startups/2012/03/amazon-kiva-systems-acquisition-facts.html.

25 Chaitanya Ramalingegowda, "Famous Failures: The Grocery E-Tailer that Raised Over $800 Million and Went Public Before Filing for Bankruptcy, September 16, 2014, https://yourstory.com/2014/09/webvan-e-tailer/.

26 Alistair Barr, "From the Ashes of Webvan, Amazon Builds a Grocery Business," Reuters, June 18, 2013, https://www.reuters.com/article/net-us-amazon-webvan/from-the-ashes-of-webvan-amazon-builds-a-grocery-business-idusbre95h1cc20130618.

27   Biz Carson, "The Amazon-Whole Foods Deal Could Have Killed
     Instacart. Instead, the Startup is Stronger than Ever," *Forbes*,
     December 12, 2017, https://www.forbes.com/sites/bizcarson/2017/11/08/
     amazon-whole-foods-deal-future-of-instacart-grocery-delivery/.

28   Ruth Reader, "Instacart is Thinking About a Self-Checkout System,
     Patent Reveals," *Fast Company*, March 8, 2018, https://www.fastcompany.com/
     40541370/instacart-is-thinking-about-a-self-checkout-system-patent-reveals.

29   Jessica Galang, "Instacart Acquires Toronto-Based Unata to Build More Online
     Grocery Solutions," Betakit, January 16, 2018, https://betakit.com/instacart-
     acquires-toronto-based-unata-to-build-more-online-grocery-solutions/.

30   Carson, "The Amazon-Whole Foods Deal."

31   Reader, "Instacart is Thinking."

11. A FASHION INDUSTRY REFIT

1   Abha Bhattarai, "'Retail Apocalypse' Now: Analysts Say 75,000
     More U.S. Stores Could Be Doomed," the *Washington Post*, April
     10, 2019, https://www.washingtonpost.com/business/2019/04/10/
     retail-apocalypse-now-analysts-say-more-us-stores-could-be-doomed/.

2   MarketWatch, "Stitch Fix Fumbles IPO Despite Strong Underlying
     Business," November 20, 2017, https://www.marketwatch.com/story/
     stitch-fix-fumbles-ipo-despite-strong-underlying-business-2017-11-17.

3   Lara Ewen, "Why Retailers are Going All In on Subscription Services,"
     Retail Dive, July 17, 2017, https://www.retaildive.com/news/
     why-retailers-are-going-all-in-on-subscription-services/445971/.

4   Katy Steinmetz, "Stitch Fix Has One of Silicon Valley's Few Female CEOs.
     But the Company Stands Out for More than That," *Time*, May 3, 2018,
     https://time.com/5264160/stitch-fix-has-one-of-silicon-valleys-
     few-female-ceos/.

5   Ashley Turner, "Stitch Fix Spikes After Beating Earnings and Revenue
     Expectations," CNBC, June 5, 2019, https://www.cnbc.com/2019/06/05/stitch-
     fix-q3-2019-earnings.html; David Marino-Nachison, "Stitch Fix: The Path to
     Doubled Profit Margins," *Barron's*, July 10, 2018, https://www.barrons.com/
     articles/stitch-fix-the-path-to-doubled-profit-margins-1531239413.

6   Minda Zetlin, "Stitch Fix Founder Katrina Lake was Coerced into Silence
     Over VC Justin Caldbeck's Sexual Harassment," Inc., July 2, 2017,
     https://www.inc.com/minda-zetlin/stitch-fix-founder-had-to-choose-
     between-speaking-.html; Kara Swisher and Jason Del Rey, "Stitch Fix's CEO
     Complained About The Behavior Of Embattled Investor Justin Caldbeck Years
     Ago," Recode, June 27, 2017, https://www.vox.com/2017/6/27/15880434/
     stitch-fix-ceo-justin-caldbeck-complaint-katrina-lake-sexual-harassment.

7   Katrina Lake interview by Guy Raz, "Stitch Fix: Katrina Lake," in *How I Built This with Guy Raz*, podcast, April 2, 2018, https://www.npr.org/2018/06/07/598302861/stitch-fix-katrina-lake.

8   Chris George, interview by author, 2018.

9   Ibid.

10   Ibid.

11   Shawn Gold, "2% of Our Customers Really Hate Us," Medium, May 31, 2016, https://medium.com/@shawngold/2-of-ur-customers-really-hate-us-6ac201bc25ac.

12   Sam Biddle, "The Biggest Scam in Online Fashion," ValleyWag, September 27, 2013, valleywag.gawker.com/the-biggest-scam-in-online-fashion-1410935207; Sapna Maheshwari, "The Dark, Scammy History Of JustFab And Fabletics," BuzzFeed, September 24, 2015, https://www.buzzfeednews.com/article/sapna/justfab-the-billion-dollar-startup-with-a-dark-past.

13   Rebecca Greenfield, "Inside Rent the Runway's Secret Dry-Cleaning Empire," *Fast Company*, October 28, 2014, https://www.fastcompany.com/3036876/inside-rent-the-runways-secret-dry-cleaning-empire.

14   Nathalie Remy, Eveline Speelman, and Steven Swartz, "Style That's Sustainable: A New Fast-Fashion Formula," McKinsey & Co., October 2016, https://www.mckinsey.com/business-functions/sustainability/our-insights/style-thats-sustainable-a-new-fast-fashion-formula.

15   Sarah Perez, "Gwynnie Bee is Bringing Subscription Clothing Rental to Traditional Retailers with Launch of 'CaaStle,'" TechCrunch, March 22, 2018, https://techcrunch.com/2018/03/22/gwynnie-bee-is-bringing-subscription-clothing-rental-to-traditional-retailers-with-launch-of-caastle/.

12. BRICKS AND BYTES—ONLINE HITS THE STREETS

1   Keiko Morris and Eliot Brown, "WeWork Surpasses JPMorgan as Biggest Occupier of Manhattan Office Space," *Wall Street Journal*, September 18, 2018, https://www.wsj.com/articles/wework-surpasses-jpmorgan-as-biggest-occupier-of-manhattan-office-space-1537268401.

2   Maya Kosoff, "How WeWork Became the Most Valuable Startup in New York City," *Business Insider*, October 22, 2015, https://www.businessinsider.com/the-founding-story-of-wework-2015-10.

3   Angela Moon, "Wework Gets $2 Billion after Softbank Cuts Planned Investment," January 8, 2019, https://www.reuters.com/article/us-wework-m-a-softbank/wework-gets-2-billion-after-softbank-cuts-planned-investment-idUSKCN1P210H; Eliot Brown, Maureen Farrell, and Anupreeta Das, "WeWork Co-Founder Has Cashed Out at Least $700 Million Via Sales, Loans," July 18, 2019, https://www.wsj.com/articles/wework-co-founder-

has-cashed-out-at-least-700-million-from-the-company-11563481395; https://www.bloomberg.com/news/articles/2019-09-16/ wework-is-said-to-likely-delay-ipo-after-valuation-plummets.

4   Eliot Brown, "How Adam Neumann's Over-the-Top Style Built WeWork. 'This Is Not the Way Everybody Behaves,'" *Wall Street Journal*, September 18, 2019, https://www.wsj.com/articles/this-is-not-the-way-everybody-behaves-how-adam-neumanns-over-the-top-style-built-wework-11568823827.

5   Kate Clark, "WeWork CEO Adam Neumann Steps Down," TechCrunch, September 24, 2019, https://techcrunch.com/2019/09/24/ report-weworks-adam-neumann-to-step-down-as-ceo/.

6   Herbert Lash, "WeWork's Starry Valuation Dazzles Landlords, Reaffirms Doubters," Reuters, May 10, 2019, https://www.reuters.com/ article/us-usa-property-wework-value/weworks-starry-valuation-dazzles-landlords-reaffirms-doubters-idUSKCN1SG1VD; Konrad Putzier, "WeWork's Mounting Lease Debt Looms Over IPO Plans," *Wall Street Journal*, June 18, 2019, https://www.wsj.com/articles/ weworks-mounting-lease-debt-looms-over-ipo-plans-11560855601.

7   Troy Wolverton, "WeWork is Setting up a $2.9 Billion Fund to Buy Buildings that It Will Lease To Itself," *Business Insider*, May 15, 2019, https://www. businessinsider.com/wework-ark-fund-to-buy-commerical-properties-2019-5.

8   "WeWork Economic Impact Report," WeWork Newsroom, press release, May 8, 2018, https://www.wework.com/newsroom/ posts/2018-wework-economic-impact-report.

9   Matthew Yglesias, "The Controversy over WeWork's $47 billion Valuation and Impending IPO, Explained," Recode, May 24, 2019, https://www.vox. com/2019/5/24/18630126/wework-valuation-ipo-business-model-we-company.

10 Ainsley Harris, "Is WeWork Worth $40 billion or $3 billion?" *Fast Company*, July 3, 2018, https://www.fastcompany.com/90179736/ is-wework-worth-40-billion-or-3-billion; Jacqui Frank, "Scott Galloway: WeWork is Arguably the Most Overvalued Company in the World," *Business Insider*, May 15, 2017, https://www.businessinsider.com/ scott-galloway-wework-overvalued-company-world-2017-5.

11 Stephanie Neal and Richard Wellins, "Generation X—Not Millennials—is Changing the Nature of Work," CNBC, April 11, 2018, https://www.cnbc. com/2018/04/11/generation-x--not-millennials--is-changing-the-nature-of-work.html.

12 "WeWork Co-founder Pushed Aside in $5B SoftBank Takeover," CBC, October 23, 2019, https://www.cbc.ca/news/business/ wework-softbank-takeover- 2qqqq1.5332147.

CONCLUSION

1   Andria Cheng, "The Subscription Box Industry is Getting More
    Crowded than Ever," *Forbes*, May 30 2018, https://www.forbes.com/sites/
    andriacheng/2018/05/30/the-subscription-box-industry-is-getting-more-
    crowded-than-ever/; Ashwin Ramasamy, "How Big is the Global Subscription
    Box Industry?," Hackernoon, April 18, 2018, https://hackernoon.com/
    how-big-is-the-global-subscription-box-industry-4b8dcb756937.

2   Adam Levinter and Jesse Horwitz, "47: Hubble Contacts—Changing the
    Culture of Contact Lenses," March 27, 2019, in *E2: Entrepreneurs Exposed*,
    hosted by Adam Levinter, podcast, http://entrepreneursexposed.libsyn.
    com/47-hubble-contacts-changing-the-culture-of-contact-lenses.

3   Jessica Dumont, "Instacart Slashes Membership and Delivery Fees,"
    Grocery Dive, Nov. 28, 2018, https://www.grocerydive.com/news/
    instacart-slashes-membership-and-delivery-fees/543180/.

4   Daphne Howland, "Restoration Hardware Declares Membership Model 'a
    Success,'" Retail Dive, March 29, 2018, https://www.retaildive.com/news/
    restoration-hardware-declares-membership-model-a-success/520274/.

5   David Feldman, "Loyalty Myths: Is Breakage Good?" Medium,
    March 15, 2017, https://medium.com/@dfcatch/loyalty-myths-is-
    breakage-good-873950da26dc.

6   Brian Dumaine, "It Might Get Loud: Inside Silicon Valley's Battle to Own
    Voice Tech," *Fortune*, October 24, 2018, https://fortune.com/longform/
    amazon-google-apple-voice-recognition/amp/.

Index

*Figures indicated by page numbers
in italics*

access subscription, 4, 21–23
Adidas, 183
Adobe Systems, 5, 46, 98
advertisement. *See* marketing
affiliate marketing, 97–98
AI (artificial intelligence), 47, 83–84,
    207–8. *See also* Alexa; Einstein
air pods, 103
Alba, Jessica, 5, 130, 134–36
Albertsons, 7, 157, 160, 168
Alexa, 42, 47, 117, 164, 207–8
Alibaba, 48–49, 84, 205
Amazon, 31–49; introduction,
    31–32; Alexa, 42, 47, 117, 164,
    207–8; Amazon Web Services,
    42–49; beginnings, 32–34;
    customer focus, 31–32, 33, 34–35,
    171, 203; dot-com bubble and
    bond issue, 35–37; in food and
    groceries industry, 41, 154, 155,
    163–64, 167, 170, 171–72; growth
    by, 13–14; impact on legacy
    retail, 41, 124; IPO, 34; Kiva
    Systems acquisition, 167; labour
    violations, 53; long tail and,
    10–11; Netflix and, 39–40, 67;

physical locations, 194;
smart technologies, 207–8;
storytelling by, 143–44;
Subscribe and Save program,
5, 40–41, 164; Whole Foods
acquisition, 155, 163, 164,
168, 172; working with instead
of competing, 15–16.
See also specific services
Amazon Echo, 42, 117, 207
Amazon Fresh, 163–64, 167, 170
Amazon Go, 164, 194
Amazon Marketplace, 43
Amazon Music, 42, *113*, 117–18
Amazon Prime: customer service and
expectations, 15, 32, 171; loyalty
programs and, 204; overview,
37–38; subscribers, 3, 14, 172;
value proposition, 41–42
Amazon Prime Now, 170
Amazon Robotics, 167
Amazon Web Services (AWS), 42–49;
introduction, 42–43; beginnings,
43–44; cloud computing services,
44–45; competition from Alibaba,
48–49; customers, 45–46; energy
industry and, 47–48; government
clients, 47; predictions for future,
46–49

AMC Theatres, 205
Amram, Yosi, 107
Anderson, Chris, 11
Anmuth, Doug, 66
Antioco, John, 58–59
Apple, 35, 53, 103, 206
Apple Music, 7, 103, 104, 112, *113*
apprenticeship, 88–91
Ariely, Dan, 26
artificial intelligence (AI), 47,
    83–84, 207–8.
    See also Alexa; Einstein
Atlassian, 72
AT&T, 65–66
Audi, 6
Audiam, 114
Automattic, 81, 98
automotive industry, 6–7, 121
Avon, 124

Banana Republic, 202
banking industry, 100
BarkBox, 18, 131–32
Barna, Hayley, 123
Barnes & Noble, 34, 205
Barry, Hank, 107–8
Beauchamp, Katia, 123, 130, 131
beauty industry, 122–31; Birchbox,
    122–24; comparison between
    Birchbox and IPSY, 129–31; IPSY,
    125–29; legacy companies, 124–
    25; subscription model and, 202
Bed Bath & Beyond, 205
beer, 121
Benioff, Marc: Amazon and, 46;
    background, 73; customer focus,
    80; on future of Salesforce, 83;
    on innovation, 69; inspiration for
    Salesforce, 73; on opportunities,
    82; personality and activism,
    78; purchase of *Time* magazine,

82–83; on securing funding, 76;
    on V2MOMS, 74; on workplace
    culture, 79, 80
Benz Patent Motorcar, 121
Bessemer Venture Partners, 95, 156
Bezos, Jeff: on Amazon Prime,
    37; background, 32; creating
    Amazon, 33, 34; customer focus,
    31–32, 35; groceries market and,
    163; Kiva Systems acquisition,
    167; on Prime Video and Netflix,
    39; purchase of *Washington Post*,
    41, 82; storytelling by, 143–44
BigCommerce, 86, *99*
billing. *See* negative option billing
Birchbox, 122–24, 125; introduction,
    122, 142, 202; challenges facing,
    131; comparison to IPSY, 129–31;
    copycat brands, 125, 130; data
    usage, 203; disruption of beauty
    industry, 124–25; as inspiration
    for Bulu Box, 133; market share,
    127; physical locations, 122–23,
    130, 176, 194; value proposition,
    123–24; Walgreens partnership,
    4, 123, 193, 194
Block, Keith, 83
Blockbuster, 13, 52, 54, 55,
    58–59, 124
Bloomingdale's, 202
Blue Apron: introduction, 154;
    beginnings, 142, 156; challenges
    facing, 161, 162–63; Costco
    partnership, 160; environmental
    concerns and, 161; IPO, 162;
    value proposition, 4, 155
Blue Bottle, 202
Boni, Albert, 17
Boni, Charles, 17
Bonobos, 194
Boo.com, 36

Book of the Month Club (BOMC),
  17, 18–19, 122
Borders, Louis, 36, 166
Bovet, Marc-Antoine, 157, 158, 159
Box, 72
BoxyCharm, 125, 202
Bradford, Andrew: *American
  Magazine*, 19
Brandshare, 188
breakfast industry, 157–58
brick-and-mortar stores. *See*
  physical stores
Broadcast.com, 36
Brooks, Ian, 160, 161
Bryson, Chris, 169
Bulu Box, 132–34

cable companies, 28–29
Cahillane, Steve, 159
Caldbeck, Justin, 177
Calm, 6
Camberos, Marcelo, 129
cannabis, 101–2
car companies, 6–7, 121
Carnegie, Dale: *How to Win Friends
  and Influence People*, 71
Carnivore Club, 14–15
Casper, 142, 193
Cave, Edward, 19
CD Baby, 115
cell-phone providers, 100
Chambers, Paul, 180
Chewy.com, 18
Chicago Bar Company, 159
China, 48–49, 84
Christensen, Clayton: *The
  Innovator's Dilemma*, 69
churn, 64, 147, 159, 176
cloud computing, 5, 44–45, 46–47,
  48–49, 75, 81. *See also* Amazon
  Web Services

Colson, Eric, 178
Columbia House (Columbia Record
  Club), 18, 24–26, 29, 64, 203
Comcast, 65–66
Commerce Planet, 27
Computer Literacy, 32, 33
consumer protection agencies, 26, 27
cosmetics. *See* beauty industry
Cosmopolitan, 20
Costco, 135, 154–55, 160, 164, 168
coworking. *See* Regus; WeWork
Crosby, David, 114, 115
Cuban, Mark, 36, 157
culture, workplace: Salesforce,
  78–80; Shopify, 89–90
curated subscriptions, 4, 18
customer lifetime value (LTV), 147
customer loyalty and retention:
  "1,000 True Fans," 9–10, 12,
  13; basis in relationship and
  customer service, 2, 12–13, 15,
  63–64, 146–48; churn, 64,
  147, 159, 176; Dollar Shaving
  Club, 146, 147–48, 201;
  Gentleman's Box, 181; Instacart,
  169, 204; lock-in effect, 100–
  101; loyalty programs, 204–6;
  meal-kit subscription boxes,
  161; Netflix, 63–64, 100–101;
  Salesforce, 100; Shopify, 100,
  101; Spotify, 112
customer relationship management
  (CRM) software, 70, 72, 83
customer service: Amazon, 31–32,
  33, 34–35, 171, 203; Fabletics,
  182–83; importance of, 2, 191,
  203, 208; negative option
  billing and, 28, 29; for retention,
  147–48; Salesforce, 80–81;
  Shopify, 99–100

data, 62–63, 118, 178–80, 202–3
Deering, Erin, 85
Dibadj, Ali, 150
digital assistants, 47.
    See also Alexa; artificial
    intelligence; Einstein
digital music players, 121
Disney, 65–66
Dixon, Mark, 197
Dollar Shave Club (DSC), 139–51;
    acquisition by Unilever, 7, 135,
    145–47; beginnings, 140–41;
    comparison to Gentleman's
    Box, 181; comparison to Gillette,
    148; comparison to Harry's,
    141; customer retention, 2,
    146, 147–48, 201; data usage,
    203; disruption of Gillette and
    Schick, 124, 149–51; e-commerce
    context, 141–43; growth and
    online market share, 4, *144*,
    144–45, 201; marketing, 1–2,
    148; storytelling and, 143–44;
    Subscribe and Save model, 5;
    value proposition, 2, 139–40
Dominguez, Frank, 76
dot-com bubble, 35–36
Douglas, 136
Dr. Dre, 107
Dreamforce, 81
Dropbox, 7, 45, 81
Dubin, Michael, 1–2, 139,
    140, 145, 148, 150
Dunkin' Donuts, 6

e-commerce, 26–27, *99*, 141–43,
    154, *192*. *See also* Shopify
The Economist, 20
Edgewell Personal Care Co., 150,
151, 201
education system, 90–91

Einstein (Salesforce AI software),
    47, 81
Ek, Daniel, 104, 109–10,
    111, 112, 117
Ellie, 183
Ellis, Craig, 85
Ellison, Larry, 73, 76
Endy, 193
energy industry, 47–48
engagement, 63–64, 112.
    See also customer loyalty and
    retention
Epic Provisions, 159
Equinox Fitness, 22
Evernote, 81

Fabletics, 140, 182–83, 203
Facebook: advertisements, 62, 70,
    143, 204; brand reputation, 53;
    comparison to Amazon, 35;
    as fast follower, 121; meal-kit
    subscription advertisements, 161;
    as news outlet, 153; Sean Parker
    and, 109; Spotify partnership,
    111–12; voice recognition
    technology, 206
Fair Financial Corp., 6
Fanning, John, 105, 107
Fanning, Shawn, 105–6
Farbman, Seth, 118
fashion, 173–89; introduction,
    173–74; Amazon's Prime
    Wardrobe, 186–87; challenges
    for legacy retailers, 187–89;
    changes in clothing prices vs. all
    goods, *174*; Fabletics, 182–83;
    The Gap, 188; Gentleman's Box,
    180–81; Gwynnie Bee, 185–86;
    Le Tote, 186; Nordstrom's Trunk
    Club, 175–76; personal shopping
    services, 175–76; rental model,

183–86; Rent the Runway, 183–85; Stitch Fix, 174–75, 178–80; subscription challenges, 202; sustainability issues, 185

Federal Trade Commission (FTC), 26, 27, 29

financial industry, 153

Fink, Dave, 140–41

Finkelstein, Harley, 87

Fleiss, Jennifer, 184

Flynn, Erin Morrison, 174

Food and Drug Administration, 134

food and groceries, 153–72; introduction, 153–55; Amazon in, 41, 154, 155, 163–64, 167, 170, 171–72; breakfast industry, 157–58, 159; delivery services, 165–70; healthy snacks, 158; Instacart, 154, 165–66, 167–70, 171, 204; meal-kit subscription boxes, 155–63, 171; online grocery sales, *154*, 155; organic food, 154–55; personalization, 172; value proposition of new services, 170–71

Ford, 121

Franklin, Benjamin: *The General Magazine and Historical Chronicle*, 19

freemium model, 6

Fresh Patch, 122

Friendster, 109, 121

Galloway, Scott, 199

The Gap, 173, 188, 202

Gartner, Inc., 72, 202, *207*

Gavigan, Christopher, 134

General Mills, 157, 159

Gentleman's Box, 180–81, 203

The Gentleman's Magazine, 19

George, Chris, 180, 181

Germany, 88–89

Gillette, 6, 124, 139, *144*, 145, 148, 149–51

Global Market Insights, 206

GlossyBox, 125, 130, 202

GNC, 205

Gold, Shawn, 182

Goldenberg, Adam, 182

Goldenberg, Daniel, 115

Goldfarb, Jennifer, 129

Google: advertisements, 62, 70, 143; brand reputation, 53; cloud computing and, 48; comparison to Amazon, 35, 43; smart technologies, 207; voice recognition technology, 206; web browsers and, 121

Google Assistant, 47, 207

Google Play Music, *113*

Graze, 4, 158, 202

Greenwald, Ellen, 125

Griesel, Thomas, 157

groceries. *See* food and groceries

Gross, Bill, 73

Gwynnie Bee, 185–86

Gymboree, 13, 173

gym memberships, 22

Haji, John, 180

Harris, Parker, 76

Harry's, 4, 139, 141, 150, 151, 201

Hastings, Reed, 54, 56, 57, 58–60, 62, 63, 64

H. Bloom, 122

HBO Go, 66

Headspace, 6

health industry: Bulu Box, 132–34

Hefner, Hugh, 20

HelloFresh, 154, 155, 156, 157, 160, 161

Hershey's, 159

Hewlett Packard, 6, 149–50
Hix, Josh, 156, 157, 161
Home Chef, 160
The Honest Company, 5, 130,
     134–37, 140, 202
Horwitz, Jesse, 204
Hoseanna, 122
Hu, Simon, 48, 49
Hubble Contacts, 204
HubSpot, 70, 72, 81, 140, 202
Hudson, Kate, 182
Hudson's Bay Company, 193
Hulu, 7, 52
Hunsicker, Christine, 185
Hunt, Neil, 55–56
Hyman, Jennifer, 184, 185

IBM, 43, 48, 75, 95, 121
Indochino, 174, 193
influencer marketing, 126, 128–29
Infusionsoft, 70
Instacart, 154, 165–66, 167–70, 171,
     204
Instagram, 204
IPSY: introduction, 4, 122, 125,
     142, 202; beginnings, 127–28;
     comparison to Birchbox, 129–30,
     131; continued growth, 129; data
     usage, 203; disruption of beauty
     industry, 124–25; influencer
     marketing and, 126, 128–29;
     market share, *127*; Open Studios
     (OS) initiative, 128–29; value
     proposition, 126
IWG, 198

Jarrett, Paul and Stephanie, 132–33
Jassy, Andy, 44, 49
J.C. Penney, 13
Jenson, Warren, 36
JolieBox, 130

Jones, Michael, 140
Jones, Nick, 22–23
Jones, Richard, 115
Jope, Alan, 146
JustFab, 4, 182. *See also* Fabletics

Kane, Sean, 135
Kardashian, Kim, 135
Karim, Jawed, 60
Katz-Mayfield, Andy, 141
Kellogg, 157, 159
Kelly, Kevin, 9–10, 12, 13
Keto Krate, 158
Khan, Shakil, 110
King, Howard, 116–17
Kiva Systems, 166–67
Klister Credit, 93
Kroger, 154, 160, 163, 164, 168
Krueger, Brian, 32

LA Fitness, 22
Lake, Katrina, 174, 176–78
Lake, Scott, 92, 93
L Catterton, 136
Lee, Brian, 135
Left, Andrew, 97–98
legacy companies: Amazon's
     impact on, 41, 124; in beauty
     industry, 124–25; disruption
     of, 12–14, 153; in fashion, 173,
     187–89; meal-kit acquisitions
     by, 159–60; in men's grooming
     industry, 149–51; partnerships
     with, 193; storytelling challenges,
     143; subscription offerings, 202;
     switching to subscription, 16;
     traditional shopping model, 2–3
Legalzoom.com, 135
Le Tote, 186, 187
Lightspeed Venture Partners, 177
LinkedIn, 5, 109, 153

Little Leather Library (LLL), 17, 18
lock-in effect, 100–101
long tail, 10–11, *11*
L'Oréal Paris, 130
Lorentzon, Martin, 104
Lott, Ray, 108
loyalty programs, 204–6
Lululemon, 183
Lütke, Tobias: apprenticeship
    background, 88–90; beginnings
    of Shopify, 92–94; leadership
    of Shopify, 87–88; on Spotify
    growth, 86

Macy's, 13, 130, 202
magazine industry, 19–20, 25
Magento, 86, 98, *99*, 142
Mang, John, 151
marijuana, 101–2
marketing: affiliate marketing,
    97–98; data usage by Spotify, 118;
    Dollar Shaving Club, 1–2, 148;
    influencer marketing, 126, 128–
    29; reduction through working
    with Amazon, 15–16; using
    Google and social media, 70, 142–
    43, 204. *See also* sales
Mary Kay, 124
McCarthy, Barry, 56, 58
McKean, Bruce, 94
McKean, Fiona, 92
McKelvey, Miguel, 195–96
meal-kit subscription boxes, 155–63;
    acquisitions by legacy companies,
    159–60; beginnings and growth,
    155–57; challenges facing, 160–
    63, 171; customer retention
    issues, 161; environmental
    impact issues, 160–61; food
    quality issues, 160; niche food
    areas, 157–59

Mehta, Apoorva, 165–66, 168
men's grooming industry.
    See Dollar Shave Club
Metallica, 107
Microsoft: cloud computing and,
    43, 48; comparison to Salesforce,
    77; sales software and, 75;
    subscription services, 5, 202;
    voice recognition technology,
    206; web browsers and, 121
Minor, Halsey, 76
Moellenhoff, Dave, 76
Mountz, Mick, 166–67
MuseFind, 126
Music-Appreciation Records, 18
music industry: Columbia House
    (Columbia Record Club), 18,
    24–26, 29, 64, 203; early
    development, 23–24; music
    streaming, 103, *113*, 116;
    Napster, 105–8. *See also* Spotify
Musk, Elon, 62, 136
MyDogBowl, 122
MyLittleBox, 130
Myspace, 121, 140
Mystery Tackle Box, 122

Napster, 104, 105–8
NBCU, 66
negative option billing, 25–29;
    by cable companies, 28–29;
    by Columbia House, 25–26;
    consumer protection oversight,
    26, 27; definition, 25; legitimate
    use of, 27–28, 29; by online
    retailers, 26–27
Netflix, 51–67; introduction, 3,
    51–53; Amazon's Prime Video
    and, 39–40, 67; Amazon Web
    Services and, 45; beginnings,
    53–55; Blockbuster and, 58–59,

124; brand reputation, 52–53; cash flow issues, 61–62, 64, *65*; comparison to Amazon, 35; competing services, 65–66; customer retention, 63–64, 100–101; data usage, 62–63; distributor problem, 57; future challenges, 64–67; IPO, 59–60; long tail and, 10–11; online streaming, 60–61; original video content, 61; subscribers, 52; subscription model, 55–57; value proposition, 52

Netscape, 36, 121

Netsuite, 70

Neumann, Adam, 195–96, 197, 200

newspapers, 153

Nike, 60, 202

Nilsson, Jessica, 157

Nordstrom: Casper and, 193; The Honest Company and, 135; Trunk Club, 7, 174, 175–76, 187

Nordstrom, Erik, 176

Oatbox, 157, 158, 159, 203

omni-channel, 159–60, 191. *See also* physical stores

online businesses. *See* e-commerce

Oracle, 48, 70, 72, 73, 75, 77

organic food, 154–55

Ottawa, 87, 95

Overstock.com, 205

Pandora, 112, *113*, 117

Papas, Ilia, 156

Parker, Sean, 105, 106–7, 109, 110–11

Payless, 13, 173

payment systems, 95–96, 142

PayPal, 96

personal brands, 71

pet industry: BarkBox, 131–32

Phan, Michelle, 125, 126, 127–28, 129–30

Phillips, John, 93

physical stores: Amazon, 194; Birchbox, 122–23, 130, 176, 194; challenges with, 193–94; comparison to e-commerce, *192*; partnerships with legacy retailers, 193; shift to by e-commerce start-ups, 191–93; shift to by large e-commerce companies, 194–95; Shopify, 101, 194–95; WeWork, 195–200

Pirate's Booty, 159

Pitch Prize, 177

Plated, 4, 7, 155, 156, 157, 160

Plaxo, 109

Playboy, 20

The Playboy Club, 21

podcasts, 118–19

Porsche, 6–7

Price, Jeff, 114

Prime Music, 118

Prime Pantry, 41, 164

Prime Video, 39–40, 67

Prime Wardrobe, 186–87

Procter & Gamble, 136–37, 150

QVC, 131

radio, 118–19

Radiohead, 108

Raider, Jeff, 141

Randolph, Marc, 54, 58

Ray, Tim, 14–15

Raz, Guy, 177

Regus, 197, 198–99

Rent the Runway, 174, 183–85

Ressler, Don, 182

Restoration Hardware, 205

Rich, Robert, 12
Richardson, Eileen, 107
Richter, Dominik, 157
ride along, 17–18, 125
ride-sharing services, 153
Ritter, Jordan, 105, 106
Rodrigues, Carl, 91
Rolling Stones, 115

SaaS (software-as-a-service),
    5, 72, 84, 202
Sacca, Chris, 177–78
Saehan Information Systems, 121
sales: churn-and-burn mindset,
    74–75; customer relationship
    management (CRM) software, 70,
    72, 83; history of, 71–72; personal
    brands, 71; university programs
    in, 69–70. *See also* marketing
Salesforce, 73–84; introduction,
    70, 202; AI-driven tools, 83–84;
    Alibaba partnership, 84; Amazon
    Web Services and, 46; beginnings
    and growth, 76–78; Benioff's
    purchase of *Time* magazine and,
    82–83; customer focus, 80–81,
    203; Fink and, 140; future of,
    83; inspiration for, 73; IPO, 77;
    launch timing, 73–74; lock-in
    effect and customer retention,
    100; price-to-sales ratio, 98;
    V2MOMs (vision, values, methods,
    obstacles, and measures), 74;
    value proposition, 75; workplace
    culture, 78–80
Salesforce Ventures, 81, 98
Salzberg, Matt, 156
SAP, 72, 77
Sarandos, Ted, 57, 64
Saverin, Eduardo, 109
Saxheim, Max, 17

Scherman, Harry, 17, 18, 19, 122
Schick, 139, 149, 150, 151
Science Inc., 140–41
Sephora, 6, 124, 125, 130, 202
Sequoia Capital, 109
Seventh Generation, 135
sexual harassment, 177–78
Sheeran, Ed, 115
ShoeDazzle.com, 135
Shopify, 85–102; introduction,
    85–88; beginnings, 92–94;
    cannabis partnerships, 101–2;
    critiques and challenges, 97–98;
    customer focus, 99–100; growth,
    86–87, 95; IPO, 97; lock-in effect
    and customer retention, 100,
    101; Lütke's apprenticeship
    background and, 88–90; Lütke's
    leadership, 87–88; payment
    system issues, 95–97, 142;
    physical locations and dynamic
    checkout, 101, 194–95; share of
    e-commerce market, *99*; Shopify
    Plus, 86; value proposition,
    85–86, 94
Shriram, Ram, 109
Siebel Systems, 72, 77
Sisley, 130
smartphones, 96, 121, 167
smart speakers, 42, 206, *207*
smart technology, 206–8.
    See also artificial intelligence
snack bars, healthy, 158
SoftBank Group, 6, 195, 196, 197,
    199–200
software-as-a-service (SaaS),
    5, 72, 84, 202
Soho House, 22–23
Son, Masayoshi, 196
Soundcloud, *113*
Spaces, 198

Spotify: introduction, 103–4; beginnings, 110; competition with Amazon Music, 117–18; critiques from music industry, 113–15; customer engagement, 112; Facebook partnership, 111–12; future prospects, 117–19; growth and future prospects, 112–13; paid subscriptions, 3, *113*; podcasts, 118–19; royalty payment, 112–13, 114–15; Spotify for Artists, 115, 119; value for artists, 116–17; value proposition, 104, 110–11

Square, 96

Starbucks Coffee, 203–4

Stitch Fix: introduction, 4, 173, 174–75; comparison to Prime Wardrobe, 187; data usage, 178–80, 202–3; growth and growth factors, 176, 178; leadership, 176–78; value proposition, 175, 188

storytelling, 143–44

Stripe, 96–97

Strong, E.K., Jr.: *The Psychology of Selling Life Insurance*, 71

Subscribe and Save program (Amazon), 5, 40–41, 164

subscription-based economy: introduction and conclusion, 1–8, 201–8; Amazon, 31–49; challenges in, 38, 203–4; comparison to traditional shopping, 2–3; customer focus, 2, 191, 203, 208; data usage, 202–3; disruption of legacy companies, 12–14, 153; Dollar Shave Club, 139–51; exclusivity and access, 21–23; fashion, 173–89; finding the right product, 202; food, 153–72; growth in, 3–4, 7, 201–2; history of, 17–29; long tail and, 10–11; loyalty programs, 204–6; negative option billing, 25–29; Netflix, 51–67; number of online shoppers using, 8; sales and Salesforce, 69–84; shift to physical locations, 191–95; Shopify, 85–102; smart technology and, 206–8; Spotify and music industry, 103–19; subscription boxes, 121–37; switching to, 16; value proposition, 14–15. *See also specific topics*

subscription boxes, 121–37; introduction, 121–22; BarkBox, 131–32; Birchbox, 122–24, 125, 129–31; Bulu Box, 132–34; disruption of beauty industry, 124–25; Gentleman's Box, 180–81; The Honest Company, 134–37; IPSY, 125–29, 129–30, 131; meal-kit subscription boxes, 155–63

Sun Basket, 161

Survey Monkey, 81

SweatStyle, 183

Sweaty Betty, 183

Swift, Taylor, 114, 115, 117

Switzerland, 90–91

Taleb, Nassim Nicholas, 90–91

Taranto, Nick, 156, 157

Target, 131, 135, 170, 193

television, 153. *See also* Netflix

Tesla, 48, 62, 136

Thiel, Peter, 109

Thornton, Matthew, 66

Thrive Market, 4

Time (magazine), 82–83

Toledo, Will, 116
Toys "R" Us, 13
Triangl, 85
Trump, Donald, 82–83
Trunk Club, 7, 174, 175–76, 187
Tunecore, 115
21st Century Fox, 46
Twitter, 45, 153
Tzuo, Tien, 7

Ulta, 130
Unata, 168–69
Under Armour, 6, 183
Unilever, 7, 135, 145–47, 158
United States of America, 47
UrthBox, 158

Viking Global, 131
voice recognition technology, 206

Walgreens, 4, 123, 193, 194
Walmart: Beauty Box, 6, 125, 130;
    Birchbox and, 131; Bonobos
    acquisition, 194; delivery service,
    170; in food and grocery industry,
    154, 163, 164; kids' subscription
    boxes, 188; subscription
    offerings, 202
Warby Parker, 142, 191–92, 193, 194
Warren, Cash, 135
Warrillow, John, 14
Washington Post, 41, 82, 173
Webvan, 36, 166, 167
Weed, Keith, 145
WeWork, 195–200; introduction,
    195; beginnings, 195–96;
    business model, 197; IPO and
    other challenges, 196–97,
    197–200; paying members and
    occupancy, 195, 198; property
    holdings, 198

Whole Foods, 135, 155, 163,
    164, 167–68, 172
Windsor, Richard, 47
Wixen Music Publishing, 114
WooCommerce, 98, 99, 142
Wordpress, 98

Yahoo!, 36
Yazdani, Bobby, 76
Yorke, Thom, 114
YouTube, 60

Zappos, 167
Zendesk, 72
Zoom, 81
Zuckerberg, Mark, 109, 112
Zuora, 7
Zynga, 109, 176